Byzantine Fortifications

Protecting the Roman Empire in the East

Nikos D. Kontogiannis

Pen & Sword

MILITARY

AN IMPRINT OF PEN & SWORD BOOKS LTD
YORKSHIRE – PHILADELPHIA

First published in Great Britain in 2022 by
PEN & SWORD MILITARY
an imprint of Pen & Sword Books Ltd
Yorkshire – Philadelphia

ISBN 978-1-52671-0-253

Typeset by Concept, Huddersfield, West Yorkshire, HD4 5JL.
Printed and bound in India by Replika Press Pvt. Ltd.

Pen & Sword Books Ltd incorporates the Imprints of Aviation, Atlas, Family
History, Fiction, Maritime, Military, Discovery, Politics, History, Archaeology,
Select, Wharncliffe Local History, Wharncliffe True Crime, Military Classics,
Wharncliffe Transport, Leo Cooper, The Praetorian Press, Remember When,
White Owl, Seaforth Publishing and Frontline Books.

For a complete list of Pen & Sword titles please contact
PEN & SWORD BOOKS LTD
47 Church Street, Barnsley, South Yorkshire, S70 2AS, England
E-mail: enquiries@pen-and-sword.co.uk
Website: www.pen-and-sword.co.uk
or
PEN & SWORD BOOKS
1950 Lawrence Rd, Havertown, PA 19083, USA
E-mail: uspen-and-sword@casematepublishers.com
Website: www.penandswordbooks.com

Contents

Glossary

Alternating brick and stone masonry see *Opus mixtum*.

Arrow loop (arrow slit) – A narrow window in a wall or tower through which arrows and crossbow bolts could be fired. They usually have a fan-shaped section, with a vertical long and narrow slit on the exterior, which opens inwards. More evolved types could include a combined form with a vertical slit, a stirrup lower part, etc. They could either be set in an **embrasure** or simply pierced through the thickness of the wall or in a **crenel** of the **battlements**.

Ashlar masonry – Regular-shaped dressed blocks set in even horizontal rows.

Ballista – A large, projectile engine, resembling a giant crossbow, which fired large wooden bolts or iron-headed bolts.

Barbican – A fortified open court, or any form of outwork, built to protect the area in front of a gate.

Bastion – A solid, protruding construction intended to withstand cannon fire; it basically replaced the function of a medieval tower. The earlier experimental forms appeared in the 15th century and had evolved into a fully fledged defensive system by the mid-16th century. The term has also been arbitrarily used to denote any solid, angular projections from curtain walls (especially in ancient fortifications).

Batter (also **talus, scarp, glacis**) – The sloping base of a wall, tower or moat. Although it was widely adopted (and known) in fortifications after the second half of the 15th century for defence against cannon fire, it was also present in medieval fortifications. Its function could be due to static reasons, such as reinforcing the foundations and lower parts of the structure; to defensive reasons, such as preventing the use of scales by attackers or to withstand ramming and mining attempts; to offensive reasons, such as facilitating the rebound (ricochet) of missiles thrown from the battlements or machicolations (an idea suggested by Viollet-le-Duc).

Battlements – The upper end/line of fire of a medieval fortification running along the **wall-walk**. It is usually formed with alternating built parts (known as merlons) and gaps (known as crenels, hence **crenellations**, used for the whole battlement zone). This form allowed defenders to fire against the attackers through the crenels and find cover behind the merlons. When the walls were under attack, crenels could be blocked with wooden planks (known as shutters); in evolved specimens the shutters could be rolled along horizontal beams set on corbels on the exterior of the merlons. The top of the merlons could have various forms: horizontal and flat, horizontal with triangular section, swallow tail, saw-toothed, etc. An alternative form of battlements has a continuous wall (known as **parapet**) with fire positions (embrasures) at regular intervals.

Blind arcade/arches – A row of arches added to the inner side of the walls and supported on pilasters. There could be many reasons for the presence of a blind arcade, including to create a wider wall-walk above the arcade and facilitate the movement of defenders; to spare construction material; or to create a lower line of fire, below the battlements, with embrasures opening in between the arches.

Buttress – An independent stone support (usually in the form of a built pillar). It was usually added in cases where a structure (wall or tower) needed to carry extra weight, such as a built roof or vault.

Cannon-hole – An opening in the wall for a gunpowder-operated weapon (whether portable or immobile). In early cannon-holes (late 14th to late 15th centuries) the form is similar to an **arrow slit**, with the outer opening being circular, oval, rectangular or 'key-shaped'. Different, more evolved, forms appear from the early 16th century onwards.

Casemate see **Embrasure**.

Cistern – A tank (either closed or open) for capturing and storing (rain)water. In most cases it is subterranean or occupies the ground floor of a tower.

Cloisonné masonry – A masonry style with dressed (usually porous) stones framed by thin, red bricks. It appears in the 10th century and continues in several variants until the end of Byzantium.

Conduit see **Cribwork**.

Corbel – A block projecting from a wall to work as a support for a superstructure.

Countermine see **Mine**.

Counterscarp see **Moat**.

Crenellations see **Battlements**.

Cribwork (also **Timber-frame**) – A structural system in which wooden beams were embedded, connected and arranged within masonry so as to create a framework/skeleton. This tie beam belting/lacing gave the structure connectivity and plasticity, especially in the earthquake-prone eastern Mediterranean. It appears almost consistently from the 11th century onwards (with the earliest recorded examples in the 10th-century walls of Rentina). In the medieval period the beams were not visible on the surface of the walls, a feature that changed in the later centuries. Where the wood has deteriorated, its presence can easily be detected thanks to the rectangular shells ('conduits') it left behind.

Curtain wall – The part of a wall between two towers or bastions.

Donjon (also **Keep**) – A tower-house used by feudal lords in medieval Europe and the Levant. It could be either part of a wider fortification (in which case it would be the most formidable structure, standing at the highest point), or stand isolated.

Drawbar – The large horizontal beam of wood used to lock a gate.

Drawbridge – A hinged bridge that can be raised to block a gateway or lowered to cover a section of the moat. Usually operated via chain and winches.

Earthworks – A fortification constructed out of dirt, usually with raised volumes of earth encircling an area or creating external obstacles. It could be combined with wooden palisades and trenches.

Embrasure – A conch or splayed opening in a wall for an arrow loop, an ordinary window or an early cannon-hole. It gives defenders room to stand and manoeuvre. With the introduction of evolved cannon, fire positions opening through thicker masonries required larger, more massive and elaborate arrangements (dealing, for example, with the smoke or the recoil), known under the generic term 'Casemate'.

Flanking fire (also **Enfilading fire**) – A fortification principle denoting the ability to protect the **curtain wall** from its adjacent protruding structures (towers and **bastions**). The flanking ability of each tower depends on the number and positioning of its fire positions (arrow slits, ballista openings, cannon-holes), their range of fire, the distance from the neighbouring tower.

Forewall see **Outer wall**.

Machicolation(s) – A protruding closed platform, supported on **corbels** and set on the upper part of the walls/towers. It has holes in the floor, through which defenders could attack those at the base of the walls. There are many variations: the simplest is a **box machicolation**, supported on two or three **corbels** and usually set above gates or tower corners to protect blind spots. A more evolved type, usually dated from the 14th century onwards, covers the whole length of walls/towers. In Western Europe this latter type supposedly replaced an earlier wooden variant (a wooden gallery on beams, known as hourding or brattice). Machicolations could also be supported on arches or **buttresses**.

Mine and Countermine – A mine is a tunnel dug under a castle by attackers in an attempt to cause a partial collapse of a wall or tower, by setting fire (or, later on, exploding) the wooden supports of the tunnel. The defenders could countermine by digging into the attackers' mine and exterminating the enemy diggers before they could complete their work. Fortifications founded on solid bedrock or surrounded by a **moat** were secure from mining.

Moat (also **fosse**) – A ditch wholly or partially encircling a fortification. It may be dry or filled with water (temporarily or permanently), although in the East Mediterranean water moats were rare. A moat achieves various aims: it holds enemy siege machines away from the main walls; it increases the relative height of the walls and discourages climbing; it prevents mining; and it is a source for building materials, especially when dug into bedrock. The sides of the moat are usually angled and smooth to prevent climbing: the side below the walls is the

scarp, and the outer one is the **counterscarp**. Above the counterscarp there can be an advanced line of defence, with a **parapet** and fire positions (fr. *chemin-couvert*, it. *strada coperta*).

Murder hole – A relatively simplified form of **Machicolation,** consisting of an opening on the roof of a passage that allowed defenders to shoot at enemies passing below. It was usually set either in front or directly behind a gateway. When set in front of a gate, it could also serve to prevent enemies from destroying the doors.

Open-back Tower (also **Half tower**, **Open tower**, **Open-gorged**, *ouvert à la gorge*) A tower, usually rectangular, whose back is left unbuilt (open) so that if attackers seized part of the walls, the tower could not be used against the defenders. This principle was already followed in Classical/Hellenistic fortifications. In Byzantine times it was used particularly for the towers of the outer walls.

Opus mixtum (also **Alternating brick and stone masonry**) – A masonry style with alternating bands of stone (or **rubble**) masonry and bands of brick. The technique presents several variants, dating from the Roman period down to the last years of Byzantium. Its form depends on the number of brick and stone courses, their consistency and their elements (whether using whole or broken bricks, dressed or unhewn stones, whether the brick bands span the whole thickness of the wall or simply cover the façade, etc.). A variant with a single brick row is known as **Alternating brick**.

Outer wall (also **antemural**) – A defensive line consisting of a lower wall outside the main enclosure. It was used in fortifications set on flat terrain. The aim was to keep the enemy as far as possible from the base of the main wall so as to prevent climbing, ramming and mining. It also secured a second exterior line of fire. As a concept it was first introduced in the Hellenistic period. An evolved type, known as 'concentric fortifications' or 'double-castrum' was introduced in Europe and the Levant during the 13th century.

Parapet – A continuous wall section protecting a line of fire (either at the top of the walls or on the ground).

Pendentive – A spherical triangle which helps the transition between a circular dome and a square base on which the dome rests.

Peribolos – Greek word for enclosure, court or ward.

Portcullis – A wooden grill/lattice (often iron-clad) that is raised or lowered to open or block a gate entrance. It is fitted on grooves curved on the gate jambs, and it is operated via a chain and winch from above the gate.

Postern Gate (also **Sally Port**) – A small gate used as a secondary entrance or emergency exit. It usually opened on the side of, or next to, a tower for added protection. Postern gates intended for sudden attacks opened on the right side of towers, so that the exiting soldiers would be holding their shields towards the enemy line.

Putlog holes – Small, usually rectangular, holes in the façade of a masonry intended for the horizontal poles or beams (putlogs) of scaffolding. In most cases, once construction was finished, the holes were filled in.

Ram (also **tortoise**) – A battering ram is a siege engine designed to break open the walls or splinter wooden gates. In its simplest form it consisted of a large log carried by men. When suspended in a mobile shelter, so that the carriers were protected and allowing for more distance to thrust it against the walls, it was called a tortoise.

Recessed-brick masonry (also **concealed-brick** or **hidden-brick**) – In this masonry style, when laying courses of bricks, each alternate course was set back from the face of the wall and covered with thick mortar. In this way the joints seem much thicker than the bricks. The technique appeared in the 11th century and continued until the 14th century, with some variants.

Rubble (also *opus incertum*, see also *opus mixtum*) – Masonry style using rough unhewn stones, irregularly placed with mortar and smaller stones (or broken bricks) in the joints.

Scarp see **Moat**.

Spout – A tub- or lip-shaped projection on the roof of a building that serves as an outlet for rainwater, conveying the water away from the side of a building and thereby preventing the water from eroding the masonry.

Squinch – A construction whose purpose was to fill in the upper angles of a square room so as to create a circular (ovoid or even octagonal) base for a domical vault.

Tortoise see **Ram**.

Trebuchet – A stone-throwing catapult that was powered by a counterweight. Used by both defenders and attackers, it was more accurate and had a greater range than the earlier torsion-powered catapults. The trebuchet became widely used from the 12th century onwards. Due to its weight, it required solid platforms when mounted on towers.

Wall-walk (also **catwalk**, **allure**) – A corridor along the top part of the walls allowing the defenders to circulate. It is defended by **battlements** or a **parapet** on the exterior, and by another lower wall (known as a parados) on its inner side. It is accessed either from staircases from the interior of the fort or from nearby towers.

Introduction

This handbook is intended to give a general overview of the fortifications of the Eastern Roman State, also today known as the Byzantine Empire (a term attributed much later, and never used by contemporaries), or Romania (a name widely used in Western sources).[1] It aims to cover the fortifications that were executed, financed, or built with the consent (or the tolerance) of a central authority, whose official ideology was the continuation of the Roman Empire in the East. This can prove somewhat ambiguous at times, as for example in the period after 1204, when different states aspired to continue the Byzantine/Roman line of succession.

I started from a number of questions – when were the fortifications built, how were they constructed and decorated, and how could they be understood in terms of defence and military technology? In the course of my study, I understood that it would be futile, and indeed boring, to speak of the monuments alone, without integrating them into the defensive system they were meant to serve; in other words, without asking the questions about who made them, who manned them, and why, since, in the words of Oedipus, 'a vacant fort is [simply] worthless . . .'[2]

For many of these issues, however, there may not be adequate answers, at least not for all the periods and regions of the Byzantine Empire. And these two words, 'periods' and 'regions' are the first problems to consider when dealing with a state that survived for more than a millennium covering an area that fluctuated from virtually the whole Mediterranean basin down to a single city (Constantinople) and some distant territories. Chronological and geographical boundaries that would help delineate the notion of the Byzantine Empire have been a continuous struggle for Byzantine studies as a whole. Multiple versions and periodizations have been proposed over more than 200 years of scientific research. In the English-speaking world one of the earliest notable efforts was Edward Gibbon's *The History of the Decline and Fall of the Roman Empire*. Gibbon saw the Byzantine era as a direct continuation of the Roman Empire, and despite the fact that his view is no longer accepted or considered valid, the interest it created for the Eastern Roman State remains undimmed until today.

Currently, there seems to be a general consensus on a tri-partite division (with an added interim part): an **Early Period** (also known as Early Christian, Protobyzantine, or Late Antiquity) covering roughly the period from the 4th to the 7th century (its precise end date fluctuates since the eastern provinces of Syria, Palestine, Egypt and North Africa were only gradually lost to the Arabs); an intermediate era, previously known as the Dark Ages, and currently referred to as the **Transitional Period**, which extends from the late 7th century up to the first half of the 9th century; a **Middle Period**, starting at the mid-9th century and finishing either at the late 11th century (including parts of the empire lost to the Seljuks) or 1204 (covering the rest of the empire which was dismantled during the Fourth Crusade); and, finally, a **Late Period**, in which a number of polities co-existed, each aspiring to the imperial legacy while struggling at the same time to extend their territory or avoid annihilation.

The end of the Byzantine Empire is usually set in 1453, when Constantinople, a shadow of its former glory, was finally taken by the army of Mehmet II the Conqueror. However, the last remnant of Byzantine polities in the Balkans (known as the Despotate of Morea) was only conquered in 1460 and its counterpart in Asia Minor (known as the Empire of Trebizond) did not fall until 1461, thus sealing the end of autonomous Byzantine rule.

The beginning date of Byzantine history is even more difficult to pinpoint, since there was practically no division point or severe change that would help distinguish it from the former Roman times. Even if most scholars (and especially historians) opt for 330 (the inauguration of Constantinople) or 395 (the final division of the two parts of the Roman Empire),[3] on closer look it seems that each discipline in the spectrum of Byzantine studies finds eventually its own dating system. And this is done according to the internal socioeconomic changes that gradually altered the fabric of the Roman establishment and brought about distinctive new conditions. Theologians and architectural historians have already integrated the 3rd century into their accounts as a necessary first stage, based on the existence and spread of Christianity. Numismatists, on the contrary, go further down in 496, when Anastasios implemented a new coinage system that would prove stable and remain in use for centuries to come.

When it comes to fortifications, one should bear in mind that they are always part of a defensive system and a set of practices that depend primarily on the territory they are expected to cover, the available resources, and the enemy they have to face. The vital concerns of central authorities are to deal with threats, to defend borders, and to protect the population within them. This means that the main factors for large-scale changes in fortification patterns come usually in the form of a dramatic appearance of new enemies or changes of borders, usually following periods of relative stability. Reacting to these factors influences the way in which the state organizes its fortifications as part of its defensive system, channels its revenues into building up its military, defensive and intelligence capabilities, and deploys them to protect certain areas, usually those most exposed to enemies.

Taking this into consideration, we come up with a more 'organic' way to envisage the later centuries of the Roman Empire and the transition point to Byzantine history. It seems that from the mid-3rd century, when the Roman state faced a series of external attacks and internal disruptions, new defensive conditions were gradually implemented, whose concrete form lasted for at least a century, up to the end of the 4th century. Within this framework all major centres of the empire received substantial fortifications, though the primary concern remained with the frontier territories. This system, usually known as Diocletian-Constantinian, although it took advantage of pre-existing fortifications, was significantly different from the earlier defensive strategy; that had focused solely on the frontier *limes*, the primary concern of the army from the times of Augustus down to the mid-3rd century.

The Diocletian-Constantinian system was in turn partially remodelled in the 5th century when the Balkan territory of what was then the eastern part of the Roman Empire required its own defences. In fact, the first period when we can talk about Byzantine or East Roman fortifications should start at the moment when there is a definite East Roman State patrolling its borders and protecting its lands. This was the case only after the state was divided between the two heirs of Theodosios I in 395; this division did not simply introduce administrative reforms within a single system – it involved a definite separation of the empire into two states with separate administration and defensive policies. This is particularly true for the Balkan provinces where there was a massive fortification programme in the early 5th century, one that was intended to defend against the Gothic menace, or even an attack from the Western Roman Empire.

The eastern frontier of the empire, however, did not experience any such change of borders. In fact, the fortifications of the Eastern Roman frontier seem to have survived without significant changes from the Early Roman conquest of the area down to the time of its loss to the Arabs. Indeed, when it comes to fortification strategy in the eastern provinces, the Early Byzantine period can simply be considered as a continuation of the Diocletian-Constantinian period.

In the 6th century this same system was extended in order to include new territories added to the Eastern Roman Empire as part of Justinian's conquests (North Africa and Italy). It was supposedly further strengthened by a new string of fortifications, if one is to believe the court author Prokopios.

Following the immense territorial losses at the end of Late Antiquity, in the 7th and 8th centuries (Transitional Period), the Empire was basically confined to the larger part of Asia Minor, along with Balkan and (continuously shrinking) Italian territories. However, many issues are still unsolved as to the extent of its real or nominal authority over these lands. The new territorial reality that was consolidated in the course of the 7th century led ultimately to a new defensive system, whose aim in Asia Minor was to contain Arab raids and counteract their military tactics, and in the Balkans to regain imperial control over invaded territories and counteract Bulgarian aggression. Some of these goals had been achieved by the end of the 8th or early 9th century, by which time the Empire had a reorganized military and administrative system. Recent research on many fortified sites is rapidly changing our earlier ideas on which places were walled at the time and how they functioned.

The 9th century emerges as a period of stability, growing prosperity and reinforcement at all levels, usually interpreted as a preparatory period for the great achievements of the next century. When it comes to fortifications, the early 9th century saw a series of robust public works aiming mainly to consolidate the power bases of the empire, the largest of these programmes being the one initiated or completed by Michael III in Asia Minor. These works were not a response to an enemy assault (as was the case with the 7th- and 8th-century walls), but were put into place as a visual proof of the state's renewed vitality, a vitality that was expressed by the great territorial expansion that followed in the next two centuries. Yet the 9th-century state remained to a large extent confined to the restricted borders it had had from the early 7th century onwards, with some additions (in the Balkans) and even losses (such as Crete). We will therefore include the 9th-century fortifications as part of this Transitional Period since the works corresponded to a consistent defensive strategy.

The Middle Byzantine Period should be divided into two parts: the first covers from the 10th until the 3rd quarter of the 11th century. It is usually known as the Macedonian Renaissance, named after the dynasty that held on to power for an extended period during a time of expansion and prosperity in all sectors of life. At the end of it, however, the state practically collapsed under the weight of the civil wars and the establishment of the Seljuk states in Asia Minor. Even though the notorious Battle of Mantzikert (1071) seems to have had less strategic importance than is usually attributed to it, the annihilation of Byzantine control in Asia Minor was a fact.

The second part, from the end of the 11th century until 1204, is usually known under the name of the ruling Komnenos dynasty. The Byzantine Empire of this period was a notoriously changed state, which saw the building of walls as the basic factor of its defence. The amount of money and effort spent on castle building during this period is virtually without precedent, considering the restricted resources available. This also reveals the general insecurity prevailing in all the territories of the Empire. This was coupled with a radical change in its social organization – power was bestowed on large aristocratic families which controlled large estates and private armies.

The Komnenos system survived for as long as the central authority had the means to control centrifugal forces, to demonstrate a will to defend territory, and to put into the field a military force equal to that of its adversaries. The collapse of this system from the end of the 12th century was marked by separatist moves aiming to create independent states. The final blow was given by the Fourth Crusade (1204), the Latin conquest of Constantinople and the dismantlement of the remaining territories which were distributed among the Franks and Venetians.

Late Byzantine history is an intriguing and complex system of parallel stories of states, each acclaiming itself as an heir to the Empire. The Empire of Thessaloniki, the Empire of Nicaea (later in Constantinople), the Empire of Trebizond, the Despotate of Epirus, the Despotate of Morea and the Duchy of Neopatras were all political entities ruled by members related to the former Byzantine dynasties, which arose at some point as continuators of the Byzantine Empire. Next to them were several other states, like the Latin Empire of Constantinople, the Second Bulgarian Kingdom and the Serbian Empire, whose rulers also claimed to be Emperors of the Romans. Problems of political ideology, changing boundaries, constant wars for survival, and rising and falling dynasties were all bound in an extricable web for a period of almost three centuries; a web that was eventually to be dissolved by the Ottoman conquest.

These socioeconomic conditions led to the building of literally thousands of fortifications, in every form and every part of the Balkans, the Aegean and Asia Minor (that is, along its western and northern littoral). The difficulty in this case is what to consider as a proper Byzantine fortification, since almost all territories passed at some point under the rule of people who claimed to be Byzantine emperors. The constructions we see, built by conflicting parties, are indistinguishable, following Late Medieval war technology. We have to wait until the 15th century in order to see fortifications in the Aegean world that would have distinctive features pointing to the identity of their builders, such as Venetians, Ottomans, and Hospitallers. For our case, therefore, we will restrict ourselves to those fortifications which can be ascribed with some certainty to Byzantine rulers and their followers, either in the Balkans or in Asia Minor.

By that time, however, the last remnants of the Byzantine Empire are usually considered as a lost cause, deprived of economic and military momentum, and simply trying to delay the inevitable. Yet, until their very last days, the Byzantines were repairing and reinforcing their walls. These final fortifications tell a somewhat different story; rather than showing resignation, they demonstrate a degree of sophistication and reveal a knowledge of the latest improvements carried out in Western Europe.

When one encounters the history of the Byzantine Empire, one sees how the state in every period evolved, transformed, and adjusted its institutions and its ideology, along with its size, internal organization, external policies, and enemies. However, at the same time it preserved its own identity and notion of continuity, hence we are correct in speaking of the same political entity, the Eastern Roman State acting as a continuation of the Roman tradition. The fortifications were a state symbol of strength and survival against its adversaries, an earthen boundary protected by the heavenly forces that preserved the Empire from the barbarians. This book is a modest effort to study and interpret the physical remains of these monuments.

However fascinating the history of Byzantine fortifications may be, it also involves a number of difficulties owing to the fact that more than a dozen states presently occupy the territories of the Empire, often inimical to one another; this means in practical terms that scholars of one region usually ignore all that has been done in another, with their accounts addressed merely to their local audience. Hence the necessity to take a general look at the subject, to try to combine data from various areas, and finally establish a concrete image of the defensive state of Byzantium at any given moment.

Nevertheless, there has been an increasing volume of studies focusing on individual sites, in older or more recent times, of generic or more detailed form, reaching either general chronological conclusions ('the castle was Byzantine') or, more rarely, solid documentation of different construction periods. Indeed, this book will only deal with published material, and the aim is to bring together all the available material for a given period of time. It will therefore deal also primarily with those examples where scientific work reached conclusions as to their date of construction, and their periods of use, and sites where these publications contain details as to architectural and defence features, such as masonry style, battlement shapes, arrow loop types and measurements, etc. Unfortunately, despite the huge number of preserved sites, only a small percentage fulfill these criteria, but there is still enough information to make the compilation of this book possible.

To the best of my knowledge, there has been a single predecessor, a first attempt to produce a general overview of Byzantine fortifications: the well-known, though usually inaccessible, composite account by Clive Foss and David Winfield, entitled *Byzantine Fortifications: An Introduction*. This is one of the most peculiar and intriguing books, including in reality two separate accounts. The first is by David Winfield, who gave a general overview and a sketchy reference to the Asia Minor castles he considered to be Byzantine, based on his remarkable personal research. The second part, written by Clive Foss, dealt first explicitly with the walls of Constantinople and Nicaea, and then went on to give a general examination of some Asia Minor fortifications (mainly in its western part). Despite the shortcomings, this is the most widely referenced source for Byzantine fortifications. It was admirably seconded by Foss's extensive record of publications on Byzantine fortifications of western Asia Minor, as well as by the concise article by A.W. Lawrence, 'A Skeletal History of Byzantine Fortification'.

Among many other scholars dealing with particular aspects or periods of the Byzantine military record, one cannot avoid mentioning some of the great mentors of our times, on whose efforts this handbook heavily relies: the likes of James Crow, Denys Pringle, and John Haldon, along with the representatives of an older generation, such as Donald Nicol and Antony Bryer. I have particularly profited from the unwavering support of Michael Heslop and his first-hand knowledge of medieval fortifications. The late Slobodan Ćurčić completed his *opus magnus, Architecture in the Balkans from Diocletian to Suleyman the Magnificent,* alas shortly before his demise. With this invaluable resource for any student of the Middle Ages in the eastern Mediterranean, fortifications attained at last their proper significance, and were superbly examined within their socioeconomic context.

Having started the compilation of the book back in 2009, I profited greatly over the years from, and would like to recognize, the help I received from friends and colleagues; although names are too many to mention, their support is humbly acknowledged, with the shortcomings of the final result remaining the sole responsibility of the author.

PART ONE

THE EARLY BYZANTINE PERIOD

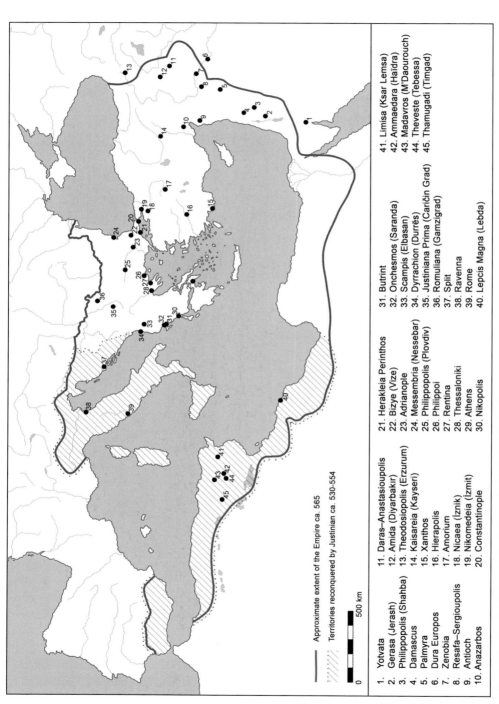

1. Yotvata
2. Gerasa (Jerash)
3. Philippopolis (Shahba)
4. Damascus
5. Palmyra
6. Dura Europos
7. Zenobia
8. Resafa–Sergioupolis
9. Antioch
10. Anazarbos

11. Daras–Anastasioupolis
12. Amida (Diyarbakır)
13. Theodosiopolis (Erzurum)
14. Kaisareia (Kayseri)
15. Xanthos
16. Hierapolis
17. Amorium
18. Nicaea (İznik)
19. Nikomedeia (İzmit)
20. Constantinople

21. Herakleia Perinthos
22. Bizye (Vize)
23. Adrianople
24. Messembria (Nessebar)
25. Philippopolis (Plovdiv)
26. Philippoi
27. Rentina
28. Thessaloniki
29. Athens
30. Nikopolis

31. Butrint
32. Onchesmos (Saranda)
33. Scampis (Elbasan)
34. Dyrrachion (Durrës)
35. Justiniana Prima (Caričin Grad)
36. Romuliana (Gamzigrad)
37. Split
38. Ravenna
39. Rome
40. Lepcis Magna (Lebda)

41. Limisa (Ksar Lemsa)
42. Ammaedara (Haïdra)
43. Madavros (M'Daourouch)
44. Theveste (Tebessa)
45. Thamugadi (Timgad)

Approximate extent of the Empire ca. 565

Territories reconquered by Justinian ca. 530–554

0   500 km

Map 1. The Empire during the Early Byzantine Period with the place-names mentioned in the text.
(Source: Görkem Günay, based on Haldon, The Palgrave Atlas of Byzantine History)

Chapter 1

The Late Roman Defences
(3rd and 4th centuries)

What Was Before: The Early Roman Times

The Roman State, as consolidated in the years of Julius Caesar and Augustus, included practically the whole Mediterranean basin and the larger part of Europe.[1] All these territories were filled with pre-existing fortifications of various dates, size, construction techniques and purposes. At the same time, the unification of these areas under a steady government, especially after the end of the civil wars, made many of these walls obsolete. The Roman State from the 1st to the early 3rd century adopted a different defensive policy from its predecessors, who had opted to actively use fortifications as part of their efforts to defend themselves. The government focused on safeguarding the state, acknowledging at the same time that further expansion would be unmanageable. Whether this was a conscious decision, usually attributed to Augustus, or the result of many factors is still a matter of debate.

In any case, the army was restructured and most of the legions were moved to the frontiers; they were transformed into frontier garrisons, policing the borders and securing the *Pax Romana*. This led over time to the creation of a huge network of frontier zones, known generically under the term Limes.[2] In reality, in each area the Roman strategists opted for a system of barriers that was cost-efficient, and manageable, but in no case was it impenetrable. They created a border zone, especially in more vulnerable places, which in times of peace facilitated communication, trade, and tax collection, while in times of peril it allowed time for the Roman defenders to regroup, relocate forces, and counterattack. In many places, these defences consisted of linear fortifications with moats, external obstacles, walls made of local materials (wood, turf or stone), guard towers and sentry stations; the latter usually followed the famous 'playing card' plan, which imitated the standard layout of Roman military camps.[3]

The most famous of these linear fortifications is, of course, Hadrian's Wall in Britain, the construction of which consolidated the pre-existing situation along the northern borders of this province.[4] It was in turn succeeded by Antoninus's wall further north, and reused later on. Elsewhere, the Fossatum Africae, the German and Danube Limes, and the Easter Frontier fortifications were parts of the greater scheme for the protection of the Empire.[5] This immense defensive system (whether it was centrally controlled or not) – its effectiveness, provisioning, purpose, and results – has been the subject of countless theories and controversies. General assessments usually fail to show the constant mobility in the frontier zone – the raids, wars, destructions, rebuildings, advances or withdrawals of an army, whose numbers, divisions and movements varied greatly according to the wider political or strategic situation.

When it comes to the defensive elements of the Roman walls themselves, one key observation strikes the viewer: their simplicity and lack of provision for active defence (such as flanking fire from regularly spaced towers, multiple platforms to fire from, double walls, posterns for assaults, etc.), particularly given the fact that Rome had inherited an array of Hellenistic fortifications which had attained, at least in the most refined examples (such as the walls of Rhodes, Perge, Messene) and the related military manuals, a degree of sophistication that remained almost unsurpassed until the invention of gunpowder.[6] The Roman walls of this period were simply constructed as field bases, points from where the army would conduct open-field operations. They were designed to offer basic protection, but never to sustain prolonged sieges by a formidable adversary. The only such adversary – the Persian Empire – lay to the East, and in that field of action Rome used pre-existing fortifications with minor adjustments. This is how we can interpret the basic defences of the many 'playing card' forts along the Roman borders, which lacked projecting or gate towers.

The reintroduction of these active defensive elements (seen in full force from the 3rd century onwards) was often envisaged within an evolutionary scheme from simpler to more complex forms:[7] corner and gate towers were first observed in German forts restored by Marcus Aurelius after the Marcomannic Wars. These towers, however, had no enfilading power since they were built far apart from one another; they were probably intended to strengthen feeble parts of the forts, like the gates or the rounded corners. The same tendency continued in the Severan period, with truncated gates on the one hand and semicircular or U-shaped gate towers on the other. Still these forts were not designed to withstand a siege, but simply protected the barracks of a field-operating army from unexpected attacks.

At the same time, existing city walls within the empire were usually neglected, with settlements developing outside their old boundaries. New enclosures or monumental city gates were built as part of city embellishment, or as a mark of imperial favour and elevation to city status, with little regard for their defensive capability. This was the case, for example, in the Hadrianic extension of Athens (only its gate survives), or in the 1st-century walls of Gerasa (Jerash, Jordan).[8] Few active fortifications were built within the imperial territory, and then only as a response to specific threats: for example for a number of Thracian cities, such as Philippopolis (Plovdiv, Bulgaria), and Bizye (Vize, Turkey), because of their proximity to the northern borders, especially during the Marcomannic Wars.[9]

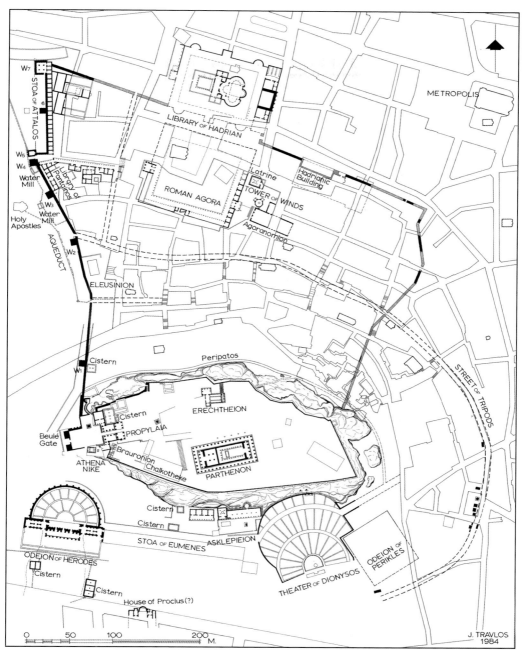

Plate 2. Athens. Plan of the Late Roman fortification and the Acropolis.

(*Source*: American School of Classical Studies at Athens: Agora Excavations)

Plate 3. Athens. Late Roman fortification wall, c. A.D. 280–290.
(*Photo*: American School of Classical Studies at Athens: Agora Excavations)

The fortification of **Thessaloniki** (Greece)[38] consists of three areas: the fortified city, the citadel and the (much later) Fort of Heptapyrgion (Seven Towers) (*see* Plate 4). The city walls rise from the sea in the south to the citadel hill to the northeast. Their plan is trapezoid and their length is c. 8km. Where the ground is level there is an outer wall and a main wall with triangular towers set closely together. The section on the side of the hill was strengthened mainly with rectangular towers. It remains unknown whether the outer wall ran along the entire length of the walls or was restricted to only the most vulnerable parts; in any case it was a weak construction. The presence of a moat, mentioned in the sources, has not been verified. The triangular towers of the city walls present a unique case: they are solid projections that are neither separate structures nor rise above the walls (they could also be described as bastions or buttresses, *see* Plate 5). Their form, number, and positioning are not so well preserved in other Byzantine sites.

This fortified complex presents a series of building phases whose chronology poses problems. The earliest structure that is currently preserved is the inner side of the city walls; this was in fact an earlier enclosure, regulated by rectangular towers. Later on it was deemed weak and it was reinforced both internally and externally with the addition of rectangular buttresses. Then the whole complex was reshaped by adding much stronger structures to its outer face (the wall with the triangular towers). Several different techniques were used in this new construction: some parts were built with schist stones set in regular courses and alternating with three to five bands of brick, while others have a façade covered

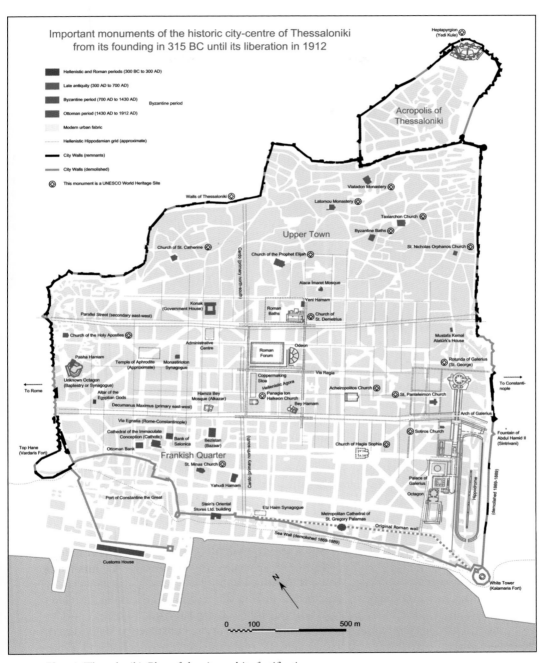

Plate 4. Thessaloniki. Plan of the city and its fortifications.
(*Source*: https://commons.wikimedia.org/wiki/File:Thessaloniki_historic_city_centre.svg)

Plate 5. Thessaloniki. The city walls. (*Photo*: Anastasios Tantzis)

with superimposed bands of brick arches that are strictly decorative; the base of a third part of the wall is made of reused marble seats which probably came from the Hippodrome.

The citadel was added later in the same period to the north of the city's existing fortification; this is proved by the towers of the intermediary wall, which project towards the citadel rather than towards the city. In its most vulnerable section, triangular and rectangular towers succeed one another.

As for its date, the earlier (inner side) enclosure of the city walls is attributed to the mid-3rd century (*c.*254) and connected to barbarian invasions. Its reinforcement has been dated to the first half of the 4th century. The restructuring of the walls, however, has been interpreted in various ways. Ćurčić has linked the building of the walls with Galerius, who took up residence in the city. He believed that the curtain wall east of the city, with the giant triangular towers, was erected as a single enterprise, along with the nearby Hippodrome and the palace. Most scholars, however, favour a later date,[39] linking the erection of the walls to a dedicatory inscription in the east part of the city to an official named Ormisdas. The identity of this individual, and therefore the date of the construction, is disputed: two dates have been proposed, namely the time of Theodosios I (Tafrali, Velenis), at the end of the 4th century (since Ormisdas is specifically mentioned as 'having clean hands', which was thought to mean that he did not participate in the massacre of the Thessalonicans ordered by Theodosios I), or later on, in the mid-5th century (the date proposed by Spieser and Vickers). The brickstamps of the outer wall have been used as evidence for a date in the mid- or third quarter of the 5th century (Rizos).

As mentioned above, one of the new architectural features of this period was the construction of **new imperial cities**.

Romuliana (Gamzigrad, Serbia)[40] was constructed by Galerius in memory of his mother Romula. It had a basically rhomboidal form, covering 4.8ha, with two main gates (east and west). An earlier system of walls was quickly deemed insufficient, and was superseded by a much larger fortification, whose dimensions and character are almost unique for this period, the reasons being mostly symbolic and hierarchical. Twenty oversized polygonal towers (six on the sides, each measuring between 25 and 30m) were added to the wall, and the corner towers were significantly larger than the rest. The two gates had multi-storeyed, elaborate façades, protected by twin towers, a design reminiscent of both imperial palaces and forts.

The so-called Palace of Diocletian at **Split** (Croatia),[41] built *c.* 300, is currently identified as a new imperial city rather than a self-standing palace, as it was considered in earlier literature (*see* Plate 6). Its rectangular plan and inner disposition resemble those of a Roman military camp, with many parallels in the eastern provinces of the empire. This layout, along with the numerous mason's marks of Syrian origin, bespeaks of eastern Mediterranean workshops employed in this scheme. The city is protected by a massive enclosure reinforced by sixteen towers; those protecting the three gates (in pairs, one gate on each side) are all octagonal, while the rest are rectangular. The façade of the gates is decorated

Plate 6. Split. The 'Palace of Diocletian'. (*Source:* Public domain)

with arcaded tiers with columns on corbels. The interior of each gate formed a square, open-air courtyard with tall three-storey fighting platforms on all sides, and a second gate leading into the city.

Constantinople (Istanbul, Turkey)[42] was inaugurated in 330, and was destined to be the centre of the medieval state that continued along the lines of the Roman Empire in the East. However, there is little physical evidence from the Constantinian period; the largest surviving monument is the Hippodrome (despite its erroneous attribution by earlier research to Septimius Severus). Its enclosure seems to have formed a wide arc running along the peninsula from the Sea of Marmara to the Golden Horn. Along the shore lines (Marmara and Golden Horn) the 4th-century walls took advantage of the pre-existing 2nd-century walls. As for its landward side, we can only tentatively trace the line of the walls on the soil, since not a single stretch has so far been identified. From sources we know of the main gate at the end of the Via Egnatia (known as the Golden Gate), and a secondary one (the Deuteron Gate) leading to the road to Adrianople, Serdica, Naissus and Sirmium.

As well as these major fortifications, a number of smaller fortresses – military outposts strategically located along the main roads crossing the Balkans or along the Danube frontiers – have been investigated archaeologically over the years. This building activity was necessary as Roman forces retreated to the Danube line, which would henceforth be the natural barrier of the empire. In many cases, these were earlier Roman camps (of the 'playing card' shape) that were rebuilt in stone but retained their symmetrical planning, with added features such as corner towers.[43]

One of the forts where a large part of the fabric is preserved is the castrum of **Scampis** or Scampa, *c.*320 (Elbasan, Albania, *see* Plate 7).[44] Scampis lay halfway between Dyrrachion (Durrës) and Ohrid (North Macedonia) and controlled traffic on the Via Egnatia. Covering an area of *c.*10ha, it has an almost perfect rectangular plan with petal-shaped towers (some rectangular) on the sides, and fan-shaped ones at the corners. It had two symmetrical and corresponding gates (east and west), protected by twin towers and leading to inner defensive courtyards. In the next century it was turned from a military outpost into a settlement.

Another such military outpost was **Rentina** (Greece),[45] which guarded the entrance to a gorge, and was crucial for traffic along the Via Egnatia and access to Thessaloniki. The first fortification consisted of a pentagonal citadel and a fortified enclosure with two gates. It was perhaps built with support from neighbouring Arethousa and at the time was named Artemision.

A number of isolated forts (turris) have also been attributed to this period.[46] Most were located along the Danube, in the modern border areas between Serbia and Bulgaria and in Hungary. They seem to have been simple watch towers, surrounded by an enclosure wall. They were designed to observe strategically important passes, and send warning signals when necessary.

Plate 7. Scampis (Elbasan). View of the walls. (*Photo*: author)

Fortifications in the Eastern Provinces

Substantial walls dating from the period survive in only a few inland cities of the eastern provinces; some of them (such as Nicaea, Nikomedeia, Ankyra, Xanthos, and Philippopolis)[47] have been the subject of extensive research.

The walls of **Nicaea** (Iznik, Turkey)[48] were built after the Gothic raid in 259. The works started under Emperor Gallianus and, according to inscriptions surviving above the Lefke and Yenisehir gates, they were completed by Emperor Claudius Gotticus in 268–269 (*see* Plate 8). They form a single enclosure regulated by towers. The walls are built in a strong rubble masonry interrupted by brick bands. They were around 4m thick and reached a height of 9m, with a wall-walk accessible through staircases built on the inner side. It seems that there was a single defence line at battlement level. Special attention was paid to the gates, which were both monumental (with arched openings made of ashlar blocks) and also well defended, with inner defensive rectangular courtyards.

The towers, built at intervals of *c.* 60–70m, had an all-brick facing covering a rubble core. They are U-shaped, with a diameter of 8–9m, and bond to the wall. A small gate opens to the left side (to the outside viewer) of each tower for attacks launched by the defenders; in that, they follow a well-known Hellenistic practice. No other openings are externally visible and therefore the towers had to be defended from their top level. Mention of the use of catapults during the Arab

Plate 8. Nicaea (Iznik). The Lefke Gate. (*Photo*: David Hendrix)

siege of 727 implies the existence of a flat roof for the installation of such machines. The presence of a moat outside the walls is probable, though its earliest mention dates from the 11th century.

Nikomedeia (Izmit, Turkey)[49] held a strategic position at the head of a deep gulf on the coast of Bithynia, and was the start point of the land route linking the Aegean coast with central and eastern Anatolia. Diocletian chose the city as his capital and carried out a large-scale construction plan in order to create here an imperial centre, a new Rome.

These works included the erection of massive and very long walls which extended to a length of more than 6km surrounding the citadel and the rough hills above the city, and down to the coast. They were designed to cover not only the inhabited areas but also the hills that control access from the north, as well as to secure a water supply. Only a small part of them is preserved today, together with a tower still standing to a height of *c.* 10m, in the area to the north of the later Byzantine fort. The rest of the walls have been consumed by the expansion of the present city. Nothing is known of the sea walls that undoubtedly must have existed.

Many different masonry styles have been observed in the preserved parts of the fortification. The commonest one has a façade built with roughly hewn stones, set in irregular zones, and a core of uncut stones with white lime mortar, smaller stones and large bricks. They are interrupted at regular height intervals of *c.* 1m by bands of bricks that continue throughout the wall thickness. There are four bands of neatly placed bricks. In fact this masonry is very similar to the earlier Roman walls of Nicaea.

The Nikomedeia walls were not maintained for a long time. They were abandoned either after the 7th century, or much earlier in the 4th century, once the capital was transferred to Constantinople. A provincial city could not afford a huge defensive enclosure, especially since it was far away from the borders and there was no apparent need for them. They were probably damaged during the 358 earthquake, and whether they were used afterwards is unknown.

The city of **Philippopolis** (Shahba, Syria),[50] the birthplace of Emperor Philip (r. 244–249), was (re-)founded shortly after his accession to the throne. The city acquired a bulky enclosure *c.* 3.5km in circumference, in the form of an irregular quadrilateral, partly following the contour of the terrain. The walls were strengthened with square towers at regular intervals (40–50m), projecting from both faces of the enclosure. The corner towers and those flanking the main gates were circular. The enclosure was pierced by four identical gates, each with a central archway flanked by two smaller arches. These gates led to the colonnaded streets and buildings of the settlement, many of which were left unfinished when the emperor died. The walls were built with large, well-cut stone blocks from local bedrock.

Of the eastern frontier fortifications, only a few major sites preserve parts of their defences. The walls at **Amida** (Diyarbakir, Turkey),[51] though later transformed and largely rebuilt, can be recognized both on stylistic grounds and from some Greek and Christian inscriptions (*see* Plate 9). They are still preserved to a length of 5.5km, and consisted of the main wall, with a width of 4.5m and height of 8–12m, and the outer wall (thickness 1.8m, height 2m). The towers, with a diameter of *c.* 15m, projected for *c.* 12m. Solid buttresses jutted out from the walls between the towers. Their width was *c.* 2m and their projection *c.* 1.8m. Three of the four monumental gateways had three passages, and were flanked by huge U-shaped towers; there are traces of blind arches on the interior side of their walls.

The defensive features of Amida have provoked a vigorous discussion about the evolution of the fortification systems of the Early Byzantine Empire. Gabriel attributed them to Constantius II between the years 324 and 337. Others have recognized them as Justinianic, while Crow has identified two phases between the 4th and 6th centuries. The city was the largest Roman stronghold on the Persian frontier and it played an important role in all the conflicts down to 639, when it was conquered by the Arabs.

The Roman frontiers from the Euphrates through Syria and Transjordan and down to the Red Sea are currently understood as a series of north–south routes on the fringes of the desert, regulated by square forts (*quatriburgia*), towers and small towns.[52] At the end of the 3rd century the region was heavily strengthened,

Plate 9. Amida (Diyarbakır). *View of the walls.* *(Photo:* Daniel C. Waugh)

and the route through Syria (connecting Damascus, Palmyra, and Sura) was known as *Strata Diocletiana*, because Diocletian had played a major role in its construction. Most of these fortifications have simply been recorded and further work on their dating has not been undertaken; some of them, though, have been thoroughly researched and they include work from later periods (such as El-Lejjun in Jordan and Resafa in Syria).[53]

One of them was the legionary fortress at **Palmyra** (Syria),[54] which was dated to the Diocletian era. During this period the city received a new wall circuit that enclosed a huge area (*c.*120ha). A separate monumental military fort was erected within the walls, occupying the northern – highest – part of the city. It included major monuments as well as the headquarters of the *Legio I Illyricorum*. In this way the entire urban area became a military centre for the defence of the empire.

Further south, the major fort at **Yotvata** (Israel)[55] guarded the road from Gaza to Aila. This was another *quatriburgium* with four corner towers projecting from tall, thick walls. Its construction at the end of the 3rd century was confirmed based both on numismatic evidence and on an inscription. The latter attributed the construction of a wing and a gate to Emperor Diocletian. The fort was placed next to a major water source with an elaborate channel system serving its distribution.

fighting techniques corresponded to the respective capabilities of the enemy they had to confront. Cavalry equipped with long spears and protected by laminated armour first saw use by the Sarmatians, Parthians and Sassanid Persians, before being adopted by the Roman army. The introduction of the bow, a typical Hun weapon (the northern enemy of the state during this period), led to a new kind of fighter: the 'composite' or 'compound' horseman, who could fight with both spear and bow.

Eventually the army was completely reorganized; horsemen took precedence, in place of the heavily equipped infantry of earlier periods. This change is usually attributed to the Justinianic period. The new horsemen were widely used in Belisarios's campaigns and later on by Maurice. Some scholars have even gone so far as to propose that this innovation in the art of war gave Byzantium an advantage against the Avars and Persians, and contributed to the Byzantine victories during the late 6th and early 7th centuries. An important innovation of this period (late 6th or 7th century) seems to have been the use of stirrups, almost certainly adopted from the Turkic Avars.[22]

A protracted debate has taken place around the appearance and military use of the traction-powered artillery piece, known usually as the traction trebuchet (as opposed to the counterweight trebuchet introduced in the 11th and 12th centuries).[23] This was basically a beam pivoting around an axle powered by handlers pulling ropes. Its use was first recorded in the late 6th century during the Avar-Slav siege of Thessaloniki. The machine would obviously have been in use earlier on, yet it remains unknown when and by whom it was introduced. During or slightly before the 6th century, torsion-powered artillery (such as the onager) gradually went out of use, while tension machines (large ballistae) were operated continuously.[24]

In any case, the Byzantine army of this period was an effective, well-organized body, whose main fighting unit was the 'composite' horseman fighting with both spear and bow. He was supported by heavy and lightly armed infantry, along with groups of allied forces. In times of peace, these army units would probably be stationed in the fortifications of the great cities of the empire; in times of conflict they would fight from the fortresses of each war zone. They were combined with local guards and the limitanei along the borders, who served as the permanent garrisons of frontier defences.

The temporary or permanent use of fortifications to counter enemy threats in each period was especially true for linear fortifications (a type widely used in this period), which required large and well-equipped forces. When Justinian withdrew the professional forces from the Thermopylae walls and replaced them with local militia (non-professional guards provided by the cities), he was accused by Prokopios of weakening the defences, resulting in their collapse and raiding by barbarians. However, Prokopios's text shows that there existed locally organized militias provided by the population which participated in the defence of their territory, although they would otherwise be hard (even impossible) to detect based on surviving evidence.

Indeed, what is clear from the sources of this period is the (real or intended) strict control and command exercised by the central authority in Constantinople. Even though the emperor himself rarely fought (with the exception of Maurice and Herakleios), he had to ensure that no general could become powerful enough to challenge his status. In the same way, all the fortifications were – in theory – constructed and commanded by the centre. Whether imperial authority sanctioned local initiatives and *fait accompli*, or indeed fully controlled the war effort, is in most cases hard to prove.

The same also goes for the logistics of war: through the sources we get the impression of an ever-present emperor overseeing the recruitment, supply, and armament of his fighting forces. In any case, it seems safe to assume that both food supplies (through the institution of the *Annona militaris*) and armament (through the construction of various *fabricae*) were provided by the state, through a system whose origins date back to the 4th century.[25] This obviously worked in a different way in the various border territories, which were more easily managed and where logistics could be covered by local sources (such as Egypt, Syria and Palestine).[26] Yet it was remarkably sophisticated in other areas, for example in the case of the complex network that provisioned the Danube garrisons and fortresses: victuals from the in-kind taxes (*Annona*) owed by the producer provinces (Egypt, Syria, South Asia Minor, etc.) had to be collected, stored, and transferred over long distances.[27] This system had far-reaching socioeconomic results for the internal markets of the empire and archaeological evidence (shipwrecks, amphorae, etc.) helps us reconstruct these networks of production and distribution.

When it came to recruitment, whether voluntary or compulsory, selective or massive, it seems again that a variety of solutions were put forward depending on the state's needs at a given moment.[28] It is through this process, fortuitous and local, rather than controlled from a distant capital, that we should understand the renewal of military skills brought to the army through the recruitment of warlike people (even erstwhile enemies). Indeed the Byzantine army of this period was an innovative force that allowed experimentation in tactics and strategy; the same is partially true when we consider the fortifications this army manned.

Fortifications

From the 5th century onwards a large fortification programme seems to have been put in place in the Balkans, although this view is not shared by all scholars.[29] According to a decree bearing the signature of Emperor Theodosios II, all cities should be fortified, and responsibility for the whole scheme was given to the *magister militum* Herculius. Constantinople, Thessaloniki, Hexamilion, Corinth, Sparta, Butrint, and Onchesmos (Saranda) are usually included in this programme, which may have continued into the next century, through the efforts of Anastasios and Justinian (see below).

Two reasons are put forward for this massive endeavour. According to the first, it was initiated after the shock given to the ancient world by Alaric's sack of Rome in 410, and its purpose was to secure the Balkans against similar raids. The Gothic and Hunnic migrations and wars had a serious impact on the population and the government, and fortifications were seen as a means of re-establishing peace and security. The 5th-century Hunnic successes in besieging walled cities showed that military works had to be strengthened, not only in the frontier zones (as presumably was done in the 3rd and 4th centuries) but everywhere in the Empire.[30] The second reason for the fortification programme was the threat of an attack, whether real or perceived, from the forces of the Western Roman State wanting to integrate the Balkan peninsula into the Western Roman orbit.[31]

During this period existing fortifications in the eastern provinces were maintained in their original form, and only occasionally do we hear of any new building. The case of Amorium is representative: this fortification was attributed to an imperial donation which aimed to enhance the city with public buildings rather than protect it from attack.

At the end of the 5th century Emperor Anastasios is credited with a number of new fortification programmes as part of his much-admired policy for protecting the state. Some of them were intended to enhance the places where they were carried out as well as improving their defences; for instance, the walls of Durrës (Dyrrachion), his native town, were coupled with an imposing amphitheatre. The erection of the Long Wall of Thrace was praised by all contemporaries as a necessary protection for the immediate surroundings of the imperial capital. Along the eastern borders with Persia, Anastasios embarked on a massive fortification programme, erecting numerous new fortifications or repairing existing ones (most, alas, known only from written sources), the most prominent among them being Daras.[32]

Justinian is credited by Prokopios with the erection of countless fortifications in all the provinces. Despite the debate about the patronage of these works, it seems that Justinian actively pursued a strategy of fortification building as part of his wider defensive policy, perhaps continuing in the footsteps of Anastasios.[33]

Were they part of a far-reaching strategy or simply a means to economize forces? The fact remains that among surviving monuments, many can be ascribed to this age, either in the Balkans (for example the restoration of Hexamilion) or in the eastern provinces (Zenobia and Resafa). The most cohesive fortification programme credited to Justinian remains the one implemented once the North African province was reoccupied, which is well documented in surviving in situ inscriptions. Some other defences appear to be unrelated to a wider fortification strategy, such as the walls of the Sinai monastery and a number of smaller walled settlements. This was especially evident in the Balkans, where the walls may have compensated for the lack of adequate garrisons.[34] It seems Justinian was trying, with the least possible effort, to avoid conflict on his northern frontier while he was actively engaged on the eastern and western borders of the empire. His policy of buying off the barbarian tribes, or turning them against each other, proved on the whole unsuccessful. The various fortifications were unable to function properly without garrisons, and Slavs and Huns raided all the way down to Thermopylae and the Corinth isthmus.

One unusual feature of this period is that we have for the first time information concerning architects (named as μηχανικοί in the sources) employed to design fortifications.[35] Chrysis of Alexandria built the walls and the city of Daras, while the walls of Zenobia were restructured by two young architects, John of Constantinople and Isidore the Younger. This was not perhaps the normal practice, which explains why we have no similar evidence from earlier or later periods. The buildings concerned should be considered as 'extraordinary' commissions, given to people of elevated status and education in science and mathematics, who were deemed able to meet the specific challenges these projects represented. In this we can detect the pattern followed by Justinian in the case of Hagia Sophia, Constantinople, where he employed Anthemios of Tralles and Isidore of Mileto. For the bulk of the remaining monuments, however, anonymous, local master builders and their workshops (known variously in the sources as 'architectones') were commissioned but never recorded in surviving evidence.

Fortifications in the Balkans

In the Balkan provinces of the empire the surviving examples can be grouped together into specific types that were used at the same time during the period. The first group includes fortified cities. In the metropolitan city of Constantinople this meant the replacement of the earlier smaller enclosure with a work of epic proportions and sophistication that proved its effectiveness for almost ten centuries. Larger fortifications replaced earlier walls in a number of other provincial cities, such as Butrint, or were even built anew, as in Dyrrachion. However, in the majority of the cities, new walls were usually built within the circumference of the pre-existing walls. In other words, the Early Byzantine fortifications were built in such a way as to cut off part of a Roman or classical wall, creating a smaller fortified area.

The most logical interpretation is that the existing walls no longer fulfilled the needs of the population, which had either outgrown the walls or – more often – diminished. It could also be that there had been no change in the population and the aim was to enable the city to resist impending raids with smaller military forces; this would be easier to achieve if the population and the garrison defended a considerably smaller enclosure.

The size of the circumference could also be related to the identity of the defenders. If the sites were seats of large military contingents, perhaps sections of the *comitatenses*, then the necessary numbers were readily available to man extensive walls. In the opposite case, fewer numbers of people would stand a better chance of survival if defending a smaller perimeter. Indeed, the question should be answered for each case separately, provided that archaeological research can define the size of each settlement in relation to its walls (in most cases still a desideratum).

The second form of fortification comprises the long walls. These are linear fortifications of considerable length that reinforce natural obstacles by cutting off a peninsula or a mountain pass, so as to create an obstacle to raiders or armies who have neither the time nor the ability to effectively mount a siege or go around the wall. It goes without saying that this category of fortifications is again connected to the sort of enemies the state had to face, that is, those moving overland and almost never threatening the safety of naval communications, which remained firmly in the hands of the Byzantines. The long walls of this period can be seen as a revival of the linear fortifications of Early Roman times. However, Roman fortifications were very differently conceived. They were built across the borders of the empire and their course took advantage – wherever possible – of the terrain, rivers, high ground, etc. The goal was practical as well as symbolic. The walls represented the physical boundary of the empire, continually manned and serving as a meeting place between the inhabitants of the empire and the barbarians beyond. Early Byzantine walls are always found within the imperial territory, and their aim was to cut off the advance of the enemy. This does not make them less monumental. Of all the monuments antiquity has bequeathed us, the Long Wall of Thrace was the most impressive linear fortification of mainland Europe, comparable only to Hadrian's Wall in Britain. The continuous manning of these walls, however, is questionable, and frankly illogical, since a wall such as the one at Hexamilion was only rarely attacked in the course of the 5th century. Left without garrisons, such walls could be easily overcome by raiding parties or invading forces.

Finally, a number of small fortified settlements (forts, fortified hilltops, watchtowers, island forts) are slowly being investigated archaeologically and documented (as in the areas of Epirus).[36] Their interpretation always needs to take into account regional requirements and the nature of the landscape: that is, those factors that have influenced their construction and use at a particular moment. Usually contemporary sources remain silent about these works, with the exception of Prokopios, who recorded the numerous forts Justinian built along the northern frontiers of the Danube river. As mentioned above, the emperor had instigated a policy of confrontation and containment against his northern enemies, based on numerous strongholds spread over the northern provinces. It is certain that, although their builders cannot be identified, these sites constituted a vast category of fortifications, one that will be further investigated in future.

Of the Balkan cities whose walls have been attributed to this period, the most important group includes the walls of Constantinople, along with a number of civic centres in Thrace which were in the vicinity or in direct contact (through the Via Egnatia or the sea) with the capital. As previously mentioned, many researchers attribute the main phase of the walls of Thessaloniki to the early or mid-5th century.

In **Constantinople**[37] the earlier Constantinian walls, which enclosed the peninsula on which the city was built, were extended in the early 5th century in order to incorporate a large area to the west. Significant effort was given to the mainland side, where the walls stretch to a length of *c.* 5.7km in a curvilinear line from the Golden Horn to the Marmara Sea (*see* Plate 10); the original line between the Tekfur Saray and Golden Horn was later altered and is now completely lost). The sea walls on both sides of the peninsula, however, simply continued the line of the Severian and Constantinian walls, and were a relatively weak curtain, regulated by rectangular towers; small parts of those earlier walls survive.

The Theodosian land walls are composed of three integral parts: an inner (main) wall, an outer wall and a moat (*see* Plate 11). The broad moat was protected on the city side by a low parapet with crenellations. Behind this parapet lay the first line of defence, in front of the outer wall. The outer wall with its towers protected the second line of defence, an area known as the precinct ($\Pi\varepsilon\rho\acute{\iota}\beta o\lambda o\varsigma$), with a width of *c.* 15–20m. Behind it lay the main wall with its massive towers. The whole defensive zone had a width that varied between 27 and 55m.

This defensive system survives in full only in a few stretches, and on closer inspection it seems that its history was much more complicated and perhaps less systematic than was first thought. For example, the moat probably did not cover

Plate 10. Constantinople. View of the land walls. (*Photo:* David Hendrix)

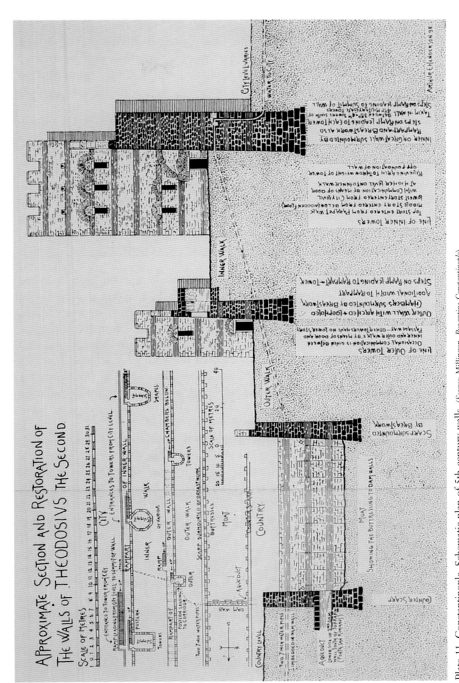

Plate 11. Constantinople. Schematic plan of 5th-century walls. *(Source: Millingen, Byzantine Constantinople)*

the complete length of the walls – it may not have been built as part of the original plan – and whether it was a water or dry moat is still uncertain. Similar questions exist for some parts of the outer and inner walls, which were in any case extensively rebuilt in later periods. There are also parts that were rebuilt for no apparent reason (such as the part known as *Sigma*), or simply disappeared (such as the whole north section).

In any case, in its preserved part the main wall (μέγα τείχος) was 5m thick and 12m high. It had a single platform to fire from at the battlement level, with its crenels reaching *c.*2m high (few if any of the original crenels have survived). The intervals between towers were *c.*70–75m. There were ninety-six towers, of which seventy-six were rectangular and twenty polygonal (almost all were repaired, replaced, or added in later periods). The towers were not structurally bonded to the wall and they stood 18–23m high. They had two vaulted storeys above ground, with no communication between them. They offered three lines of fire, with arrow slits (first storey), openings for ballistae (second storey), and a crenellated terrace fit for catapults (third storey).

The outer wall (ἔξω ἡ μικρόν τείχος) was 2.20m wide and 8m high, and had ninety-six alternately rectangular and semicircular (U-shaped) towers (again largely rebuilt). They were 15m high and 5m wide. They had two inner levels, a vaulted room with arrow slits and a roof with battlements above. Each of these towers was placed midway between two towers in the main wall, in order to maximize the flanking fire from the two lines of walls. The outer wall had two lines of defence: the lower had a series of blind arches, each with an embrasure for bows or hand-ballistae (largely altered in later centuries). The arches supported a wall-walk with battlements for the second line of defence. The outer wall was rather slender (0.50–1.15m.) and relatively weak.

The land walls were pierced by seven large gates and four smaller ones, while a large number of posterns opened at the sides of the towers (of both inner and outer walls); the latter enabled surprise attacks by the defenders against the besiegers. The main gates were always set between two towers and were combined with respective gates at the outer wall. The most monumental structure was the Golden Gate (Χρυσή Πύλη) with two rectangular towers protecting a triple-arched gateway (*see* Plate 12). The whole façade was covered with ashlar marble blocks, and sculptures decorated the roofs above the gate, which boasted gold-plated doors.

With the exception of certain key points, such as the Golden Gate, the land walls are almost uniformly constructed with a masonry of alternating layers of five courses of brick (extending through the thickness) and several courses of ashlar (a façade over a packed rubble core).

The sea wall across the Golden Horn has an equally complicated history, since it was an extension of pre-existing Constantinian and Severian fortifications, and at the same time was linked to isolated enclosures whose purpose and history are

Plate 12. Constantinople. The Golden Gate. (*Source*: Koç University – GABAM Archive)

difficult to decipher, such as the walls surrounding the area of Petrion (Fener), and the suburb of Blachernae (Ayvanserayi). The Golden Horn wall seems to have been a rectilinear curtain regulated by rectangular towers. Its height was *c.*10m and its length was *c.*5km. It had 110 towers; only two of its gates survive.

The seaside wall of the south coast of the city (the Sea of Marmara) is preserved to a larger extent. It had a total length of 8.5km and in its course it included the enclosure protecting the port of Agios Eleutherios (Yenikapı, with a perimeter measuring 1.1km). From the Marmara wall thirty-six main or secondary gates are preserved wholly or partly, together with 103 towers and tower projections. Originally it had 188 towers, many of which were rebuilt and repaired countless times over the centuries.

As for the date and history of the Constantinople walls, the current belief is that the land walls were probably conceptualized at the end of the 4th century (during the reign of Theodosios I, when the Golden Gate could have been independently built as a triumphal arch), construction started towards the end of Arkadios's reign (r. 383–408) and finished *c.*422 during the reign of Theodosios II (402–450). In 439 Theodosios II ordered the construction of the sea walls of the Golden Horn and the Marmara; responsibility for the scheme lay with Kyros Panopolitis, who was at the time the praetorian prefect. Throughout the 5th and 6th centuries there were numerous mentions of collapse and rebuilding due to earthquakes, for example in 447, 554, and 557. The fifty-seven towers destroyed in the earthquakes of 447 were rebuilt under the command of Constantinos, another praetorian prefect.

Very close to Constantinople lay the coastal city of **Herakleia Perinthos** (Marmara Ereğlisi, Turkey),[38] the main centre of the province of Europe during Late Antiquity. Parts of the walls that once surrounded the lower city are still

Plate 13. Herakleia Perinthos (Marmara Ereğlisi). Lower city walls next to the basilica.

preserved in good condition (*see* Plate 13). They are built with bands of bricks alternating with stones (the façades partly covered with ashlar blocks). Large U-shaped and pentagonal towers reinforce the curtain. The walls and towers are bonded together and belong to a single construction phase. The upper city walls were built with all-brick masonry. Two solid pentagonal towers were located 60m apart.

Four brickstamps from the lower city walls date them to the early 5th century, perhaps as part of the imperial policy of securing the route towards the capital. The upper city towers were probably of late 5th/early 6th-century construction.

On the Black Sea coastline of Thrace one of the most important naval stations was **Mesembria** (Nessebar, Bulgaria).[39] It occupied a promontory and so was a highly defensible position from the mainland. The site was surrounded by walls during the classical period, but they were extensively restructured in the middle to late 5th century. They were built following the *opus mixtum*, alternating bands of bricks and stones. On the side opposite the land, where the main (west) gate was situated, the walls were built on a double line (with main and outer walls), strengthened by rectangular and semicircular towers. The gateway was flanked by pentagonal towers, and consisted of a portcullis and a double-leaf gate. The construction of the walls is usually attributed to Emperor Anastasios.

Along the Via Egnatia, a couple of fortifications in Western Thrace (such as Komotini and Drama, Greece[40]), from which few parts are currently remaining, have been identified as military forts or small settlements, built perhaps in the early 5th century. The city of **Philippoi** (Greece),[41] on the other hand, was a major station along the Via Egnatia. The earlier Hellenistic city drew its prosperity from its pivotal position between Thessaloniki and Constantinople. The antique city walls followed an irregular layout, encircling an inner grid plan with streets connecting the wall gates. In this period the ancient Hellenistic wall was reconstructed and doubled with the addition of an outer wall. The latter was a simple curtain with no visible towers (at least in its preserved parts). It is assumed that it covered only the southern, more vulnerable, part of the enclosure. Due to extensive spoliation, there is little left standing; it was probably built with alternating bands of bricks and stones, using spolia in its construction. As to its date, it is usually attributed to the 5th or 6th century.

Among the fortified sites of the central Balkans attributed to this period (such as Golemo Gladište, North Macedonia)[42] extensive research has taken place in the newly founded city of **Justiniana Prima** (Caričin Grad, Serbia, *see* Plate 14),[43] the birthplace of Justinian. The city was formed of three interconnected walled sections (citadel, upper and lower town) covering the long and narrow shoulder of a plateau. The roughly circular citadel occupied the summit of the hill and protected the cathedral and episcopal palace; it was in fact a fortress within the fortress, protecting its occupants not only from exterior enemies, but perhaps

Plate 14. Justiniana Prima (Caričin Grad). Plan of the settlement. (*Source*: Vujadin Ivanišević)

also from the town population. The citadel was surrounded by the upper town, whose main section lay to the east and southeast, housing a number of administrative buildings. The lower town included a residential area, a bath-house and churches. The building sequence of these three entities is still contested, although they were all probably constructed within a restricted time frame. Three monumental city gates regulated traffic between the enclosures and opened to colonnaded streets. The main eastern gate was situated within a concave façade wall, flanked by a pair of projecting square towers. The south gate was flanked by pentagonal towers. By 535 Justinian had made the city the capital of an archbishopric and seat of a praetorian prefect. It continued to grow after the age of Justinian until it was overrun by invading Avars and Slavs in the early 7th century, and was abandoned.

A number of cities on the western Balkan littoral (situated in the Epirus Vetus and Nova provinces, in modern Greece and Albania), from north to south Dyrrachion, Onchesmos, Butrint, and Nikopolis, acquired enclosures during this period, each of them usually connected to an imperial initiative.

Dyrrachion (Durrës, Albania)[44] is located in one of the most important harbours along the Western Balkan littoral and served as the gateway to Italy along the Via Egnatia. The new walls surrounded a smaller part of the city than the older Roman walls, but their design and construction were most impressive (*see* Plate 15). They were strengthened with rectangular, circular and pentagonal towers. Their masonry was solid brick, which makes them stand out as exceptional, high-quality, work. Ćurčić attributed this either to the availability of

Plate 15. Dyrrachion (Durrës). View of the walls. (*Photo*: David Hendrix)

bricks from the older Roman walls or to the strategic importance of the city in the communication networks of the empire. The new walls were sponsored by Anastasios, who was a native of the city.

The seaside city of **Onchesmos** (Saranda, Albania),[45] another Hellenistic settlement, saw extensive additions during the Late Roman period, among them a fortification wall which defended only a portion of the city (a perimeter of *c.*850m). The walls followed the general layout of a pentagon. They were strengthened with circular, rectangular and pentagonal (prow-shaped) towers, set at regular intervals (26–27m apart). The remains of staircases led to a battlemented walkway. The north side was protected by an outer wall, which is documented in old photographs. The presence of a moat has been suggested. The surviving parts of this fortification, with a thickness of 2–2.50m, are built with a mortared rubble core and façades made of roughly hewn limestone blocks set in courses.

The wall has been attributed to the period of Emperor Anastasios (491–518). A destruction layer has been located in monuments (such as the city's basilica) as well as in some of the towers; it is dated to the time of Justin II (565–578) based on numismatic evidence. The excavator connected the city's destruction with a Slavic raid in 586–587. Afterwards, the city declined.

Butrint (Albania)[46] occupies a small peninsula formed by the Vivari channel, situated in the straits of Corfu. The citadel is at the highest point on the peninsula and the city occupied the area running down to the channel. During this period the whole settlement was fortified and only the far side of the channel was left outside the walls. The walls contained an area of 16ha, much larger than the older fortification of the 4th century BC which surrounded the citadel hill and a part of the hillside.

The walls were constructed entirely with rubble masonry, with no distinction between core and façade. In their course they have integrated older structures, which is evident in the southwest side by the Vivari channel, where a building of the 1st or 2nd century AD was used as part of the wall. In the wall to the west of the Channel Basilica is the sea gate, built upon a pre-existing street which entered the city from a strong Hellenistic gate that survived in the older precinct. Much of the Early Byzantine wall has been destroyed in the course of later building.

It seems that large sections of the old citadel walls were rebuilt or repaired. The gates of the old precinct were maintained, though repaired, which means there was a degree of continuity in the city's road system. The Lion Gate, where an ancient sculpture was reused to create a much smaller doorway, belongs to this period (*see* Plate 16).

The walls were erected in the 5th century, perhaps in the third quarter. Excavation proved that the walls on the channel side were dated to the late 5th or early 6th century, probably in the reign of Anastasios or Justinian. At the same

Plate 18. Hexamilion. The Byzantine forttress, view of the northeast gate. (*Photo:* N. Kardulias)

shallow, comprising a ditch cut in bedrock or soil, in which a layer of mortar was set. The wall was built in horizontal layers, and this is obvious in the core masonry, where each layer can be clearly seen. The core was not formed by stone rubble thrown in the gap between the façades; rather, the stones were laid in layers and then filled in with mortar. The façades were made of rectangular stones cut from the local Corinthian sandstone. The dimensions of the stones varied between 1.2 and 1.6m in length and 0.4 to 0.7m in height. Broken pieces of brick and lime mortar filled the voids. Layers of bricks were not used in any part of the original structure; where bricks have been found they must date from later repairs, probably carried out during the time of Justinian.

A feature of Hexamilion is the use of spolia from the nearby sanctuary of Poseidon and other ancient buildings in the area. This was for both practical and aesthetic reasons. It is also interesting to note the incorporation of pre-existing walls, for instance in the Roman baths at Isthmia, where the north wall was reinforced and used as the Hexamilion wall.

Archaeological research identified a total of sixty-eight towers; a few more may have been destroyed or have not yet been located. All were rectangular, with the exception of the towers at the gates of the fort. Those at the southeast gate were semicircular, while the ones at the south gate were externally octagonal. Usually the towers did not have an entrance at ground level and access was at first-floor level from the adjoining wall-walk. Most towers would have had a flat roof supported on a first-floor vaulted ceiling as platforms for ballistic machines. Towers were regularly constructed at relatively close distances (40–50m) in places where they were most vulnerable to attack. Many towers were not structurally bonded to the adjoining wall.

According to Prokopios, a series of forts reinforced the Hexamilion. The only one preserved is that of Isthmia. The aim was double: on the one hand to house the guards and on the other to serve as a meeting point and refuge for the defenders. The Isthmia fort is of irregular shape, with a length of 210m (north–south) and a width of 100–200m (east–west). The walls followed the fluctuations of the ground. A gate opened at the northeast side, and its towers functioned as observation posts looking out towards the area to the north. The fort covers an area of *c.*27ha and reflects the size of the garrison that camped within. Gregory estimated the manpower of the Isthmia fort at around 2,000, some staying in the fort, others living in Corinth or Acrocorinth.

Hexamilion was built in a single construction period in the time of Emperor Theodosios II. Its construction was supervised by Herculius (408–412), the praetorian prefect for Illyricum. It was abandoned in the mid-5th century, and afterwards the walls and towers functioned as residences, as shown by the female burials discovered there. The earthquakes of 522 and 551 probably reduced the defensive capability of the line. During Justinian's reign in 548–560 repairs were made, mainly at the northeast gate of the fort. According to the surviving *tabula ansata* inscription, Victorinus, probably the praetorian prefect of Illyricum, supervised the works. The goal was to reinforce the fortifications so that they could be defended by fewer soldiers. At the end of 6th and until the mid-7th century Hexamilion continued to be inhabited, but it is not known whether the inhabitants were soldiers or civilians, and they may have stayed there sporadically. Slavic ceramics were found in four places during the excavation.

To the north of Hexamilion, at the famous site of Thermopylae, there was another linear barrier, known as the **Dhema Pass** (Greece),[54] guarding the Oite-Kallidromos passage and securing the whole of central Greece. The fortification complex was constructed to exploit the naturally defensive characteristics of the pass and included two separate barrier walls at a distance of *c.*150m apart, a walled garrison stronghold, two (probable) signal or watch towers, and a massively constructed main portal or gateway (conjectural). All the buildings were made of mortared rubble using irregularly shaped stones, while pre-existing masonry was reintegrated into the Byzantine structure. The stronghold was roughly circular, covering *c.*0.5ha. One watchtower is circular, and the other is rectangular. The original portal was destroyed; it has been replaced by a wall with crenelles and a walkway covering a narrow gateway.

Based on C14 dating samples, two major construction periods have been suggested: the first in the second half of the 4th century and the second in the first half of the 5th century. It seems that both phases used the same construction techniques. Cherf considered the Dhema Pass as part of a local system of mountain fortifications which defended the southern tip of the Balkan peninsula.

He considered the 5th-century phase to be contemporary with the Hexamilion and the Walls of Constantinople. During the 6th century the Dhema Pass was described by Prokopios in the 'Hunnic' invasion of 539. The walls were valiantly defended, yet overcome. Afterwards Justinian ordered that a permanent garrison of 2,000 professional soldiers should be stationed there, replacing the limitanei of old.

Another linear wall was situated on the northern end of the **Kassandra** peninsula (Greece),[55] cutting off access to the western 'foot' of the Chalkidiki. The wall extended for *c.*1.2km and was intended to block the narrowest entrance to the peninsula from the north. There was a gateway at its centre. Only small parts of it are currently visible. According to Prokopios, Justinian rebuilt the wall after the destruction of the nearby city of Kassandreia by the Huns in 540.

The most monumental of these works was undoubtedly the **Long** or **Anastasian Wall** of Thrace (Turkey),[56] which lay at a distance of 65km to the west of Constantinople and stretched in a curvilinear formation from the Marmara to the Black Sea (*see* Plate 19). Its original length was *c.*45km; today less than half of it remains. It took advantage of the natural topography of the ground, and it followed the shortest route that made sense from a defensive point of view.

Research has been conducted on the central part of the wall, to the north and south of the modern junction of Derviş Kapı. This stretch is 3km long and has eighteen towers and one small fort. To a lesser extent the surviving northern section, as far as the Black Sea, has also been recorded. The defences had the

Plate 19. The Long Wall of Thrace. Detail of the walls. (*Photo*: James Crow)

following parts: a moat, the linear wall strengthened with towers, and a system of rectangular forts placed along the wall.

In Derviş Kapı, in front of the wall, there were well-preserved traces of a V-shaped moat that made use of a pre-existing quarry. It had a width of 11.13m and was placed 30m west of the wall; it is presently preserved to a depth of 2.5m. In the north parts of the wall, where the location was more naturally defensible, there was no moat.

As for the wall itself, in the part close to Derviş Kapı the masonry is made with a façade of (roughly) rectangular ashlar calcareous blocks with a rather hard lime mortar used as the binding material. The core is rubble, and bricks were used only for arches and vaults. The towers were pentagonal/prow-shaped, semi-circular, rectangular or polygonal. The form and distance of the towers varied greatly according to location. In the more vulnerable parts the towers were closer together, as in the south part of the wall, since the main access from the west was through the south side of the peninsula and the Via Egnatia. The thick vegetation and the rough terrain to the north prohibited the movement of large armies.

The most impressive towers are pentagonal, projecting almost 11.5m from the wall. Smaller rectangular towers often come in between them, projecting a mere 2m from the wall; these seem to have been an exclusive feature of this wall. Perhaps in the interior they housed double staircases for climbing to the wall-walk, allowing access to the walls and towers.

The distance between the towers varies from 80 to 120m, with the minimum being 60m and the maximum 150. Observations of this part of the wall suggest that originally there were at least 340 towers for the whole 56km length of the wall. The larger towers were probably intended to house catapults and would end up with a battlemented terrace; two interesting aspects of the towers are the triangular stones from the battlements and the complete absence of tiles.

In some parts the wall stands to a height of 5m, while in its northern part, as far as the Black Sea, it is often preserved to a height of *c.* 3m. It is estimated that the original height was more than 10m, with a width of *c.* 3.3–3.5m. One section of the wall, to the north of Derviş Kapı, had blind arches on the inner side that probably supported the wall-walk. In this section the width of the wall is smaller, 1.6–1.8m, reaching a total of 3.10m with the arches. The arches are 3.15m across, and their original height would have been *c.* 4.4m. It is possible that there was originally a double series of arches set one above the other, but the upper ones were destroyed, together with the adjoining wall. The total wall height to the wall-walk is calculated to be more than 10m.

As for the forts that would house the guards, in the part from the Black Sea down to the south of Derviş Kapı a total of six forts were recorded, set at distances of *c.* 3.5km apart. All the forts were built on the inner side of the wall. They were rectangular and had facing gates on opposite sides. The use of blind arches on the inner ground level is also attested in the forts.

was connected to a pre-existing citadel and acquired its present triangular form probably in the period after 545. The emperor commissioned two young engineers for the job, John of Constantinople and Isidore of Miletos the younger.

The fortified settlement of **Resafa-Sergioupolis-Anastasioupolis** (Syria)[63], built around the shrine of the popular St Sergios, included an oasis in the Syrian desert with many underground water sources. The walled area is a trapezoid; its defences consist of earthen outworks (with a rampart/dyke and a shallow moat) and a built enclosure that survives almost to its full height (*see* Plate 21). It is strengthened with large towers, rectangular, pentagonal, and circular (at the corners), all set at regular intervals. These alternate with smaller rectangular turrets, open-gorged and allowing for direct communication with the wall-walk. The main entrance is a monumental structure with a broad gate for carriages to pass through; three of the main gates are protected by an outer wall (barbican). The enclosure walls are solid up to a height of 6m, where they form a series of open vaults on the inner side. Defenders could circulate through the vaults, which also served as defensive positions for archers. At the top of the walls there is a continuous parapet with arrow slits (and no crenellations).

The site was inhabited from the 8th century BC to the 13th century AD. The settlement flourished from the late 4th century AD onwards due to the popularity of St Sergios. The earlier sections of the walls were built at the turn of the 6th century AD and were a lavish structure; they were concluded in a more functional way in 503–526; earthquakes, along with extensive adjustments in the built parts, happened perhaps during the period 532–540.

As well as frontier sites, a number of **inland civic centres** (such as Hierapolis, Amorium, Caesarea, Anazarbos and Antioch) were provided with impressive fortifications during this period and these have attracted the attention of researchers.

The city of **Hierapolis** (Pamukkale, Turkey)[64] lies on a Phrygian plateau overlooking the valley of the Lycos river. The walls enclosed not only the commercial centre (agora) but the whole former Hellenistic city. There were no walls on the west side of the city, where the abrupt slope served as a natural boundary. The course of the walls followed the original grid plan of the city, even though they used at least two buildings that had been damaged in the 4th-century earthquake, and destroyed a number of water-pipe lines when building the walls. The masonry of the fortification incorporated large quantities of well-cut material from earlier monuments that were in the agora, like the stoa and the Early Roman theatre, as well as other buildings that lay in ruins. It had twenty-four square towers, two main gates and a number of side gates.

The towers are solid, with no internal rooms, at least in their surviving parts. The main gates lie at both ends of the (main) Frontinus Street (*see* Plate 22). They are similar in shape, with a relatively narrow opening surrounded by two

Plate 21. Resafa. View of the walls. (*Source:* https://www.flickr.com/photos/sillie_r/)

Plate 22. Hierapolis (Pamukkale). The Frontinus Street and the North Gate. (*Photo*: Görkem Günay)

powerful rectangular towers. Above the horizontal lintel there is a relief arch. Decoration in the form of an eight-ray star or reused Roman lion and Medusa heads were probably placed for apotropaic purposes. The wall had a width of 2.50m; its original height remains unknown (although a part in the south side of the agora is preserved to a height of 4.10m).

The enclosure was, in all probability, built in the early 5th century, a sign of the insecurity that reigned in the area as a result of barbarian invasions. Its use continued into the first half of the 7th century, when it was damaged by an earthquake.

The city of **Amorium** (Hisarköy/Afyon, Turkey)[65] was a large settlement: it is estimated that its inhabited area covered more than 50ha. The city lay on the south military road that connected Constantinople to the eastern borders, passing from Dorylaion (Eskişehir) and Ikonion (Konya) to the plains of Cilicia. The area was divided into two sectors, the upper city and the lower city (*see* Plate 23). The upper city occupied a hill, 5ha in size and *c.*20m. high, the result of continuous habitation from prehistoric times. The lower city lay to the south and east of the hill.

The walls of this period surrounded the whole lower city circumference; this huge length was their primary feature. Only their course is preserved, with foundation stones visible throughout the area. A small part with a gate has been excavated at the southwestern side, and based on that we can estimate that there was a single line of fortifications with no outer wall, reinforced with towers and dotted with gates along its perimeter. In the excavated part the lower courses of

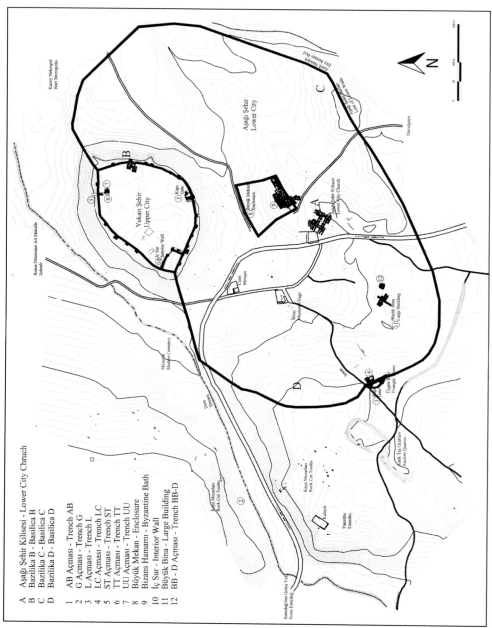

A Aşağı Şehir Kilisesi - Lower City Chruch
B Bazilika B - Basilica B
C Bazilika C - Basilica C
D Bazilika D - Basilica D

1 AB Açması - Trench AB
2 G Açması - Trench G
3 L Açması - Trench L
4 LC Açması - Trench LC
5 ST Açması - Trench ST
6 TT Açması - Trench TT
7 UU Açması - Trench UU
8 Büyük Mekan - Enclosure
9 Bizans Hamamı - Byzantine Bath
10 İç Sur - Interior Wall
11 Büyük Bina - Large Building
12 BB - D Açması - Trench BB-D

Plate 23. Amorium (Hisarköy). Plan of the fortifications. (*Source*: Amorium Excavations Project)

the wall are made of large, well-cut blocks, while the upper parts are built with courses of smaller stones with rough fronts. No spolia or reused material from the Roman town or the cemeteries has been observed in the structure. A second similar wall on the inner side of the rampart was interpreted as a retaining element, or for enclosing the area with the staircases that would lead to the wall-walk and the battlements.

The gate had an opening of *c.* 4m and a horizontal lintel of well-cut stones that were connected together with angles. The lack of thresholds or holes for door frames led to the conclusion that perhaps there was a portcullis falling from above. The gate was protected on its right by a large triangular tower that would have been multi-storeyed originally. Another similar tower also existed, perhaps on the other side of the gate. A barbican, a small outer wall creating a small yard in front of the gate, was uncovered outside the tower.

The refoundation of Amorium is attributed by later sources to the Emperor Zeno (474–491). Specimens of wood from the excavated tower were dated to shortly after 487, thus placing the tower's construction in the late 5th century (during the reign of either Zeno or Anastasios). The masonry of the walls points to a date between the mid-5th and mid-6th centuries, and it is very similar to the first phase of the basilica excavated in the lower city. They were probably erected at a time of peace, since there was time to quarry new material and to complete the work. The fortification of Amorium, a grandiose monumental construction, can therefore be confirmed as the result of imperial sponsorship.

In the city of **Caesarea** (Kayseri, Cappadocia, Turkey)[66] the walls of the Byzantine (and later Seljuk) city are found in the centre of the modern settlement, preserved in many parts throughout their course. Based on differences in the masonry, two parts can clearly be discerned: the north and the south. The north part of the walls has a façade of large and well-cut blocks of volcanic rock. It comprises a series of rectilinear ramparts reinforced with rectangular towers built at intervals of 40–50m. In some cases they are open at the rear (open-gorged), and probably contained the staircases that led to the wall-walk. The walls reached a height of at least 15m, and their width was *c.* 2m. On the inner side solid buttresses (1.60m wide) support a series of double arches. Therefore the wall at wall-walk level would have had a width of 3.50m.

Only a small section of the south part of the enclosure survives, at its east end. Its width is 2.50m. It is built with reused material, and has triangular towers at intervals of 25m. The towers probably had an inner five-sided room and in some places had arrow slits on the second floor. The ascent to the wall-walk was through staircases at the inner side of the wall, and the wall stands uniformly to a height of 5m above ground, but with no indication as to its original height.

Based on written sources, the Hellenistic and Roman cities were without walls until 241 AD, when a large wall was built; it was documented by numismatic evidence and an inscription. Parts of this enclosure have been identified recently in the hills surrounding the city. In the third quarter of the 4th century St Basil complained about the ruined state of the fortification. According to Prokopios, in the mid-6th century Justinian reduced the immense enclosure, cutting off many parts built on the hills and reinforcing the remaining parts. Two different dates have been proposed, both tentative, for the surviving parts (north and south): according to the first, the north part was constructed in 241, while the south part is attributed to Justinian. The second, which seems to be more widely accepted, attributes the north wall to Justinian, and suggests that the south wall is Seljuk in date.

Anazarbos in Cilicia (Turkey)[67] was an important Roman metropolis, covering an area of *c.* 100ha. It followed an orthogonal grid system, with a monumental colonnaded street, oriented north–south. The city acquired two rings of walls. The first enclosed almost the entire Roman city; it is only partially preserved and usually dated to the 4th century (the reign of Theodosios I). The second set of walls was more impressive and is fully intact in its lower levels, but it protected a significantly smaller inhabited area. The fortification consisted of three elements: a fortified ditch, an outer wall and a main wall. The main wall was strengthened with eighty rectangular towers set very close together. The outer wall also formed the inner side of the ditch, and its main features were small rectangular retaining pillars (buttresses).

The fortification was constructed with huge limestone blocks, except for the upper parts of the main wall, where smaller stones were used. All the material came from the surrounding buildings; for example, the south part of the main wall was built entirely of stone seats from the nearby theatre. Both walls incorporated an impressive triumphal arch (2nd century AD), which stood independently at the end of the city's colonnaded street and became a monumental city gate.

Various dates for the second ring of walls have been proposed: either that the parts with the large blocks were Byzantine, while those with the smaller ones were 12th- to 14th-century Armenian constructions; or that two phases (the first with the ditch and outer wall, and the second with the main wall) should be dated to the 9th and 10th centuries, while under Arab occupation. The latest research, however, supports a date in the 6th century (during the reign of Justinian).

Of the monumental walls that defended the Syrian metropolis of **Antioch** (Antakya, Turkey)[68] very few traces still remain today. Original parts were depicted in 18th-century engravings and later photos. The walls covered a substantial area: they followed the mountain line of Mt Silpius, at the peak of which lay the citadel, and then descended to the plain below. Their features are some of the best examples of the period: tall rectangular and polygonal (pentagonal/prow-shaped or heptagonal) towers protected a high curtain. Parts were built with alternating brick bands and stone blocks, while other parts used ashlar masonry. In one section the inner (upper) part of the walls was supported by blind arches.

The gates had monumental façades and were flanked by towers; the Beroea Gate seems to have been protected also by an outer wall (or barbican?). Based on the visual record, Crow has attributed some of the parts to the early 5th century.

Fortifications in the North Africa[69]

In the territories conquered by Justinian in Africa (the exact limits of these territories is a matter of debate), the fortification system that was created differed from the older Roman one.[70] The Byzantines did not concentrate their power in frontier strongholds, nor did they reuse the older Roman defences (generically known as the *Fossatum Africae*), which, in any case, lay outside the reoccupied territories. Instead they spread their forces throughout the area and maintained a network of forts that functioned as strongholds for the army and as refuges for the population. Set next to earlier Roman settlements, with access to water and land resources, these military bases allowed the Byzantine forces to deploy quickly and to defeat marauding Berbers. The defence-in-depth system employed in Africa in fact followed the defensive strategy applied in all other imperial lands.

The main difference from the rest of the empire was that most of the 6th-century African fortifications were not improvements or adjustments of pre-existing defences but were constructed from scratch, often reusing readily available building material. Many of the surviving monuments have a single construction phase – often identified by dedicatory inscriptions – as many of these sites were not reused in later periods. These fortifications align with Late Roman military practice while also meeting local needs and conditions.

Based on size, Pringle divided the fortifications into three categories:[71]

1. Large forts, citadels or walled cities. The plans are, in most cases, rectangular with projecting towers, following the quadriburgium type of ancient Hellenistic prototypes, also used in the Diocletian-Constantinian period. There are also examples where the wall creates angles/indentations, another characteristic that has existed since Hellenistic times.
2. Small forts intended to house a larger garrison but with a size less than *c.* 1.5ha. Their plans are typically rectangular, with rectangular projecting towers, usually placed at the corners, again following the quadriburgium type.
3. Smaller constructions, such as isolated towers, which were usually rectangular. In Africa there are hundreds of *gsur* or *ksour*, fortified habitations that date from the 3rd to the 7th centuries, although some continue well into the Islamic era. Only three such towers can be securely dated to the 6th century based on epigraphic material. They probably served as barracks for the garrisons that would patrol the neighbouring settlements.

It is interesting to note that most of these fortifications were similarly constructed, with façades of ashlar masonry (often reused from earlier Roman sites) covering a rubble core. The walls had a thickness of *c.* 2.5m and reached a height of *c.* 10m. They rarely had additional works, such as outer walls and moats. Most towers were rectangular, with very few exceptions (circular and hexagonal). This lack of elaborate defensive features has been regarded as a sign of limited economic resources or as a statement about the perceived weakness of the expected attackers (the Berber nomadic groups).

Among the walled cities, **Ammaedara** (Haidra, Tunisia)[72] is one of the best preserved. It was located on the route from Carthage to Teveste. The Byzantine citadel was at the centre of the older Roman city; it is an irregular quadrilateral, measuring *c.* 125 × 195m, with its walls reaching, at points, a height of 7–8m (*see* Plate 24). All the towers are square, except for a single circular one. The wall-walk that ran around the top of the walls was carried on blind arches along the east and (part of the) west sides. The masonry includes a lot of older structural material on the façades, covering a rubble core. Vertical joints between the wall sections have been interpreted as the work of different workshops. Prokopios mentions that it was walled by Justinian.

The city of **Theveste** (Tebessa, Algeria)[73] overlooked the relatively fertile plain of Merdja and functioned as a market centre for the wider area. It was also strategically located along four major communication lines. The walls, *c.* 2m thick and rising to a height of 9–10m, enclosed a large, roughly rectangular area

Plate 24. Ammaedara (Haidra). View of the walls. (*Photo:* Julian Myles Fidler)

(290 × 260m); they were built with ashlar façades and a rubble core. The wall-walk was carried on blind arches at some sections and on corbels on others. The enclosure was flanked by fifteen rectangular towers, spaced *c.* 95m apart and rising to heights of *c.* 16m. At the side between each tower and the adjacent wall there were 'corbelled chambers' (perhaps box machicolations?), which were square (*c.* 1.20m) and could be entered from the wall-walk. Pringle interpreted them as observation posts or latrines. They could also double as machicolations.

Three gates were recorded, but either they have not survived or they have been altered significantly. The main (west) gateway (also known as Porte de Solomon) was a vaulted passage, flanked by two rectangular towers; it had a double-leaf gate on the outer face and a portcullis on its inner side.

According to a currently lost inscription, the walls were constructed by the Patrician Solomon (probably in the period 536–544) and set in the gateway that blocked the Caracalla Arch. The walls were largely intact until the French occupation (1851), after which they were remodelled to fit the needs of a garrison town; parts were demolished in the mid-20th century.

Lepcis Magna (Lebda, Libya)[74] was an important ancient port at the mouth of the Wadi Lebda, yet by the 5th century it had been deserted. Archaeological work has revealed two defensive walls, both surrounding a small area around the harbour. It seems that the outer enclosure (covering an area of 44ha) was quickly abandoned (and dismantled) in favour of the second, more reduced one (28ha). The pre-existing Severan forum was included in both and was probably turned into a redoubt, likely the seat of the military commander.

The walls are strengthened with rectangular towers, many of them flanking the city gates. There is no sign of an outer wall or a moat. Their masonry is solidly built with reused blocks, and there is no differentiation between the core and the façades. The fact that both walls are similarly built indicates a single building phase, during which the plans were changed in favour of the reduced fortifications.

Lepcis Magna is described by Prokopios, and its walls are attributed to Justinian, along with a palace and a church; the enclosure was probably completed by 543, when Dux Sergios lured in and slayed the local leaders.

One of the best-preserved fortresses in Africa is **Thamugadi** (Timgad, Algeria).[75] It occupied part of a former Roman colony that had been abandoned during Vandal rule. The Early Byzantine fort occupied the area to the south of the older Roman city; it was chosen due to the presence of a natural spring (known as *aqua septimiana felix*), and a Roman cistern was included in the enclosure. The fort is rectangular, with inner dimensions of 111.25 × 67.50m (*see* Plate 25). The sides and corners are protected by eight rectangular towers, one of which houses the main gate (at the centre of the north side).

The walls have a thickness of *c.* 2.50m and are preserved to a height of over 15m in certain parts. They are constructed with façades from well-cut stones – mostly

Plate 25. Thamugadi (Timgad). Interior view of the Byzantine fort. (*Source*: Sellami Mohamed Tewfik)

reused ancient material – and a core of rubble masonry. The towers were accessed from the ground floor of the interior of the fort and at first floor from the wall-walk (or external ladders) since the tower floors were not linked in the preserved examples. Not all towers were structurally bonded to the adjoining walls, which has been accredited either to different workshops working side-by-side or to the construction of different parts of the fort happening at different rates or at different times.

The main entrance opens at the ground level of a tower-gate on the mid-north side. The tower projects from the wall by 6.55m. The entrance had two doorways 7.50m apart. The external one is closed with a portcullis; the internal one is a two-leaf door secured by a horizontal bar. Small rooms in the walls around the gate were interpreted as places for installing the portcullis mechanism. Lesser gates were constructed on all sides of the fort.

Prokopios attributed the fortress to Justinian. During excavations three identical inscriptions were found, which probably adorned three of the four gates. Based on their text, *Cibitas Tamogadiensis* was constructed by the patrician Solomon in the 13th year of the reign of Justinian and Theodora (1 April 539 to 1 April 540). It continued being used up to the first half of the 7th century, since the last testimony is an inscription from the reign of Constantine III in 641.

Madavros (M'Daourouch, Algeria)[76] also lay on the road from Carthage to Theveste. The Byzantine fortress was constructed at the centre of the city and occupied part of the Roman forum. Its plan appears somewhat odd because it includes a semicircular side. It has been shown that they started building it as a larger rectangle (measuring 38 × 63m), but during construction they decided to use the semicircle of a destroyed Roman theatre for the foundations of the northwest wall; it ultimately covered an area of 0.17ha. Three of the fort walls are internally articulated with blind arches, which supported the walkway at a height of *c.* 11.50m above ground level. Rectangular corner towers flanked the south and east corners. The main entrance was a tower-gate, with two gates, situated midway along the south-east wall. The outer gate still preserves a bilingual foundation inscription above its lintel. According to the inscription, the fort was again the work of Solomon (who was both military and civil governor of Byzantine Africa), in the period 534–544.

The surviving parts of the fort are constructed with ashlar façades over a rubble core, both of which make use of reused material from earlier buildings. Pre-existing structures were also used as foundations and incorporated into the walls.

Limisa (Ksar Lemsa, Tunisia)[77] was a small fort occupying a hill 500m above the Roman city. It is almost square in plan, with a side length of *c.* 30m, strengthened with four towers at the corners. It is one of the best-preserved monuments in North Africa. Except for the south-east wall, the remaining fortress stands at its original height. The walls, with a thickness of *c.* 2.20m, rose to a height of 10–12m, ending with a battlemented walkway. They were built with ashlar façades and a rubble core. All towers had four storeys and wooden floors, although their dimensions and arrangements differ. The fort, based on a displaced inscription, was probably constructed between 585 and 600, during the reign of Maurice.

Chapter 3

What Makes an 'Early Byzantine' Fortification?

This chapter offers an overview of the structural and defensive features that the fortifications of the Eastern Roman Empire shared from the 3rd to the 6th century. These features make them stand out from earlier and later works, and eventually helped architectural historians to date these structures to this period. However, none of these elements was used only in this period or only in this part of the world, since they all belonged to a grand repertoire developed globally as a response to the offensive weapons available in the pre-gunpowder era. One has to bear in mind that every fortification is constructed in response to the power of the expected enemy and does not always reflect, therefore, the wealth or sophistication of the builder. It is therefore the combination of a number of defensive attributes, when envisaged within their historical framework, which can lead us to assign a specific structure to this historical period. This is especially true in cases where historical sources are silent and researchers have to rely solely on the preserved walls. In a number of such sites a Late Roman/Early Byzantine date has been ascribed purely on the basis of the construction/defensive features (as in the case of Drama, Greece, which was probably a military installation that later turned into a city).[1]

Masonry – Construction Materials

The main characteristic of Early Byzantine masonry is the continuation of the Roman tradition of distinguishing between the core and the façades of the wall. In most places the cores are of rubble masonry, with uncut or roughly hewn stones mingled with lime mortar. The advantage of mortared rubble is that it applies less pressure to the surrounding masonry. When connected to the façades with stretchers/binders in a masonry known in antiquity as *emplekton* (header-and-stretcher), the walls could be both thinner and higher. Height augmented the range of ballistic machines; at the same time, since the expected enemy usually lacked artillery, the walls did not have to be quite so thick.

However, different façade techniques appear in the same provinces, and at present it is not known what the determining factor for this choice was. Therefore, the general rule usually found in older architectural handbooks (that the Balkans, western Asia Minor and the capital were using stone and brick, while the eastern provinces used solely ashlar stones), although largely reliable, has to be applied cautiously when it comes to fortifications.

It is true that in the **Aegean provinces** (the Balkans, western Asia Minor) one of the most common masonry styles is a rubble core and a stone façade, both intersected by horizontal brick bands[2] that act as a structural bonding system. The façade can be covered by a variety of stones (from roughly hewn to well-cut), depending on the importance of the fortification or even the importance of different sections of the same fortification (if visible or centrally placed). The walls of Constantinople and Thessaloniki are largely built with this system, and the same is true of Nikopolis. Bricks are extensively, almost invariably, used for the vaults (i.e., within towers), as well as for any sort of arched construction.

However, in the Golden Gate of Constantinople, the walls are covered with ashlar marble blocks. Parts of the Thessaloniki walls are constructed entirely with bricks, both façade and core; they are also decorated with successive arches that continue to the core, thus also acting as relieving arches. Furthermore, one group of fortifications was constructed without bricks but rather with raw stones in the core and well-cut ones (sometimes reused from older buildings, see below) on the façade, as in Hexamilion and Sparta, or with roughly hewn stones, as in Butrint.

In the **eastern provinces**, where the Hellenistic tradition remained strong, the construction material was also present on the façade in elaborate, ashlar masonries. Indeed, stone was the dominant material, both in the core of mortared rubble and in the carefully worked isodomic façade. Incredible examples of stone vaults are preserved in Zenobia and Resafa. In some areas, on the fringe of deserts, stone beams and slabs replaced hard-to-get wood. All the arches and arcades in the gates, the windows and the weapon-slots are made of stone. In the majority of cases, the material was locally quarried. In Zenobia and Resafa the local Gipsos alabaster was used, easily cut in square blocks. At Daras the lower parts of the walls and towers are carved on bedrock, while in Zenobia quarries are located just outside the citadel.

The use of other materials is rare. In contrast to other parts of the empire, brick is seldom encountered, either alone or in combination with stone. Bricks were mainly used for the building of vaults in cisterns or towers (Zenobia, Amida, Daras, Resafa). Tiles have been found both for buildings or towers, which would have had a wooden roof. Mud-bricks are supposed to have existed – if one believes Prokopios mentioning that Justinian replaced many mud-brick fortifications with stone. Wood was used for floors and roofs, usually sourced from the mountains of the southern Taurus and Lebanon for the southern provinces (in the cases of Zenobia and Resafa) or from the Pontic Mountains for the northern ones. Wood was also used for doors and their frames.

The initial fortifications built in **Africa** by the Byzantine army were of wood and earth.[3] When Belisarios landed, his troops constructed a palisade and a ditch to protect the encampment, and similar structures were built throughout the war.

Those fortifications destined to become more permanent installations were built with stone or, in rare cases, with bricks. Several forts were built near antique cities, which they used as quarries of ready-made material. Here as well the façades were built with ashlar masonry and the core with rubble, following up the late Hellenistic tradition.

Towers

In contrast to Early Roman towers, their Late Roman counterparts typically projected from the walls.[4] Their purpose was two-fold: they were a steady superimposed level for the installation of ballistic weapons, and they flanked the adjoining walls. Flanking fire was utilized often during this period, as seen, for instance, in the cases of gates and corner towers; some of the latter were built in such a way as to direct fire in four different directions (as in Hexamilion). Another striking feature was the variety of ground plans; in many fortifications this is all that remains, so scholars focus on why one plan was chosen instead of another. Should we search for a 'signature' plan (such as the fan- or prow-shaped) – one that perhaps should be related to a single emperor or area? Or should we look for local traditions that were possibly transferred when military units were relocated from one province to another? Who ultimately decided what form a tower should follow?

The majority of towers are rectangular or partially circular (semicircular, horseshoe-shaped, U-shaped). As a general rule, rectangular towers were usually placed along the main or outer walls, while circular ones occupied corners or flanked the gates. In addition, there are other types that deserve attention, though they are less frequently encountered.

The first type is fan-shaped towers, usually considered as a peculiarity of Constantinian-era military architecture, with examples in various parts of the empire (although unfortunately none preserved to a substantial height). We are nevertheless still in the dark as to who introduced them, where they might have originated, and why they were built. In any case, this slightly eccentric shape had no descendants in the later centuries.

In contrast, the pentagonal towers (also known as prow-shaped) had continuities in later fortifications, to the point that Winfield suggested these were the Byzantine towers *par excellence*.[5] Pentagonal was a shape recommended already by Hellenistic authors. In Late Antiquity such towers seem to have been erected in all parts of the empire (Byzantine Italy, the Balkans, Asia Minor, Syria). Ćurčić (and following him, Rizos) rightly noted that pentagonal towers seem to appear more often in fortifications of the later 5th and 6th centuries.[6] In all cases these were monumental structures that usually covered exposed ground or flanking gates.

Another exceptional group is the octagonal towers, also destined to have an illustrious tradition in later Byzantine architecture. From their earliest examples in Diocletian-era fortifications, they were attributed a ceremonial/imperial connotation. They were rare, yet in each case occupied prominent positions, and they invariably promoted a sense of power and imperial presence that went beyond their utilitarian function. As might be expected, they were used extensively on the main land wall of Constantinople. As forerunners, we could cite the various new capitals built in the Balkans during the Tetrarchy (such as at Split); further away, Constantius Chlorus added similar, still standing, towers to the walls of York, in a gesture to lend imperial prestige to the seat of the Caesar.

The towers of this period are, in principle, multi-storeyed. The ground levels often had no particular military use (as was the case in later times) or even connections to the upper floors, and they could be used separately as mere storerooms. At Zenobia they were used as stables; in Daras the graffiti leads us to believe the towers were more civic than military in nature. Access to the ground floors was through gates from the interior of the enclosure or via a ladder from the upper storey (Hexamilion). Some of the towers in Constantinople (on both the main and the outer walls) and Nicaea also had a smaller postern, typically opening on the right-hand side (from the defender's point of view). This put into practice the old Hellenistic principle (also promoted by Vitruvius) of allowing the defenders to launch assaults against the enemy by coming out from one postern and re-entering through the next tower, thereby remaining protected by their shields at all times.

The upper (two or more) floors of the towers could be used by archers or for a ballista; the use in each case is determined by the shape of the openings – slots or the rectangular type. They were covered either with vaults (barrel or domical), or with wooden ceilings. The existence of a flat, battlemented roof resting on a vault definitely points to the use of large catapults, a common practice since the time of Constantine I. However, for some towers, evidence points to a roof covering the top (as the presence of tiles in Resafa and Zenobia indicates), which obviously prevents their use for defensive purposes.

Two tower versions do not seem to conform to the above categories. The first were almost always used as smaller structures during this period (for example, at Resafa and Caesarea), and the back sides were left unbuilt. In all cases the ground plan is rectangular. The type is usually known as 'open-gorged' (or *ouvert à la gorge*), and it is again a well-known practice from Hellenistic and other earlier military architecture. In fact, it was particularly praised by Vitruvius as a way to prevent a tower, once in the hands of the enemy, from being used against the defenders of a fort.

Finally, the triangular, tower-like projections, most notably seen at the walls of Thessaloniki, have evoked a vivid discussion about how they are related to (or identified with) the pentagonal towers mentioned above. These projections, however, were not towers in the sense of a separate construction that stands out of the walls both in height and in size. They were mere projections from the wall with

Defensive Features

The positions for firing weapons in Early Byzantine fortifications were tailored to a variety of ballistic weapons and fall into distinct forms, which were widely standardized and repeated (although at present we lack any measurement studies, tables or comparisons).

Arrow loops are simple constructions with an external vertical slot, a funnel-shaped plan, and an inner rectangular opening. In many cases their sides are made of a single stone, probably for durability. To the best of my knowledge there has never been any research on the various forms of bows such structures could serve. One should also keep in mind that the exact same form has often been used for simple air or lighting reasons.

Large ballistae, able to shoot over longer distances, used openings in the form of rectangular windows, which in Constantinople are arranged on the sides of the towers to facilitate enfilading fire. One-arm catapults needed open ground and could follow the Constantinian practice of using the flat roofs of high towers to achieve greater range. However, in many cases (such as Zenobia and Resafa), researchers have proposed that the towers had roofs covered in tiles, therefore rendering them incapable of hosting such ballistic weapons.

To create the optimal conditions for enfilading fire, the distances calculated by military builders would be directly related to the weapons available. The main issue of ballistae was their inability to shoot at distances less than 50–80m. This meant that towers built less than *c.*50m apart would be dependent primarily on archers for side defence. This seems to have been the case in the eastern provinces, where towers were built closer together. When alternating larger and smaller towers (or buttresses), this could perhaps indicate an intention to combine both weapons for maximum protection (as in Amida, Daras, Resafa). However, in these structures most tower superstructures have seriously been tampered with, and no ballista windows or arrow loops are preserved, with the exception of Daras, where large windows on the upper tower floors have been connected to ballistic weapons, very similar to those of Constantinople.

The form of battlements is also largely undocumented. People tend to reconstruct – as in the (badly restored) sections of Constantinople – a familiar scheme with alternating crenels and merlons, despite the fact that in the majority of cases no surviving elements could possibly be dated to this period. An important exception is in Resafa, where battlements were constructed with a continuous horizontal parapet interrupted by fire positions. In Limisa (Africa) original crenels are thought to be preserved, reaching a height of 1.50m. In Teveste crenels survived until the 19th century and had a height of 1.50m above the parapet, which was 0.50m above the wall-walk.

Simple box machicolations supported on two or three corbels are observed in a number of sites (such as Bashir Jimal). Machicolations that could also have served as latrines are preserved at the sides of the Resafa towers. However, since they could not be precisely dated to the Early Byzantine period, they have long been considered as Islamic additions to pre-existing fortifications. The uniquely preserved machicolation above the original gate of Sinai monastery, with the tabula ansata mentioning Justinian, is proof beyond doubt that such devices were by no means an Islamic invention but rather an – at least – Early Byzantine practice. If I am not mistaken, this machicolation is the earliest known preserved specimen in military architecture.

PART TWO

THE MIDDLE BYZANTINE PERIOD

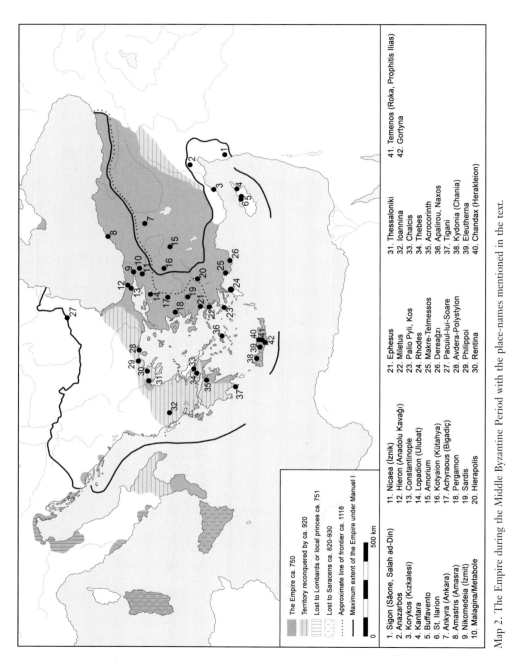

Map 2. The Empire during the Middle Byzantine Period with the place-names mentioned in the text.

(*Source*: Görkem Günay, based on Haldon, *The Palgrave Atlas of Byzantine History*)

The Empire ca. 750
Territory reconquered by ca. 920
Lost to Lombards or local princes ca. 751
Lost to Saracens ca. 820–930
Approximate line of frontier ca. 1118
Maximum extent of the Empire under Manuel I

0   500 km

1. Sigon (Sáone, Salah ad-Din)
2. Anazarbos
3. Korykos (Kizkalesi)
4. Kantara
5. Buffavento
6. St. Ilarion
7. Ankyra (Ankara)
8. Amastris (Amasra)
9. Nikomedeia (Izmit)
10. Malagina/Metabole
11. Nicaea (Iznik)
12. Hieron (Anadolu Kavağı)
13. Constantinople
14. Lopadion (Ulubat)
15. Amorium
16. Kotyaion (Kütahya)
17. Achyraous (Bigadiç)
18. Pergamon
19. Sardis
20. Hierapolis
21. Ephesus
22. Miletus
23. Palio Pyli, Kos
24. Rhodes
25. Makre-Telmessos
26. Dereağzı
27. Pacuiul-lui-Soare
28. Avdera-Polystylon
29. Philippoi
30. Rentina
31. Thessaloniki
32. Ioannina
33. Chalcis
34. Thebes
35. Acrocorinth
36. Apalirou, Naxos
37. Tigani
38. Kydonia (Chania)
39. Eleutherna
40. Chandax (Herakleion)
41. Temenos (Roka, Prophitis Ilias)
42. Gortyna

Chapter 4

The Fortifications from the 7th to the 9th Century

Introduction – The Major Conflicts

This period is usually envisaged as one of constant struggle, with the Empire turned into a militarized zone and continuously responding to attacks on all fronts. The earlier ideas of collapse, the disappearance of cities, and the disruption of economic activity, which resulted in this period being known as the 'Dark Ages', is gradually giving way to an array of conflicting – yet more objective – views, thanks also to the support of archaeological research. Despite the diverse conditions, which obviously changed substantially over three centuries, the state remained entrenched in and gradually solidified its territories covering Asia Minor, the Balkan peninsula, and parts of South Italy.

The Events of the 7th Century

As already mentioned, the first half of the 7th century brought about the complete alteration of a Mediterranean configuration that had persisted for centuries, as well as the establishment of the Arab caliphate in large parts of the eastern Mediterranean. The second half of the 7th century is viewed as a period of constant warfare against advancing Arab tribes, who almost brought the empire to the edge to extinction. The Byzantines perceived the Arabs as a very real threat; at least twice emperors considered deserting Constantinople and re-establishing the capital closer to Rome: in 618 Herakleios thought of moving to Carthage (then still Byzantine), while in *c.* 662 Constans II started his journey to Italy and then to Sicily, where he was ultimately assassinated in 668.[1]

The Arab advances continued, and Byzantine North Africa was gradually conquered (Carthage was finally lost in 698), along with Lazika and Armenia in the Caucasus area (695–709).[2] Asia Minor was constantly being raided (the earliest raid came in 647, when Mu'awiya captured Caesarea). Arabs also expanded their naval prowess, which left the islands prone to Arab raids (Cyprus in 649, Rhodes in 654), with Cyprus ending in 688 in a state of *condominium* (or no-man's land).[3] In the end Constantinople was blockaded by the Arab navy for a period of four years, from 674 to 678. The capital survived thanks to the help of a new weapon: Greek fire (see below).[4]

In Asia Minor the Byzantines were gradually able to consolidate their border with the caliphate along the Taurus Mountains. Constantine IV led a successful military expedition into Cilicia in 684–685, forcing the Arabs to pay tribute to Byzantium.[5]

Along the Balkan frontiers of the Empire the Avars were the main enemy during the 7th century, although their power was gradually waning. The conditions in the rest of the peninsula have been hotly debated: many researchers uphold that it was overrun by Slavic tribes who had no coherent political entity (keeping the area, at least nominally, a Byzantine territory), with real imperial authority confined only to the area of Thessaloniki and other coastal settlements.[6] Others believe that the Slavic incursions were more limited, perhaps restricted to the mountainous mainland, and that Byzantium retained real power in most Balkan territories. Certainly, Thessaloniki barely survived the Avar-Slav siege of 614–617, a few years before the major Avar-Persian siege of Constantinople (626); Constans II led a (proclaimed as successful) expedition in the *Sklaviniai* (Balkan areas settled by Slavs) in 658. Later on, Justinian II led another successful expedition against the Slavs (688–689) and reached Thessaloniki, where he celebrated his triumph.[7]

At the end of the 7th century a new group, the Bulgarians, moved to the Danube area. In 681, following a defeat, Constantine IV was forced to formally recognize their hold on the territory between the Balkan Mountains and the Danube. Forming an independent state centred at Pliska, the Bulgaro-Slav kingdom became the main Balkan enemy of the empire until their final defeat in 1018 by Basil II (see below).[8]

The Events of the 8th Century

The 8th century should be seen as a consolidation period, especially under the warrior leaders of the Isaurian dynasty, who were retrospectively discredited due to their iconoclast policy. The Arabs, the main eastern enemy of the empire, continued their war of annihilation against Byzantium, especially during the first half of the century. The siege of Constantinople in 717–718 was a milestone, since its failure is thought to have averted Arab expansion into Europe.[9] However, what followed was almost ritualized warfare in Asia Minor, with annual raids by the caliph's armies. Sudden attacks against cities are often mentioned in the sources (Caesarea of Cappadocia and Nicaea in 726/727), although they were seldom successful. Operations could escalate to large-scale invasions – such as Harun al-Rashid's, which reached Chrysopolis (opposite Constantinople) in 782, before concluding with a peace treaty that forced Byzantium to pay yearly compensation – and might include open-field battles (such as the important victory won by Leo III at Akroinon in 740) or, more often, focused on ravaging and pillaging the countryside. Such attacks were further facilitated when the internal politics of the

Byzantine Empire were in upheaval, as in the last years of the century, under Empress Irene (the Arab raids of 791, 798).

Yet from the mid-8th century onwards the Byzantines initiated counterattacks, with raids against northern Syria (746), Melitene (751) and Theodosioupolis (754 or 755). These border skirmishes eventually laid waste the frontier areas. However, the war against the Arabs was also fought at sea, although we have very little information about the Aegean. Arab sea raids were launched against Sicily from Ifriqya, while the Byzantine fleet won a naval battle for Cyprus in 748.[10]

On the Balkan frontier most of the information concerns the struggle against the Bulgarians. Even at the beginning of the century (712) the Bulgarian raids reached the walls of the capital, allegedly in revenge for the execution of Justinian II by Philippikos (r. 711–713), since Justinian II, before reclaiming the throne in 705, had allied himself with the Bulgarians. Later on, Constantine V is reported to have embarked on a well-thought policy, making the Thracian territories denser by sending new settlers, strengthening the fortifications, and launching regular campaigns (760, 763, 773, 774, 775). A successful campaign, ordered by Irene in 783, targeted Slavs in Macedonia and Thessaly and reached all the way to the Peloponnese.[11]

At the same time Byzantium seems to have completely abandoned its northern and central Italian possessions in the face of the advancing Lombards. Ravenna, the last imperial foothold in North Italy, was finally lost in 751, and the Pope turned to the Frankish leaders for military protection.[12]

The Events of the 9th Century

The war with the Arab caliphate, usually in the form of raids, continued in the early 9th century. Larger Arab campaigns took place in 804, 805 and 806, when armies, often led by the caliph himself, reached deep into Byzantine soil, to Cappadocia (Tyana) and Ankyra (Ankara).[13] They eventually made peace, agreeing on a treaty that included the usual (Byzantine) compensation payments.

In the Balkan territories the 9th century started with the decisive actions of Nikephoros I (802–811) to reorganize the administration of the Helladic provinces, to resettle the Peloponnese and counterbalance the Slavic population, and finally to re-establish imperial authority and presence.[14] It seems very probable that his policy also included the renewal or erection of fortifications in the new provincial centres.

Nevertheless, he confronted a formidable adversary in the face of the Bulgarian khan Krum, who destroyed a Byzantine army at the mouth of the Strymon river in 808 and in 809 occupied Serdica (Sofia) and razed the fortress.[15] Nikephoros retaliated by pillaging the Bulgarian capital, Pliska. In the 811 campaign the Byzantines again occupied Pliska but were then ambushed and completely massacred, the emperor included. In the following year Krum occupied a series of Byzantine fortresses (Develtos, Anchialos); the most important among them was the city of Mesembria (Nessebar), the main Byzantine military base on the Black Sea. Sources mention that he found a large quantity of war materials, including weapons as well as stocks of Greek fire. In 813, following an unexpected victory over the Byzantine army (that later chroniclers attributed to the mutiny of Leo the Armenian), Krum went on to besiege Constantinople.[16] We hear that on his way back he destroyed Selymbria, Adrianople, and the fortress of Rhaedestos, although Herakleia was saved thanks to its strong defences. Krum died in 814, just before embarking on another campaign against Byzantium.[17] Hostilities with the Bulgarians ceased until 894, when the new Bulgarian ruler, Symeon, attacked, allegedly over commercial disputes. The Byzantine army was defeated in 896 near Adrianople and a peace treaty was agreed.[18]

Byzantium itself experienced a serious military upheaval as result of internal strife: in particular, the revolt of Thomas the Slav against Emperor Michael II. The rebel army, gathered from all the Asian provinces, crossed to Thrace in December 821 and laid siege to Constantinople.[19] The fact that most of the navy aided the revolt, leaving the seas unchecked, also accounts for the loss of Crete to the Arabs.

This proved a major setback for the empire, and for the whole Aegean area. An independent Arab state was created there, after its capture by North African tribesmen/pirates, sometime between 824 and 827/828. Arab domination in Crete created conditions of insecurity throughout the Aegean, and the Byzantine state tried repeatedly, yet unsuccessfully, to reconquer the island; one of these operations, the naval campaign under the leadership of Theoktistos in 843, only briefly restored Byzantine control.[20] The loss of Crete was followed by the gradual Arab conquest of Sicily (starting in 826, it was only concluded in 902, with the last Byzantine stronghold falling under Arab control in 965). Yet before the end of the ninth century Byzantium was able to recover some of its south Italian territories and restore Byzantine authority on both sides of the Adriatic.[21]

From the reign of Theophilos onwards, Byzantium was, nevertheless, able to launch, for the first time, counterattacks against the Arabs both at sea and on land. Two of the caliphs led successful attacks in person, in 830–832 (capturing Lulon and Tyana) and again in 838 (defeating Theophilos at the battle of Dazimon, and destroying Ankyra and Amorium).[22] The Byzantine land forces repeatedly raided Arab lands (856, 859) and achieved a great victory near the Lalakaon river (863); they also attacked Sozopetra in Syria. Basil I continued the raids in Mesopotamia and succeeded in occupying some strongholds (Zapetra, Samosata), while failing at others (Melitene, Tarsus).[23] The same emperor reconquered Cyprus for a short period, and incorporated the island into the theme system.[24]

Sources Relevant to Fortifications

As already mentioned, many researchers now accept a 9th-century date for the works of Syrianos Magister, who was sometimes seen as a compiler of ancient authors. Among them was one of the most important Byzantine military works, known as *de re strategica/On Strategy/Περί στρατηγίας*.[25] This manual has been attributed to an anonymous writer, allegedly a mid-6th-century army engineer who wrote it during the reign of Justinian. Although the author is clearly familiar with ancient writers, it is evident that he had personal fighting experience and knowledge of fortifications and/or war-machine construction.[26]

In chapter 6 (*Defence*),[27] he gives the guidelines that a general should follow in fortifying a territory. In the following chapters he explicitly prescribes the provisions for frontier forts (ch. 9, *Forts*),[28] and he goes on to describe, in detail, civic fortifications and defensive practices (chs 11–13, *The Site for Building a City, How to Build a City, Preparations Needed to Resist Enemy Siege Machines*).[29] It is interesting to note that, in the author's mind, a 'city' is always perceived as a (small) fortress.

Army Organization

The military organization of the Early Byzantine state continued to function probably until the 660s, even though gradual changes must have started from the 650s, as a result of Arab incursions. However, the situation quickly deteriorated as these attacks were repeated on a regular basis, in addition to the Bulgarian and Slavic raids in the Balkans. Central control of materials and military units must have become harder, if not impossible. Once the centralized system of the early period collapsed, military commands and recruiting systems were reorganized on a regional basis. At the same time, the changing war tactics required both lightly armed horsemen who could easily chase after or entrap small groups of raiders during their seasonal campaigning, and contingents of infantry to guard passages and fortifications.[30]

These needs led, during the period from the 7th to the 9th century, to the appearance and the enforcement of the new administrative and military system of themes.[31] Themes were large army divisions, which were based in peripheries (eventually also known as themes). Their military (and also gradually the civic) government was controlled by a military commander, a *strategos*, directly answerable to the emperor. The system developed organically as field armies from all lost provinces were withdrawn, brought to Anatolia, and resettled in regions that supported them; eventually the field armies took their names from the regions in which they were located (*Opsikion, Armeniakon, Thrakesion, Anatolikon*). A naval division was organized in the southern Aegean, under the name of *Karabisianoi*, later replaced by coastal themes.

The goal of this system was for every large region to be able to efficiently and independently organize its own defence. The main task was to meet enemy raids with the means, weapons, and men available in the region. Theme armies and their divisions (known as *tourmai, drouggoi* and *vanda*) had to include lightly armed units that could swiftly intervene and confront small numbers of raiders.

Soldiers were recruited and paid locally, although (nominally at least) central control never ceased to exist.

Within this framework, fortifications were not only maintained but also extended to accommodate new war tactics: major cities acted as the capitals of the themes, and their citadels were protected by well-organized standing armies. It is even possible to detect how the fortifications were provisioned, with both sophisticated weaponry and manpower (as in the case of Ankyra).

At the same time, all settlement fortifications were maintained; some antique cities were even transferred to more strategic locations, so as to be able to withstand raiding armies (as was the case with Chalcis, Euboea).[32] The importance of walls for the continuation of civic life was such that from now on the word *kastron* (castle) was identified in the Byzantine vocabulary with the (alas, restricted) city itself. In times of peace the walls (apart from thematic capitals or division bases) were probably guarded by local militia, but in case of attack the theme *strategos* would dispatch regular armies to defend them (as stated in the account of the Arab siege of Chalcis, *c.* 880).[33] The key to this defensive system was the ability to follow closely the movements of raiders from the moment they crossed the borders, and to safeguard forces until the opportune moment came to either annihilate the invaders or force them from imperial soil. This realistic strategy presupposed the existence of checkpoints, guard towers, and small forts, all able to survey their territories and share information; a number of rudimentary hilltop enclosures have been attributed to this period and interpreted as the temporary refuges of the population during the yearly raids.[34]

The empire in this period had two major enemies (Arabs and Bulgarians), and this resulted, according to some scholars, in the Byzantines experimenting less with military strategies and skills. Offensive campaigns were rare and were usually carried out by units stationed near the capital and under the direct control of the emperor. The knowledge of advanced war qualities or technical skills, like archery practised by mounted units or the production of chain mail armour on a large scale, probably declined in many regions.[35] The production of weapons and military equipment was also impacted; most of the earlier production workshops appear to have been abandoned over the course of the 7th century. Yet from the story of St Euthymia's relics, we learn that Leo III ordered the establishment of an arms factory in a Constantinopolitan monastery: furnaces were constructed and armourers employed.[36]

A new weapon appeared during this period, and its first mention is linked with the First Arab Siege of Constantinople in the 670s (which later research concluded may never actually have happened): the famous 'Greek' or 'Liquid Fire', which has since acquired mythical dimensions.[37] A weapon invented by the legendary Kallinikos, it was a form of napalm, made of crude oil. It was projected from tubes that could be mounted either on towers or on the bows of warships. It seems that it was particularly adept for naval battles or against ships engaged in sieges of coastal towns (as in the case of the Russian ships that besieged Constantinople in 941 and were burned down easily from the sea walls). Constantine VII Porphyrogennetos narrates how its preparation and safekeeping remained a highly guarded state secret that should never be disclosed or fall into enemy hands; this happened when Krum occupied the military base of Mesembria (Nessebar) in the Black Sea and found Greek fire weapons in store. It is no longer mentioned after 1204, a sign that the secret recipe was lost after the Latin conquest of Constantinople. Nevertheless it was often mentioned in Western or Arab sources later on, obviously referring to weapons with similar intentions or capabilities.

The Fortifications

It is evident that in this period, when the state struggled for its survival, fortifications played a vital role in preserving the population and the authorities. With army units consistently drafting soldiers from local populations, and with all able-bodied people (men and women) ready to participate in repelling enemy raids in all imperial territories, it seems that the whole society went through a phase of militarization, with defence holding a primordial place. However, texts and contemporary written sources provide very few data on the use, erection, manning, and control of the fortifications.

We can deduct from the inscriptions preserved on the walls and the poor archaeological record that 7th- and 8th-century Byzantium erected a number of fortifications in an effort to sustain and safeguard its population against continuous raids. Most of these works concentrated on civic centres, and they featured both the repair of earlier walls and a focus on protecting a smaller part of earlier larger settlements. Whether this reflects a shrinking of the population or (more possibly) military practicalities is in most cases unknown. Furthermore, the involvement or the role of central government, theme *strategoi* and local magnates in these endeavours is also impossible to detect. The Nicaea walls, where the accompanying inscription clearly attributes the renovation to imperial intervention, is an exception to the rule. What seems to be a common feature for all 7th- and 8th-century fortifications is the abundant reuse of earlier building material, spolia, to such an extent as to be almost a mark of the era.

For the 9th century the situation is slightly different: the tide had turned against its enemies and Byzantium was reorganized, strengthened, and prepared to go on the offensive. Among the surviving monuments, we can detect a number of buildings that seem to be part of a centrally implemented fortification programme. The same defensive features are repeated in various fortifications, while inscriptions in several places praise the emperors for initiating and conducting these works. It seems that this programme started in the walls of the capital with various towers erected by Theophilos. Its main fortifications, however, were built under Emperor Michael III (Nicaea, Ankyra, Kotyaion), thus disqualifying the post-mortem negative propaganda of the following dynasty towards him. The purpose of this programme was to protect the main cities of the empire, the centres of regional government. Since there was no eminent danger, and these fortifications were not executed to protect overgrown centres, their purpose was mainly a preparatory one, to ensure the stability of central power and to enforce central authority in regions that had been thrown into civil wars by individual *strategoi* struggling for the imperial throne.

Fortifications of the Balkans and Aegean
Relatively few fortifications have been attributed to this period in the Balkans and the Aegean by earlier scholars, although this image is gradually changing thanks to recent research. For the mainland territories the discussion was, from the start, related to the problem of Slavic raids and their (unknown) settlement extension; that is, whether Byzantium lost or retained control of its Balkan provinces during these centuries, and how it gradually reasserted its dominion. This controversial issue is beyond the reach of present research. With the exception of the walls of the capital, where significant additions reflect the imperial policy to safeguard the capital, almost all mainland examples that have been dated to the 7th to 9th centuries are small fortifications intended to protect reduced settlements or military bases. Most of them are situated along the coast lines (Abdera, Tigani), and this could be linked to their role as naval stations for the imperial fleet. Civic fortifications also existed, either newly created (Chalcis) or – more often – repaired (Thebes, Thessaloniki).[38]

In the Aegean islands the discussion has focused on the danger of Arab raids and the resulting insecurity, which probably increased dramatically once Crete was turned into an Arab emirate in the early 9th century (by 827/828); a number of civic centres, usually local capitals (Naxos, Rhodes; Herakleio, Gortyna, Eleutherna and Kydonia in Crete), were fortified during this period, and their remains are gradually being identified thanks to archaeological research.

As mentioned above, the walls of **Constantinople** (Istanbul, Turkey)[39] stand apart during this period, since, along with Thessaloniki, this is the only Late Antique metropolis that remained within the confined border of the Byzantine state. The series of sieges and raids it successfully withstood instilled a feeling of divine protection to its citizens, along with a sense that as long as the capital was safe, the empire could regain all its losses and continue to exist. Enemy attacks, earthquakes, and natural erosion necessitated continuous repairs and additions, usually accompanied by inscriptions commemorating the emperors responsible for the works, as part of the imperial propaganda.

Such was the case for sections along the land walls, whose inscriptions attribute them to Emperor Leo III and his successor, Constantine V. The walls along the Sea of Marmara were reportedly strengthened and successfully withstood the Arab siege of 717–718. These works, especially near the Great Palace, were credited to Tiberios II (698–705) and Anastasios II (713–715) and made liberal use of older sculptural material from monumental buildings of the 6th century. It is during this time that we first hear of the large chain that protected the Golden Horn, stretching between the Eugenios Tower and that of Galata.

The Marmara walls were substantially rebuilt after 825, during the rule of Theophilos, with the new towers still preserving inscriptions bearing the names of the emperor and his son, Michael III. These towers resemble the construction styles of 5th-century works, with extensive use of spolia. The same Late Antique spolia reuse is also evident in the Boukoleon Palace, which was built in this period and is frequently credited to Theophilos.[40] It consisted of two wings along the sea front, built along the wall line, each with an elevated and semi-covered gallery. They were separated by a staircase and a landing bridge that led to a monumental gateway.

The most important addition, however, was the extension of the whole northeast part of the enclosure to include the suburb known as Blachernae; this extension needed to be constantly reinforced because of the location's vulnerability (*see* Plate 26). During the siege of 626 the Avars concentrated their efforts in that area to breach the walls. Herakleios, immediately afterwards, covered the whole area with a single line of wall, *c.*100m long, reinforced with blind arches on the inner side and with around thirteen rectangular towers. An outer wall, *c.*25m long, doubled the defence of the northeast corner of the enclosure; it was built by Leo V following a Bulgarian attack under Krum in 813 and was reinforced with four smaller towers. Later on, three hexagonal towers, among the most powerful ever built, were added to its land side by Michael II and his successor Theophilos in the early 9th century; two of them flanked the gate known as Blachernae. These towers were built using mostly reused stone blocks in the lower sections and whole-brick masonry in the upper structure.

It should be noted that from the end of the 7th century (Justinian II, 685–95) the Great Palace, situated in the southeast of the historical peninsula, received its own enclosure, of which no trace exists today. Henceforth, this new fort was cut off from the city and was able to stand on its own against attacks both from outside enemies and from within the city.

A few relatively small fortifications, protecting settlements and ports, have been attributed to this period based on archaeological evidence. However, their walls were either repaired later on or survive in a rather fragmentary state.

The fortified settlement of **Tigani** (Greece)[41] occupies the tip of a small peninsula, an area both naturally defensible and vital to naval routes (*see* Plate 27). Access to the castle was either by sea or from the south along a small strip of land that connected it to the mainland. This was the area protected by the walls: a rectilinear fortification reinforced by a rectangular solid tower. The masonry consists of roughly hewn stones set in irregular courses. There is practically no difference between the core and the façades.

Plate 26. Constantinople. The Blachernae walls. (*Photo*: Gokhan Tan)

Plate 27. Tigani. General view. (*Source*: Archive of the Ephorate of Antiquities, Lakonia)

The excavation of a basilica (originally dated to the 7th century and later redated to the late 10th century) in the southeast part of the fortified settlement demonstrates the importance of the settlement. It is accepted therefore that Tigani should be identified with the Byzantine castle of Maina/Μαΐνης, mentioned by Constantine VII Porphyrogennetos in his *de Administrando Imperio* (10th century).

Abdera/Polystylon (Greece)[42] was already a main port facility from the 6th century BC, under the name Avdera. During the 7th and 8th centuries the city was confined to the harbour and became a small market town. Part of the wall is built with reused stones from the ancient settlement, often without the use of bricks. The Byzantine wall was constructed upon the older classical fortification, with the addition of an outer wall. From the 9th century on the town was known under the name Polystylon, probably due to the ancient columns still visible at the site. The churches in the interior of the castle were used and repaired from the 9th to the 13th century, documenting an era of relative prosperity for the settlement.

In recent years fortifications of this period have been identified on a number of Aegean islands, proving the importance central government placed on their safety.

Excavations within the city of **Rhodes** (Greece)[43] traced the remains of the Byzantine fortress of the second half of the 7th century (*see* Plate 28). The fortress surrounded a rectangular area that later became the Hospitaller Collacium, used by the Knights of St John of Jerusalem as quarters for the brethren. It had on its south, west and north sides a main wall, an outer wall and a moat. The main wall

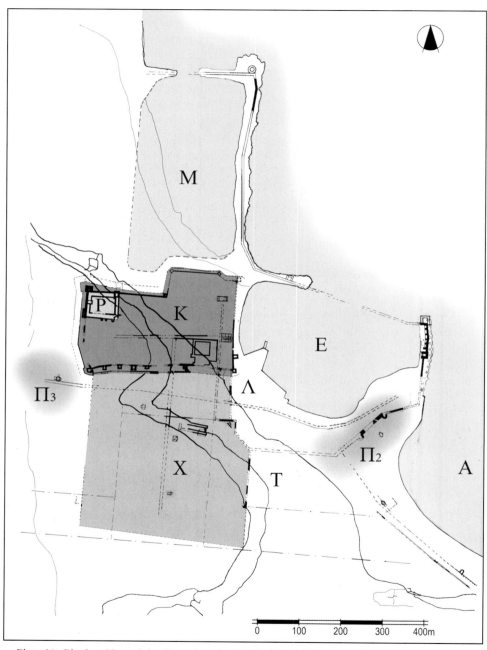

Plate 28. Rhodes. Plan of the Byzantine city. P=citadel; K=7th-century fortress; X=11th–12th-century extension. (*Source*: Katerina Manousou-Ntella)

had rectangular towers at irregular distances. The eastern side, built across the port, obviously had no moat and perhaps no outer wall either. The citadel was located in the northwest part, later occupied by the palace of the Hospitaller's Grand Master.

The towers and the main wall of the fortress were built with large porous blocks (some more than 2m long), most of them reused ancient material, with broken bricks or small stones at the joints. Both the main and the outer walls were 3–3.3m thick. On the south side there was a two-gate complex, with one opening each at the main walls and the outer walls. The corner tower of that side, measuring 12 × 9m, is preserved almost to its original height of 12.50m, missing only its battlements. The distance between the towers fluctuates between 17 and 27m.

On the south side the outer wall is also fully preserved, built with ashlar masonry. It has a height of *c.*5.10–5.20m from its talus base, which lies today beneath the street level, up to its rectangular crenels. The sloping base was 2m wider than the body of the wall and reached a depth of at least 3m. In front of the outer wall there was a moat whose existence was verified by excavations that revealed a filling of pure soil and chipped porous flicks. The moat was *c.*10m wide, judging from the surviving part to the west of the Palace of the Grand Master.

The citadel of the fortress, today occupied by the Palace of the Grand Master, was built with ashlar masonry. The 7th-century fortification can be recognized, based on masonry, throughout the palace's perimeter, including its basement, ground floor, and up to the height of the first floor. Its northwest and northeast angles were occupied by two powerful rectangular towers. Another similar tower was excavated along the northwest side.

According to Arab sources, in the last quarter of the 7th century, when Rhodes was briefly occupied by Arab forces, the city had a fortress where the local population could take refuge and organize resistance. Therefore the date for the erection of the fortress was set to the second half of the 7th century. Kollias believed, however, that only the main and outer walls belonged to this building phase; the moat and the reinforcement of the fortifications dated from the end of 1475 onwards.

The initial phase of the walled settlement of **Apalirou** on the island of **Naxos** (Cyclades, Greece)[44] has recently been attributed to this period. It occupies a steep mountain top on the island's interior. The walls cover the summit, with a maximum length of 315m (north to south), a width of 100m (west to east) and an area of 21ha. They consist of a curtain, nine towers, a gate and a later circular bastion. It was a simple construction of fluctuating thickness, while outcrops of bedrock have been organically embodied in the fortification line. Most towers were rectangular, evenly distributed and projecting from the outer wall surface, with two semicircular ones at the southwest side. The gate is centrally placed at the centre of the west side; it was positioned at right angles to the wall so that it was protected from direct assaults.

Large parts of the walls were built with roughly hewn stones, without mortar (drystone technique), while other sections have a rubble core with lime mortar. Fragments of broken tiles and amphora sherds were occasionally used for the rough coursing of the stones. Ashlar blocks were used for structurally sensitive points, such as the tower corners. Two building phases have been recognized, although their dates are hard to establish. The earliest phase, which included the whole enclosure, was attributed to the 7th century. At a later date there was an effort to improve the walls, coupled with the construction of cisterns, which would augment the settlement's capacity to resist attacks. The walls remained in active use until the early 13th century, when the area eventually came under Venetian rule.

Apalirou has been interpreted as a fortified urban site founded for the first time in the mid-7th century, and as such it is seen as a rare case for the Byzantine Empire. The complex and densely built settlement housed not only a standing garrison but also a substantial civilian population.

Similarly, a number of fortified towns on the island of **Crete** have been attributed to this period. The fortification of **Kydonia** (Chania, Greece)[45] occupied a naturally defensible hill (Kastelli) where a Hellenistic citadel once stood, overlooking a secure harbour on the north coast of Crete. Its plan is oval, following the contour of the hill, with an orientation from east to west. On the north and partly the east and west sides, the wall simply covers the rock of the hill, while on the (smooth) south side, it rises high above ground level. Excavations on the south side proved that – at least on this side – there was a moat and an outer wall. The moat was probably intended to be filled with water.

The wall had rectangular and pentagonal towers with straight segments in between. The towers did not bond to the curtain and rather rose above it. On the south side excavators discovered that the towers were built at a higher level, since the wall itself rested on an earlier Hellenistic enclosure. Two main gates opened on the east and west sides, with lesser gates north and south. The main west gate opened between two towers, of which the south one partially survives. This tower was much larger than the rest and could have played a important defensive role.

The walls were built mainly with well-cut blocks from ancient monuments, including columns, capitals, architraves, door jambs and simple rectangular blocks. The excavators dated the Byzantine fortification of Chania to the period from the mid-7th to the 8th century, based on comparisons with other similar structures. It is known that the Arabs occupied the fort following a siege in *c.* 823, after which there is no further mention of it.

Gortyna (Crete)[46] was a large metropolitan city, situated in the most fertile part of the island. During the 6th and 7th centuries the city remained unwalled and does not appear to have shrunk or been abandoned; on the contrary its large aqueduct was repaired, bringing water to at least fifty fountains and marking the dispersed settlement pattern. The only fortified part was the citadel, which occupied a hill. The walls of the citadel were strengthened with towers, one of which was pentagonal (prow-shaped). A large rectangular complex – the function of which is still debated – was built at the top of the citadel hill. A branch of the aqueduct brought water to the citadel, feeding a large open reservoir.

Various dates have been proposed for the erection of the walls, such as the end of the 7th century, following a large earthquake in 670. A lead seal of an imperial administrator from the middle of the 7th century, found in the pentagonal tower, proves that the citadel functioned as the administrative centre of the city. In hagiographic sources the citadel is known as the Fort of Drimeos.

Eleutherna (Crete)[47], in contrast to Gortyna, was one of the smallest cities on the island, located on a naturally fortified location in the northwestern foothills of Mt Ida. The Hellenistic city covered the area of two neighbouring hills (known as Pyrgi and Nisi), but it was restricted to Pyrgi from Roman times onwards. The hill was surrounded by rivers that allowed access only from the south. The erection of walls surrounding the hill must have been a significant change for the residents. Currently, only some of the towers are preserved to a substantial height. One of them is rectangular, with a side measuring *c.* 5m and a solid base. The core was constructed with rough stones, bricks, and mortar, while the façades were covered with ashlar blocks in rows with broken bricks at the joints. The surviving parts of the enclosure were similarly built, but the façades, in most cases, have fallen off or were purposely detached to reuse the blocks. This masonry style, encountered also in Kydonia and Gortyna, has been dated to the 7th century, with Eleutherna most probably dating from the early 7th century.

Fortifications of Asia Minor

The fortifications of Asia Minor that have been attributed to this period fall into two categories. The first comprises large civic and military centres. If previously fortified, then the new, 7th- and 8th-century enclosures usually occupied the citadel or a small part of the earlier walls, reducing their circumference and therefore the numbers required to man them. If these centres were without walls, then a small section was delineated with ramparts, usually in an easy-to-defend area of the city, using the available building material from older structures. A notable exception is Nicaea, whose earlier walls were greatly renovated in a more monumental masonry style, obviously for political reasons.

The reduced enclosures are not necessarily linked to a smaller population but rather to needing to be able to defend a population with a reduced number of soldiers. When these walls were built, enemy attacks were not a theoretical future possibility: they were a reality that needed to be dealt with every year, and therefore the local population had to be able to survive, even if protected by a smaller number of soldiers. Both a city wall and a citadel were added in Ankyra, signifying its exceptional role as the military centre of central Anatolia.

It should be noted that many of these centres (for example, Nicaea/Iznik, Ankyra/Ankara, and Kotyaion/Kütahya) were further strengthened in the first half of the 9th century, with a clear aim to 'upgrade' their walls and provide further means of active defence, usually with the addition of extra flanking towers. This initiative seems part of an orchestrated central policy to instill feelings of grandeur and security among the population of the empire. It was particularly evident in the monumental inscriptions that constantly reminded the locals of imperial patronage, as was also the case for the walls of the capital.

The second category of fortifications has been recorded by earlier scholars as the mountain forts and 'refuge sites of the Dark Ages'.[48] They usually comprise simple rubble constructions, built on mountaintops with no distinctive or identifiable features. Many encompass large areas with no traces of regular habitation detected. With the exception of the Dereağzı fort, no dating clues can be provided by either the masonry or the finds; their names did not survive either. Foss has proposed that we should recognize them as temporary strongholds to safeguard local populations in the face of recurring Arab raids; it is a subject that remains open to further research.

Of the major civic centres of Asia Minor that received new walls or additions during this period, only a few have been studied so far, often as part of wider excavation projects (Sardis, Pergamon, Ephesus, Miletos, Amorium, Xanthos, Patara, and Side);[49] in sites where massive walls are still standing (as in Ankyra, Kotyaion, Nicaea, Telmessos-Makre)[50] research has focused on discerning construction features in relation to masonry types.

In the case of **Nicaea** (Iznik, Turkey)[51] two new building phases have been recognized, adding to the pre-existing Roman walls. The aim was clearly to repair or reinforce the existing enclosure, which was vital to the internal communication network of Anatolia. The first building phase (8th century) included three main categories of works (*see* Plate 29): the first was the rebuilding of towers and wall sections, the second was the addition of a new, higher wall-walk (balustrade) throughout the wall perimeter, and the third was the construction of a wall connecting the southwest enclosure corner to the shore of the lake. Rebuilding was constrained mainly to the parts adjoining the Istanbul Gate, while lesser works survive near the South Lake Gate. The higher wall-walk endowed the enclosure with a higher defensive zone, by *c.*1.80m, which is largely preserved in the southern and eastern sections of the walls. Finally, the lake wall prohibited enemies from attacking the enclosure from the water.

The 8th-century works were all executed exclusively with high-quality ancient material, the majority of it former theatre seats, although many statue bases and columns were also used. The blocks were set either horizontally, to cover the

Plate 29. Nicaea (Iznik). The walls of the 8th century. (*Photo*: David Hendrix)

wall-walk surface, or vertically when used for the new crenels. This ashlar construction is well made and stands out from the rest of the masonry. It served less practical purposes – more a desire to prove the military prowess of the reigning dynasty.

The second building phase, dated to the 9th century, was more extensive. It included the addition of new towers set among the existing ones, especially on the east and south sides, between the Yenishehir and Lefke Gates. This reduced the distance between the towers by half and effectively doubled the defence capability of these exposed parts. The walls east of the South Lake Gate were reinforced from their inner side, since the original wall was probably considered too weak. The inner side, between Towers 95 and 99, was built with alternating bands of bricks and stones. Here there were blind arches that supported the wall-walk.

The new towers were constructed in two ways: those in the southwest wall (Towers 97–100) were built with a lower part of alternating bands of stones and bricks and an upper part built solely with bricks. Roughly preserved spolia were used for the tower base. These towers are built in the style of the day, reminiscent of similar examples from Ankyra.

The second group of towers – those added on the south side (the even numbers between Towers 1 and 19) – have a façade of bricks and a rubble core. They are built on a stone base of spolia, which was set sometimes in an ordered manner and other times carelessly. The towers do not bond to the adjoining wall and lack the ground-floor side gates of the pre-existing towers. They are built *c.* 2m above the

3rd-century ground level. The builders attempted to copy the 3rd-century towers, but the new ones exhibit many differences, such as thicker bricks that are set in a different way.

At the mid-height of the towers there are rooms with arrow slits or ballistae openings. These rooms are sometimes below the wall-walk level, but are more often at the same level or slightly above it, meaning that bows and ballistae were the main forms of defence. At the tower summit there would have been a flat roof with battlements for the catapults. In one case the original crenels are preserved.

In the mid-8th century Nicaea became the capital of the Opsikion theme, which extended to the northwest part of Asia Minor. The city was attacked by a large Arab force that encircled the city in 727 and levelled a section of the walls. Therefore the 8th-century building phase is dated immediately after the Arabs' departure, in *c.*730. An inscription preserved on a tower mentions Emperors Leo III and Constantine V, and, based on masonry resemblances, all similarly built sections are attributed to the same rulers (*see* Plate 30). These works were intended to repair damage from the Arab attack and to correct for the gradual rising of the ground level due to earth silting.

The second building phase is attributed to Michael III, who conducted a large reconstruction programme in 858. Many inscriptions are preserved (although none in situ), and in at least eight inscriptions the emperor is named as the builder of a tower. Although the reason for this building programme is not clarified

Plate 30. Nicaea (Iznik). The dedicatory inscription mentioning emperors Leo III and Constantine V. (*Photo*: David Hendrix)

Plate 33. Kotyaion (Kütahya). View of the walls. (*Photo*: author)

The outer wall has no towers in its surviving parts. It must have been 3–4m high and 1.60m wide. It was a relatively simple structure, built with roughly rectangular stones.

There are no written sources concerning the dating of Kotyaion's walls. It was one of the main military bases of the Opsikion theme. In 866 the local general revolted against Michael III and was confined to the Kotyaion, the first mention of a fort at the city. The first Kotyaion walls are later than the Early Byzantine period, since many spolia of that period were incorporated in the masonry. Based on masonry style and fortification features, Foss concluded that the walls probably were connected to the wider building programme of Michael III.

In the regional capital of **Amorium** (Hisarköy, Turkey)[59] walls of this period surround the upper city, an artificial oval hill with an area of *c.*5ha at a height of 20m above the surrounding ground level (*see* Plate 23). The walls followed the contour of the summit, and today only their trace is visible at ground level. They were strengthened by projecting rectangular towers, interspaced with a number of gates. At the southeast and southwest angles the walls were connected to the lower city's Early Byzantine enclosure, and therefore for some time they co-existed as part of the same defensive system.

Excavations in the upper city revealed two separate building phases for the wall. The earliest one was built with reused large blocks, taken from Roman buildings and the extensive cemeteries around the city. This building phase is visible in some parts on the hill surface but lies buried under the later enclosure in others. In the second building phase the inner side of the wall was lined with blind arches that supported the wall-walk.

From *c.*640 the city became the military centre of the army of Anatolikon and its chief, the *magister militum per Orientem*. It later became the capital of the Anatolikon theme and a key site for the defence of Byzantine territory against Arab raids. Based on excavation data, the early upper city enclosure must be dated to the early or mid-7th century and be related to the new military role of Amorium. The military authorities were stationed in the upper city, while the city continued to be protected by the lower city enclosure. In 838 it fell under siege and the walls were rendered obsolete by the armies of Chalif Al Mutasim, yet it quickly reverted to Byzantine control. At some time after 838 the destroyed upper city enclosure was rebuilt (second building phase) while the lower city walls were never used again.

Anazarbos in Cilicia (Turkey)[60] was situated along the main route through Anatolia to the eastern borders. A circuit of walls was erected around part of the urban fabric. Its south gate incorporated a late 2nd-century triumphal arch that opened to the main colonnaded road of the city. The exterior façade of the gate itself was carefully maintained.

The wall circuit was definitely built after the 6th century, based on the incorporation of spolia in the masonry. The techniques, thickness, and lack of architectural ornamentation point to a date in the 7th century. In this period Anazarbos was a critical bastion near a threatened frontier.

A single fort of this period has been surveyed at **Dereağzı** (Turkey)[61] in southeast Asia Minor. It is usually associated with the exceptional, large Middle-Byzantine church located in its vicinity and known by the same name.

The fort was constructed on the site of an ancient fortification, occupying a high, pyramid-shaped hill. It consisted of multiple sections adjusted to the topography: an outer ward with its north wall, almost 200m long, flanked with rectangular, pentagonal, and triangular towers; an inner circuit; and a citadel with a long spur wall leading to a tower that overlooked a gorge.

The walls were constructed with reused ashlar block and rubble. The fortress protected the large basin of Kasaba and guarded the route from inland to the Mediterranean coast. It was obviously an elaborate construction perhaps protecting a new settlement. The Dereağzı church is usually attributed to the 8th or 9th century, a date proposed also for the fort.

to its potential users as military leaders seeking to besiege Arab cities. The manuscript containing both texts was richly illustrated with drawings, usually copied or altered from their ancient sources.

A number of military manuals (*taktika*) are dated to the second half of the 10th century, an era of prosperity and military achievements. They are both concise and comprehensive, written with a practical spirit and with few – if any – theoretical approaches.

The text known as *Praecepta Militaria/Στρατηγική ἔκθεσις καὶ σύνταξις Νικηφόρου δεσπότου/Presentation and Composition on Warfare by the Emperor Nikephoros*[17] is dated to *c.*965 and attributed to Nikephoros II Phokas. It is written for commanders of expeditionary forces in the East and describes in detail the equipment and tactics that were deployed in the offensive wars against the Arabs. The author discusses various situations, skirmishes, pitched battles, espionage and reconnaissance. It also included details of the army's religious observances, which were considered in line with the emperor's ascetic values.

An anonymous treatise written in the 970s and known as *Περὶ παραδρομῆς/De Velitatione/Skirmishing*[18] specifically describes the style of 'guerrilla/hit-and-run' frontier fighting that had been consistently followed in the eastern borders for the previous three centuries, until the middle of the 10th century. The author was probably a high-ranking officer who was experienced in this kind of warfare and very close to, if not a member of, the Phokas family; he clearly states that he wrote the text following an order by the deceased Emperor Nikephoros II Phokas (so, shortly after 969). Next to the detailed narratives on frontier skirmishes and conflicts on the Anatolian mountainous borders, fortifications are mentioned in passing as refuges for the countryside population in times of peril, yet they are also seen, according to Haldon, as essential elements in a system for transmitting information about the movement of hostile forces.[19] Chapter 21 (*The siege of a fortified town*) deals with the preparations of fortified towns and how field forces should act to break the siege.[20]

The manual known as *De Re Militari/Ανωνύμου βιβλίον τακτικόν/De Castrametatione/Campaign Organization and Tactics*[21] has been traditionally ascribed to the general Nikephoros Ouranos and dates to the last decade of the 10th century; it is addressed to Emperor Basil II and focuses on the advances of the Byzantine army, with the emperor in command, into enemy lands, probably Bulgaria. Numbers, details and specific measurements show that the writer had himself participated in similar endeavours. One of the exceptional features of the text is that its first chapter describes, in detail, marching camps (either ideal or actual), accompanied by some (later) sketches. In the later chapters he recounts various guidelines for field armies on the move. From chapter 21 onwards[22] he gives details on siege warfare (from the point of view of the attacker) and on how to cut provisions, set camp outside the walls, lure the defenders out, attack the walls, dig mines, demoralize the defenders, etc.

Finally the *Taktika* of Nikephoros Ouranos,[23] dated to *c.*1000, is largely considered as a paraphrase of earlier authors, including the *Praecepta Militaria*; yet, especially in the chapters where he relies on the latter source, the author includes first-hand updates based on his own experience along the eastern frontiers.

Army Organization

The recovery of the Byzantine state and the switch from a mainly defensive to an offensive policy led to a change in the organization of its military units. It was understood that thematic armies could no longer act as semi-independent units and should rather be coordinated under an effective central command. The light, flexible cavalry of the 7th century could no longer satisfy the state's objectives, since it could not serve as a powerful offensive weapon. In the 10th century the military commander of the standing army, known as *Domestikos ton Scholon*,[24] increased its jurisdiction and further mercenary units were created and armed by the central government. The thematic armies were gradually reduced to mere provincial militias that served alongside the main army force during campaigns.

The appearance of standing field forces, well disciplined and drilled in battle formations, was a huge boost to the offensive capability of the Byzantine army, now closely resembling its Roman counterpart.[25] These changes are usually connected with the general (and later emperor) Nikephoros Phokas. The key features of the late 10th-century army were the following:

- a heavily armed infantry able to confront enemy forces, march long distances and function as garrison troops away from home territory;
- a heavily armed cavalry (known as *kataphraktoi*) served a sort of 'strike force' and could therefore enhance the aggressive power of the army. They would closely resemble contemporary western knights, with both the warrior and the horse being covered with armour;
- the main forces were supported by effective units of mounted and infantry archers;
- new war tactics were put into practice, along with a strict chain of command to control and contain all the forces; and
- these features were supported by a revived interest in military art, including tactics, strategy and mechanics.

Within this military system, fortifications were no longer used as defensive but rather as offensive weapons. Those within the imperial territory served as stations for the passing field army, as points in the military supply chain and as bases from which campaigns were conducted. Those occupied or constructed in newly acquired territories served to reinforce control, facilitate army circulation and support Byzantine authority.

At the same time, many of the Byzantine victories involved the successful siege of strong fortifications (such as Dorostolon in the Balkans or Tarsus and Antioch

Plate 35. Temenos. The northeast entrance.

(*Source*: Gigourtakis, 'Vyzantines Ochyroseis stin Kriti kata ti B' Vyzantini Periodo (961–1204)')

In the walls of **Nicaea** (Iznik, Turkey)[38] some towers were built using the hidden-brick technique, which is usually dated from the 11th century onwards. These masonry parts were more extensive in the upper parts of the walls, and they were reduced towards the bottom. They were constructed with the use of a timber frame (with the beam holes still visible). Schneider and Foss acknowledged them as repairs after the 1065 earthquake. In fact, the Nicaea walls must have been repaired earlier on, based on historical information: in 978 the rebel Bardas Skleros occupied the city, having attacked with siege engines and inflicting serious damage to the walls. However, the 1065 earthquake was the single worst disaster in the city's record, allegedly levelling it to the ground. Nevertheless, we assume that the walls were soon repaired, since the city successfully resisted the attack of Emperor Nikephoros III Botaneiates, although it surrendered in 1080 to Nikephoros Melissinos, a claimant to the throne. It later became the capital of the first Seljuk state in Asia Minor.

In **Amorium** (Hisarköy, Turkey)[39] the area of the so-called enclosure was investigated at the centre of the lower city (*see* Plate 23). It was a trapezoidal area surrounded by a wall. At the south side it is preserved to a length of *c.*25m and a height of up to 3.5m, with a thickness of *c.*2.35m. Its façade was structured with blocks in irregular horizontal courses with broken bricks at the joints. The core is rubble with bricks and lime mortar. Spolia pieces were used both at the core and in the façade. This wall did not stand independently. Along the inner side a series of rooms were built, also with reused older material.

In the same period an inner fort (keep?) was added to the interior of the upper city fortification. This fort, reinforced with rectangular and circular towers, occupied the southwest corner of the upper city.

As discussed above, the major event in Amorium's history was the 838 Arab siege and subsequent sack. It seems, however, that prosperity returned during the 10th and 11th centuries. Numismatic evidence dates the enclosure to the end of the 10th century or the early 11th century. The reason for the construction of the enclosure is not known, but the excavators assumed that it was built to serve a specific military function. Perhaps it was a station and supply centre for the Byzantine army during its offensive campaigns in southeast Anatolia and north Syria. It is also expected that thematic armies would have had their barracks and headquarters in the city at the end of the 9th century and during the 10th century.

The fort of **Sigon** (Saône, Sahyun, Salah ad-Din, Syria),[40] located in the Jebel Ansarieh mountains, occupies a long rocky spur (over 5ha) commanding all surrounding lands down to the coast of Lattakia (*see* Plate 36). It is divided into two plateaus (higher and lower). It is framed by spectacular ravines and is best known for its impressive Crusader walls, the breathtaking rock-cut moat, and the fierce siege it suffered from Saladin's forces. The earlier Byzantine fortress was a trapezoidal solid complex. It stood on the peak of the high plateau (at a height of

One of the more extensive and imposing additions is found in the land walls of the capital, **Constantinople** (Istanbul, Turkey).[25] This addition consists of the whole north section between the Tekfur Saray and – what remains today of – the Blachernae Palace (the so-called 'Prison of Anemas') and is commonly known as the 'Manuel Wall' (*see* Plate 37). It is a single line of defence, with no outer wall or moat. It covers a fairly steep hill and therefore any further structure would be useless. The curtain is thicker and more massive than the main wall of the earlier (Theodosian) enclosure. It is internally reinforced with buttresses that supported blind arches and is flanked by thirteen powerful towers built at close intervals (20–30m). In its south part the towers are interchangeably U-shaped and octagonal; in the north part they are only rectangular. One further rectangular tower was added in 1186–1187 by Emperor Isaac Angelos at the north end of this section, in front of the Blachernae Palace.

The Komnenian towers had three storeys. The first storey was blind, with no arrow slits or openings. Defensive measures were concentrated on the second floor (with embrasures for arrow slits and a wooden floor) and on the flat roof, which rested on solid domical vaults. These towers differ greatly from their predecessors. They are massive, reaching a wall thickness of *c.*4–5m, and are reinforced internally by buttresses. This restricted the inner space.

Plate 37. Constantinople. The 'Manuel Wall'. (*Photo*: David Hendrix)

The 'Prison of Anemas', an intriguing structure, is preserved at the north end of the walls (*see* Plate 38). This is a long and narrow building (11 × 55m), built in front of and in contact with the fortification line. Its exterior is regulated with pilasters and buttresses, corresponding to an internal series of walls (set vertically to the curtain). These in turn supported barrel vaults and ultimately created a lofty platform some 20m above ground level. In fact, what we see today was the undercroft of the Blachernae Palace, built to provide the necessary height for spectacular views towards the Golden Horn, the city and the surrounding countryside. The rectangular tower attributed to Isaac Angelos had a triple-arched opening on its upper level, presumably a loggia for appearances, with a now-missing balcony that was once supported on a series of column spoils used as brackets.

The Komnenian walls exhibit many differences in their masonry; their only constant elements are reused stone material, along with bricks, in various building techniques and combinations (alternating courses or bands of bricks and stones, rubble, cloisonné, recessed-brick, etc.). All structures use cribwork in a sophisticated and consistent way. There are also many decorative elements (such as conches with saw-toothed motifs, female busts set above the Gyrolimne Gate). Manuel I Komnenos (r. 1143–1180) is the emperor credited with building these new structures; he supposedly wanted to include the Blachernae Palace within the walls. The complex architecture and techniques employed in this area have generated many divergent theories as to its building and dating sequence.

Several sections in the walls of **Thessaloniki** (Greece)[26] were repaired over the course of the 12th century, mostly limited to damaged parts of the old city wall. The masonry of this phase consists of alternating neat courses of stones and bricks, set with regularity. Lime mortar covers all the surface abnormalities, and is also extensively used even to cover the surface of bricks and stones. A multi-coloured effect was created by mixing the red of the bricks, the green of the stone and the white of the mortar. This masonry is found at various parts (such as the tower in the southwest corner of the citadel, the wall north of the Litaia Gate, sections of the northwest wall, the tower and the wall where the city wall joins the citadel from the west, and the towers in the east wall of the citadel).

This building phase is connected to two inscriptions from the third quarter of the 12th century, located in the southwest tower of the citadel. The names mentioned in the inscriptions (Andronikos Lapardas and Michael Prosouh) are known in the prosopography of the Komnenian era (around 1167). Also belonging to this period is the inscription at the citadel tower bearing the name of Bishop Basil, identified as the metropolitan of Thessaloniki, Basil Achridinos (1145–1169).

The city of **Ioannina** (Epirus, Greece)[27] played a significant role during Alexios I's wars against the Normans. The medieval city occupied a hill next to the lake, which offered protection from at least two sides. The fortifications

Plate 38. Constantinople. The 'Prison of Anemas' wall. (*Source*: Koç University – GABAM Archive)

preserved today are, to a large extent, the work of the early 19th century. It seems, however, that in the Byzantine period there was a large enclosure with two inner citadels, each occupying a natural elevation. Of the original enclosure (probably 10th century?), which was used in the wars of Alexios, nothing remains today. Yet each of the citadels has been attributed by different researchers to this period. A strong oval-shaped tower from one of them (known as the Municipal Museum citadel) remains today. It is built with rubble masonry and still has the ground and first-floor levels. The citadel gate was flanked by two solid towers and had a two-leaf door (outside) and a portcullis (inside).

The second citadel (today known as Içkale, or 'inner castle') preserves in its interior a Middle Byzantine rectangular enclosure, *c.*0.11ha, with a circular tower at the corner towards the settlement. This tower rises to a height of *c.*13m and is commonly known as the Tower of Bohemond. Both the tower and the adjoining walls were built with ashlar blocks, probably taken from an older antique fortification.

Anna Komnene clearly states that the Norman prince Bohemond occupied Ioannina in 1082 and that he found the existing citadel to be insecure; he therefore built another one in a different part of the walls. Based on this information, we can deduce that the city was already fortified and that it already had a citadel. Which of the two is the one that was present and which Bohemond added are still up for debate.

In the city of **Rhodes** (Rhodos, Greece)[28] a new fortification was built to the south of the existing one, probably to include a part of the settlement that lay outside the walls (*see* Plate 28). The trace of this extension was located, fairly accurately, during excavations, although only segments have been found. The new fortification had a slightly irregular rectangular plan, so the city had a tripartite division: the citadel, the inner castle (fort, later collacium) and the (newly built) outer castle (city). The area within the walls had an estimated size of 17.5ha.

The new wall, with a thickness of *c.*2.14m, was built with sizeable blocks and pre-existing building material. In all its surviving parts there is evidence of the systematic reuse of material from older buildings (Hellenistic or Early Christian) in the area. Excavations also revealed that during this period repairs took place in the pre-existing fort, notably to the main wall near the Church of the Virgin of the Castle, and to the south wall, as well as to the outer wall. This building activity is currently attributed to the end of the 11th century or during the 12th, a period when the strategic position of Rhodes was updated because its port served all the passing Crusader armies on their way to Palestine.

In addition to the cities, the bulk of the fortifications attributed to the Komnenian era, as noted already, comprises hilltop forts (as in the cases of Rentina, Acrocorinth and Palio Pyli) that were destined to protect garrisons, the surrounding population or local magnates. In many instances these forts were rebuilt citadels of pre-existing towns, and also included small settlements either inside or outside the walls.

At the fort of **Rentina** (Greece)[29] the constant erosion of the bedrock brought about the destruction or abandonment of the pre-existing eastern walls, including the end tower Π1 (see above). To amend this situation the 'twin walls' were constructed: a double line of walls preserved to a considerable height and forming an obtuse angle. This double line was erected to create a barrier to enemies attacking from the eastern – weak and vulnerable – side of the settlement. During this period the western side of the walls was also externally repaired and large surfaces were covered with white slip. All these works were dated to the 12th century.

Acrocorinth (Greece)[30] acquired a new set of strong walls. As mentioned above, its plateau rises above the city of Corinth, which was the regional capital of the Theme of Hellas and later of the Peloponnese. However, Acrocorinth seems to have developed as an independent settlement and might even have been the seat of administrative and ecclesiastical authorities. The new fortification programme was one of the most important building programmes in the southern Balkans, and it is very much what one sees today. On the one hand, taking full advantage of the steep and naturally fortified sides, a simple wall (with a length of *c.*2.7km at a height of *c.*5m) surrounds the hill. Along its course, it has only two towers (one rectangular, one triangular), both on the relatively vulnerable southern side, but on all sides there are angles (pseudo-towers, able to provide flanking fire), depending on the hill's contour.

In contrast, the main access to the castle, from the west side, was heavily fortified (*see* Plate 39): there are two lines of walls (the inner one at a higher point and the outer one somewhat lower down the hillside) that meet at their ends. The outer wall was strengthened with massive towers, with the gate opening on the ground floor of a tower (with the gate axis set parallel to the line of the walls, so that the attacker had to turn in order to reach it). The presence of murals on the room above the door may point to its use as a chapel. The builders reused the ancient walls for the inner wall (with a C-form plan), and it was strengthened with six massive towers (four rectangular and two triangular). A monumental barrel-vaulted gate opens between two of these towers. Its façade is decorated with a slightly horseshoe-shaped blind arch. The gate closed with a double-leaf door on the outside and had a portcullis set further in.

The defences of Acrocorinth had simple battlements with merlons and crenels and a few arrow loops opening on the towers below the battlement level. There are two simultaneous masonry styles: the first, in more visible parts of the walls, uses large, dressed blocks (some of which were spolia) with irregular lines of bricks between the courses, while the second (in secondary places) is built with small, roughly hewn stones, cut from the local bedrock and set with bricks at the joints.

This impressive fortification programme has been tentatively attributed to Manuel I Komnenos, perhaps following the Norman raid on Corinth in 1147.

Plate 39. Acrocorinth. The fortifications of the west front.
(*Source*: Athanasoulis, *The Castle of Acrocorinth and Its Enhancement Project (2006–2009)*)

The castle of **Palio Pyli** (Kos, Greece)[31] occupies a rough hill, cut from the main mountain chain, at the centre of the island. The walls, forming three enclosures around the hill, followed the contour of the ground, reinforced with rectangular, semicircular and pentagonal towers. The only part of the castle that can be securely dated to this period is the central gateway.

This was originally a tower, with the entrance opening at its ground floor, which is the only currently surviving part. The main façade had lateral conches on both sides of the gate, decorated with brick motifs. Four massive corner pillars within the tower supported a low dome through a system of arches and pendentives. The lower part of this structure was built with spolia, roughly rectangular stones and broken bricks at the joints. The upper part was built with all-brick masonry. The inner pillars and the façade conches used the recessed-brick technique.

The castle at Palio Pyli is linked to the figure of Christodoulos, a monk of Mount Latros and later the founder of the Patmos Monastery (see below), although nothing can be attributed to his activities. In 1136 the emperor John II Komnenos bequeathed the area to the Pantokrator Monastery of Constantinople. The central gateway has been dated, based on its structural elements (brick decoration, conches and recessed-brick technique) to the late 11th/early 12th centuries. It was built either by the representative of the state, who controlled the Christodoulos estate after 1088, or by the monks of the Pantokrator Monastery of Constantinople, around 1136.

A group of three hilltop forts – St Ilarion, Buffavento and Kantara – dotting the northern part of **Cyprus** have been summarily ascribed to the Byzantine efforts (perhaps in the times of Alexios I) to counterbalance the Seljuk offensive coming from the shores of Asia Minor.[32] Parts of the original walls are currently preserved at St Ilarion, but none of these castles has been thoroughly studied.

Fortifications of Asia Minor
The territories of Asia Minor – those that remained or were gradually reintegrated into the imperial territory – served as frontier zones in the constant struggle against the Seljuk state, based first in Nicaea and then in Konya. In these circumstances, all fortifications, despite their size, should be actively seen as administrative centres, rallying points, war bases and last refuges for the surrounding population. Their limited size, in most cases, reflected the respective resources and forces the empire could spare in order to man and defend them.

Earlier civic fortifications, and especially their better defended citadels, were strengthened to instill a sense of security in the local populations. Most of these walls, if not explicitly mentioned in historical resources (as in the case of Nicaea), are often attributed to the Komnenian programme of securing the administrative centres of the empire (such as Kotyaion, Pergamon, Nikomedeia, Hierapolis and Makre-Telmessos).[33]

In **Nicaea** (Iznik, Turkey)[34] a single tower (106B) at the south part of the enclosure is attributed to the period immediately following the First Crusade. It is built exclusively with reused material that was hastily put together. Many Seljuk tombstones are included, giving us a terminus post quem.

In 1097 the Seljuk city was besieged by the Crusaders, who concentrated their efforts at the south wall; more specifically, they focused on the tower known as 'Gonatas' because the structure was already leaning due to erosion that had happened a century earlier. The Crusaders dug mines under the tower and breached it. After the capitulation, the tower was quickly rebuilt by Alexios I Komnenos as a way to bolster the newly established Byzantine control in the area.

At **Kotyaion** (Kütahya, Turkey)[35] the citadel of the city received an extensive second building phase of its fortifications (*see* Plate 33). The main features were the addition of numerous massive towers to the main wall with short distances between them, and the transformation of the outer wall to a series of constrained spaces with no obvious utility.

From the surviving sixty-three towers of the enclosure, fifty-six preserve masonry of this period, while forty-three are totally new creations. The castle of this period uses U-shaped towers with masonry of alternating courses of bricks (usually five) and stones. The new towers belong to two groups: they are either solid with one defensive surface at their summit or they have a room on the first-floor level and a flat roof. They are built at such close intervals – almost touching – that usually the distance separating them is smaller than their width. These towers occupied the whole space between the main and outer walls, even projecting beyond the latter. Nevertheless, it is clear that the outer wall continued to function, and it was neither abandoned nor changed in form.

Various styles are observed in the masonry of the new parts: some sections were built with stones of different sizes, randomly used together with broken bricks and covered with pink slip. Others present a cloisonné façade, while there are also sections with banded masonry (alternating rows of bricks and stones).

The second building phase has been dated to the Komnenian period, based on the new military technology, which the new towers indicate (see above/below), and the masonry type (bands of bricks and cloisonné). The city was lost to the Seljuks after 1071, but was recaptured by the Byzantines in the period either of John II or Manuel I Komnenos. Foss dated the rebuilding of the Kotyaion walls to the period 1120–1150, as part of the Komnenian policy to secure Asia Minor through the construction of fortifications.

In the city of **Pergamon** (Turkey)[36] Manuel I Komnenos created a new fort as part of his endeavour to strengthen the fortifications of the newly created Theme of Neocastra. The walls surrounded the old citadel. The better preserved parts occupy the foot of the hill, built above the ancient ruins with rectangular, semi-circular and U-shaped towers at distances of 30–40m. The towers had façades with lines of spolia and rough stones, with an interpolating single line of broken bricks. In places there is also a type of cloisonné. The masonry is mostly irregular, with large blocks intercepting the courses, while the lines of bricks rarely run the full length of the towers.

The wall is built in the same way. Despite the differences at certain points, the walls of Pergamon belong to the same period. Their decorative elements are distinctive, however, and evident at the more exposed parts of the walls.

In **Nikomedeia** (Turkey)[37] the old citadel walls were reused and integrated into a hill fortress. The main entrance opened in the south side, and the walls are strengthened with rectangular or circular towers. An outer wall existed in the two especially vulnerable sections. One of them lies on the slope outside the north walls, where the hill is relatively flat and easily accessible. Only a small part is preserved, although its traces can be followed for *c.*175m.

At the interior of the fortress, five towers delineate an inner ward at the northeast corner. Two of them were clearly part of the older external wall, while the others turn to the fortress interior and were added later on to create a separate defensive area. The inner ward is a triangle with sides measuring *c.*$50 \times 60 \times 70$m.

The most extensive remains, visible in almost every part of the Byzantine walls, are built with masonry styles (alternating brick, cloisonné) that are attributed to the Komnenian era. It is the most extensive reconstruction observed in Nikomedeia, unfortunately with no precise dates available. The rough cloisonné is present in many variations, which probably reflects different building phases or wall repairs. It is possible that all variations present a large reconstruction phase of the 12th century.

The text of Odo de Deuil, who visited the city in 1147, mentions that the city, and obviously the walls, was in ruins. If this was the case, then reconstruction must be dated to the second half of the 12th century and to the emperor Manuel I Komnenos.

In **Hierapolis** (Pamukkale, Turkey)[38] the fort of this period lies close to the bath area at the edge of a ravine that overlooks Pamukkale and the Lykos valley. It is possible that the walls on the ridge of the ravine were never constructed. Those towards the city are preserved in good condition, while some parts have collapsed. This side may have had a moat for added protection. The wall was built exclusively with spolia; it includes rectangular ashlar blocks, some with classical inscriptions and a number of column shafts set vertically so as to unite the inner and outer façades. A section of the walls is preserved to its original height, along with its battlements, which were later walled up. A number of staircases built along the inner façade led to the wall-walk.

The three rectangular towers had at least two floors, the upper one resting on horizontal beams and wooden planks. They were defended by arrow slits with vertical slots on the exterior, fanned inwards. One of the towers has been excavated. Signs of a fire were uncovered above the ground floor, which was constructed of thick lime mortar. The interior had been filled in, while earthquake cracks cut across all the masonry, including the ashlar blocks and the stairs of the walls.

The date of the fort's construction is unknown, but it may be attributed to the Komnenian era. Manuel I Komnenos tried to secure the area through fortifications in the years after 1150. Yet the lack of bricks in this masonry is a rarity and is not encountered in other Komnenian works. Another theory attributes the fort to Manuel Maurozomes, a Byzantine liege of the Seljuk sultan in the early 13th century. In any case, it was abandoned because of an earthquake (or not long before one). The fire uncovered within the tower produced lead coins of the Aydin Emirate, dated 1360–1390, providing a terminus post quem for the abandonment of the fort at the end of the 14th century, during the Seljuk period.

A number of forts of various sizes have been recognized in the western and southern parts of Asia Minor, intended to protect populations, secure land-sea routes and facilitate war efforts as military stations (as in the cases of Korykos, Lopadion, Achyraous and Malagina). In addition, we find the forts that guarded the entrance from the Black Sea to the Bosporos Straits. Today only the east (Asian side) one survives, known as **Hieron** (Anadolu Kavağı, Turkey).[39] The fort occupies the summit of a high hill, while a large outer enclosure (whose date is still debated) extends downwards along the sides of the hill. The fort is polygonal in plan, its length greater than 500m, while its width fluctuates between 60 and

Plate 40. Hieron (Anadolu Kavağı). View of the main entrance. (*Photo*: David Hendrix)

130m. It probably housed a large garrison. The main entrance, opening to the east, was protected by two massive circular towers (*see* Plate 40); the distance between them was less than 7m. The gate was also protected with a portcullis. In every tower there were high rooms with a cross plan and access from the ground floor through arched openings. Originally the towers had internal wooden floors that allowed access to the level with the arrow loops.

Along the inner side of the east and south walls there is a series of blind arches for the support of the wall-walk. Circular towers, smaller than those of the gate, reinforced the walls at intervals of *c.*80m or more. On the north side, which was steep and physically protected, there were neither towers nor blind arches.

At Hieron the façade of the walls is set with bands of spolia and raw stones separated by lines of bricks. At the towers of the gate most stones are roughly rectangular and set in bands of four courses alternating with seven courses of bricks. The walls on the sides of the hill are built with smaller stones, set at courses of six alternating with four or five courses of bricks. The masonry of the inner towers features rows of bricks alternating with rows of stones.

The fort of **Lopadion** (Uluabat, Turkey)[40] stood on the banks of the Ryndakos river (the Mysia valley) and defended a bridge and a land route connecting the Marmara region to the provinces of Hellespont and the Aegean. It was built in 1130 as a military camp (*aplekton*) by John II Komnenos and served as an important base in the imperial campaigns against the Seljuks.

Plate 41. Lopadion (Uluabat). View of the fortification. (*Photo*: David Hendrix)

The fortress was rectangular, measuring *c.* 475 × 150m, with towers of various shapes set to distances of 30–40m (*see* Plate 41). The gates were simple openings through the wall, and the plan has no special features or evolved defensive construction. The simplicity reflects its function as a fortified camp and meeting point for the forces that were to move against the enemy. The masonry is homogeneous. One of the preserved towers has unhewn stones and spolia in courses in its façade, with alternating smaller and larger stones. Every course of stones is separated by a single file of bricks. Broken bricks are set parallel to the bricks to fill in the joints. There are also many bricks set vertically so as to create an irregular cloisonné.

The walls are built in a similar manner, but the stones are usually small and set with large quantities of lime mortar, while the lines of bricks are set more regularly. At certain points the surface was covered with a lime mortar slip, in such a way that it covers any defects in the masonry, and especially so in the joints.

The fort of **Achyraous** (south of Balıkesir, Turkey)[41] presents an interesting masonry style. It uses rough stones of various sizes, whose courses alternate with a single or triple band of bricks. Many of the stones are set vertically, with bricks piled among them. There is also some brick decoration that creates a vivid impression; this imperial structure was clearly thought out and cared for.

The remains of **Malagina/Metabole** (in the area of Pamukova, Turkey)[42] have been identified as a Komnenian fortress rebuilt in 1145 after a Turkish raid. Part of the fortification differed structurally from the rest and was identified with this rebuilding phase. A large projecting construction with arched openings on three sides is visible from far away and has visual contact with the whole Sangarios valley. The façade is built with spolia from the nearby Hellenistic walls, and the rubble is set in courses. There is a bond with three lines of bricks at the level of the arch springing. Traces from pendentives in the interior show that the area was probably covered with a brick dome, which would have supported the platform of the floor above. Due to its size and position, the construction presented a serious threat to every attacker. The walls that connected this tower to the rest of the fortification are built with rubble and bands of bricks.

On the coastline opposite Cyprus, the gulf of **Korykos** (Kızkalesi, Turkey)[43] was an important naval crossing point. The fortifications consist of the land castle, built on the coast (*see* Plate 42), and the island castle, built on a rock in the centre of the gulf.

The land castle is almost square in plan, with two lines of walls (main and outer) strengthened with rectangular towers. This is a singular case of a concentric fortification, with obviously many diverse building phases. In its masonry there are large quantities of spolia from ancient buildings in the surrounding area. The island castle was a rectangle, with a single line of walls strengthened with semicircular towers at the corners.

The older walls of both castles have been dated to the early 12th century and attributed to Alexios I Komnenos. According to an inscription, the island castle was built partly by Hetoun I, king of Lesser Armenia, in 1251. Yet it is evident that these castles, the land one in particular, are palimpsests of various rebuildings that have not been studied properly.

Plate 42. Korykos (Kızkalesi). View of the land castle. (*Photo:* author)

In view of the lack of surviving superstructures, the proposed reconstructions for the towers of Rentina reflect an interesting selection, even though their veracity cannot be confirmed.

The Komnenian period saw a definite degree of renewal and experimentation in tower building. Even when using traditional shapes (rectangular, octagonal, U-shaped), towers from this period are robust and actively defensive. Their walls are massive, and their interior is usually covered with lowered domical vaults supported either on pendentives or inner buttresses. They are multi-storeyed, with the main defensive level concentrated at the battlement level, and arrow loops on the first-floor level. At present it cannot be differentiated between arrow loops meant for bows and those for the new portable crossbows that appeared during this period. For the battlement level, especially in the cases where it rests on massive vaults (Kotyaion, Constantinople, Hieron), it has been proposed that it was intended to accommodate the new artillery weapon, the trebuchet. Although these structures were attributed to Manuel I Komnenos, more careful consideration shows that new military technology was not simply introduced overnight. Forms and weapons were evenly disseminated in all parts of the empire without any sign of rupture from earlier tradition; it seems therefore that Byzantium did not 'adopt' a foreign trend but rather fully participated in the military advances that occurred in other parts of the world.

Another feature observed on two Komnenian examples (Constantinople, Palio Pyli) is the brickwork conches on their façades; they were slip covered and incised in such a way as to imitate decorative patterns or the masonry underneath. Similar elements are commonly seen in religious buildings of this period, and their presence in fortifications poses new questions about the aesthetics of the period.

Gates

Few gates of the 7th to 9th centuries can be securely dated. Most of them are simple openings between two towers. The one at Ephesus has two doorways, with a small distance between them. The gate of Rhodes, although only the foundation level survives, is also very illuminating since it follows Early Byzantine strategies, with a follow-up of two gates on the same axis: one opening at the outer wall and the second at the main wall, flanked by rectangular towers.

The bent gateway of the Ankyra citadel stands out for both its intriguing plan and its structural details: the barbican, the right-angled positioning of the doors, the external portcullis and the internal double-leaf door, the extreme use of spolia. It was initially seen as a *unicum* in Byzantine fortifications, for which only Islamic/eastern antecedents could be found.[3] Nevertheless, the presence of similar formations in the earlier North African fortifications of Justinian, in the gates of Amastris (quasi-contemporary with Ankyra), and in the later Balkan complexes (Mystras) proves that bent gateways were an integral part of Byzantine tradition.

Gate examples are far fewer for the 10th to 11th centuries. The north gate of Păcuiul lui Soare is a typical gate tower, with a double gate opening at its ground level and along the same axis. They are blocked with a portcullis (outside) and a one-leaf door (inside). The monumental gate of Samuel's castle at Ohrid has also been assigned to this period and is interpreted as a typical structure: it is a simple opening between two towers.

The same forms of a tower-gateway (Palio Pyli, Acrocorinth), a gate flanked by a single tower (Constantinople, Korykos), or an opening between twin towers (Hieron) are also found in 12th-century examples. In most preserved examples the doors are beneath semicircular arches, forming a relieving panel above a horizontal lintel. They also stand out for their decorative aspirations, with brick conches, sculptured lintels or brickwork façades. The Gyrolimne Gate of Constantinople, decorated with the three busts of empresses, is another *unicum* which needs further attention.[4]

Ramparts

For the period from the 7th to the 9th century there are many defensive features that show continuity with the previous era and contradict the claim of a Byzantine decline. The existence of a double line of walls (outer and inner) in a number of cases (Rhodes, Abdera, Kotyaion/Kütahya) is at first glance surprising, yet it shows that the know-how existed and that sophisticated forms of defence could readily be employed when needed. The lower parts of the Rhodes outer wall had a talus, meant to withstand artillery fire, mining, etc. This has not been observed so far in Byzantine military architecture, but it became a common practice in later medieval castles.

In the few cases where the top section of the wall survives, we usually observe a single line of defence at the battlement level; the case of Ankyra, with a place for archers to shoot from below the battlements, stands out. In a singularly preserved battlement level in the 7th-century Nicaea repairs, we observe rectangular crenels, each with a cross-wall for side protection; this is a feature prescribed in Hellenistic military literature but seldom seen in practice. Rectangular crenels also survive in Ankyra, yet in the 9th-century Nicaea towers the crenels are triangular.

In fact, very few things can be said about the curtain walls of the Middle Byzantine period, since they have received relatively little notice. A distinct change is evident again in the Komnenian era, when we see the use of blind arches on the interior side of the walls. This is consistently used in the Constantinople walls and Hieron, but also appears in provincial fortifications (Palio Pyli), making it a widespread trend that was revived in this period for reasons that remain difficult to explain at present. Blind arches were also encountered in the walls of the Daphni Monastery (see below); if they date from the 11th century, as some researchers believe, then we have there an immediate predecessor that demonstrates continuity with the Komnenian walls.

Defensive Features

The arrow loops and rectangular openings for ballistae in the Ankyra walls stand out as among the few surviving defensive features for the 7th to 9th centuries. Being structured below the battlement level, they were served by corridors within the wall. A covered gallery with embrasures is also reported at 7th-century Sardis, although not described in detail. A remarkable feature is preserved in the 10th-century walls of Rentina: a covered gallery protecting a staircase that descends from the corner tower down the cliff, all the way to the river passing beneath. Its raison d'être was contested, but the provision of water seems to have been its most probable purpose. If so, it predates the widespread use of such devices in the Late Medieval (*c.* 14th century) Balkan castles.

As already discussed, the main evolution in 12th-century Byzantium defences seems to be the introduction of two new weapons, the crossbow and the counter-weight catapult (trebuchet). The use of these weapons became extremely important to the Komnenian military machine, and their presence must have profoundly influenced the design, arrangement and structure of the walls (as was also the case in western Europe).

Historians have not yet researched in depth how defensive elements may have been altered to accommodate the positions necessary to fire a crossbow. However, it seems that the arrow slits of this period (for example, in the Komnenian walls of Constantinople) become much shorter and compact, pointing to a targeted use and potentially being adjusted for the new weapon. It may also be that a number of earlier arrow slits in the outer wall of the Theodosian curtains of Constantinople were adjusted/repaired to accommodate crossbows.

As for the trebuchet, Foss was the first to suggest that the Komnenian towers (Kotyaion, Constantinople, Hieron) were specifically constructed and acquired solid roof platforms to facilitate the use of this ballistic weapon. Since it was possible to throw a stone weighing *c.* 150kg a distance of 300m, its counterweight may have reached as much as 10 tonnes in weight. Therefore we can easily understand the need for massive towers and their differences in relation to those preceding the period.

work is known mainly from a later French translation (by Jean de Vignay), under the title *Enseignemens ou ordenances pour un seigneur qui a guerres et grans gouvernemens a faire*. Theodore himself says that he composed the work when he was in Constantinople and left it to be used by his father (Andronikos II) and nephew (Andronikos III).

Theodore covers a number of subjects but in a confusing order, always taking a personal stand and narrating from his own point of view. For example, he touches upon how to mobilize and organize armies, how to divide the spoils of war, how to plan attacks, how to use spies, etc. Yet he speaks very little of tactics, and despite mentioning that castles must be fortified, he does not say how. He states that people engaged in building walls should be fearsome of their lord, since this fear would drive them to construct better fortifications. If mercenaries are to be employed, they should come from different countries, since if they speak the same language they would be prone to plotting against their employer. Whether the author consulted older Byzantine authors or contemporary western ones is debatable.

Army Organization

The Late Byzantine period was the only period in which every part of Byzantine-held territory was open to slaughter and destruction. Conflicts were not simple frontier struggles but rather devastating calamities that affected every part of the country. Byzantium – taken as a whole – in its last period is a society at war, with no clear frontiers or distinctions between who was fighting and who was not; thus, reviewing Late Byzantine armies is a complicated endeavour.[5] The basic features of these armies were their small size and motley composition. Soldiers could be mercenaries, local farmers, conscripts or small fief holders. An army could not solely consist of mercenaries, simply because there were never adequate funds for their payment; nor could it consist solely of fief holders or small landowners since they could never campaign for long periods of time and they were bound to specific areas, their homelands.

Our information is both very fortuitous and uneven, depending on a variety of sporadic sources that rarely cover all the Byzantine states. We often have references to titles or office-holders without truly understanding what these titles represented in terms of manpower and potential. In the Empire of Trebizond, for example, the land forces were commanded by the *megas* (grand) *domesticos*, and the *megas stratopedarchis* was responsible for local troops. Foreign mercenaries and divisions were under the *megas kontostavlos*. Naval forces were commanded by the *megas doukas* (grand duke) or *amiralio*. We also have to bear in mind that the art of war was substantially altered from the 13th to the 14th century, passing from what was basically a continuation of the Komnenian army organization to a system that could be described as 'early Renaissance armies', almost identical to what happened in contemporary Italy.

For the 13th century information is forthcoming for the Nicaean Empire: the policy of the Lascarids against a variety of enemies was successful and in accordance with local conditions. They aimed to protect their borders and strengthen their fortifications by leaning mostly on local forces. They continued extensively using the *pronoia* institution, that is, grants of extensive lands or resources to influential magnates in return for military service, either in person or by proxy. Smaller land-holdings were also distributed to people who were expected to serve in either the army or the navy. Finally, mercenaries were employed, but they were used mainly in more distant expeditions, such as to the Balkans. We learn of different warrior types, such as heavily or lightly armoured horsemen, infantry and mounted archers, and of different contingents, such as the palace guards, the castle/frontier guards, etc.

Whether the same systems and divisions applied also to Trebizond and Epirus is difficult to say. In the sources we find only rare glimpses, such as when Michael I of Epirus asked Frederic II Hohenstaufen to employ mercenaries from Italy. We can only assume that, along with mercenaries, local forces would have formed the backbone of the regional armies, supported by militias that guarded cities and forts.

The continuous warfare in the Balkans, where a host of different polities (Byzantine, Frankish, Bulgarian and Serbian) fought each other, demanded enormous resources. Michael VIII Palaiologos is usually accused of utilizing all the resources of his state to support his western policy: he reinforced the Byzantine navy and used the Asia Minor military units for his European campaigns. However, this policy left the Asian provinces undefended and open to Turkmen raiders. Losing territories, and consequently the soldiers supported by them, meant that the state had to rely more on mercenaries. The army under his successor, Andronikos II Palaiologos, comprised constantly changing groups of mercenaries, combined with inadequate local forces.[6] Each time, an army was formed to confront new dangers and unpredictable situations, with no central policy or long-term results apart from survival.

Early in Andronikos II's reign a Mongolian force appeared that had been requested by his father; he used this force in his battles against Serbia. Later on he tried to install military units in Asia Minor, which ultimately revolted against him and had to be suppressed; their failure accelerated the loss of all the eastern provinces. He next turned to Alan, and then to Catalan, mercenaries.

In 1320 Andronikos II tried once more to organize permanent mercenary forces and a navy; neither venture was successful. He found himself plunged into a war with Venice and was forced to watch the Venetians burning Byzantine ships in the Golden Horn, right in front of his palace. In the ensuing period of civil wars the military strategy of John VI Kantakouzenos stood out for its simplicity and consistency: for every conflict he summoned Turkish mercenaries, as he had excellent personal relations with their leaders.

a few pockets of land were left under Byzantine control, with the exception of Morea, where the Byzantine presence continued to expand until it covered almost the whole Peloponnese (with the exception of the Venetian territories). Taking advantage of the collapse of Byzantine authority (or possibly at the invitation of some of the various factions participating in the civil wars as mercenaries), the Ottomans eventually crossed over at Gallipoli and started their conquest of the Balkans, with Didymoteichon in 1352 as the first step of an astonishingly swift expansion. Gradually the Byzantines (as all other Balkan polities) were deprived of all their lands, with the exception of the city (and immediate hinterland) of Constantinople, some coastal settlements and north Aegean islands, and the distant Morea. From this point on their main aim was self-preservation.

A surprising Ottoman setback followed their defeat at the Battle of Ankyra (1402), and the Byzantines took back some of their lost territories (such as Thessaloniki) and revoked concessions (such as renting the whole Morea Despotate to the Hospitallers). The final half century of the Byzantine state, until the conquest of Constantinople in 1453, is usually seen as a death rattle, prolonged by the constant wait for western reinforcements that never materialized.

The siege of Constantinople has been regarded as a milestone in the history of fortification technology – a successful demonstration of the devastating force that the new weapon (cannon fire) could inflict on traditional fortifications.[4] It has also been seen as equally pivotal for military changes, as the slightly later Italian wars of Charles VIII show. Certainly there have been numerous contemporary and later accounts of the events, as well as miracle stories, myths, reconstructions and depictions. It has been accorded disproportionate historical/political value (although this is changing in current scholarship), seen variously as the end of Byzantium, a milestone in Ottoman history, a struggle of civilizations, etc.

The Fortifications

This is a period of intensified military activity, with a peak in the construction of fortification structures around 1300, but building continued uninterrupted until the very end of the state (1453 for Constantinople, 1460 for Mystras). The vast majority of new structures were ultimately small in size and incorporated a spectrum of types, ranging from isolated towers built by local magnates to ambitious forts with fully explored defensive features. In addition, almost all pre-existing fortifications received repairs and modifications.

In **Asia Minor** the 13th century was one of the most creative periods of castle building, when the Lascarids were focused on securing their territories. The remains from this period are extensive; fewer examples remain from the Palaiologos era, during which the last efforts to defend Byzantine Asia Minor occurred.

The Palaiologos dynasty worked on securing their **Balkan** territories, and their building activity in this region was extremely rich in quantity, range of forms and quality. In some instances these structures were seen as part of a specific fortification programme. Such was the case of a series of fortifications around Thessaloniki, built in the three first decades of the 14th century to defend the Macedonian territories against Serbian expansionism.[5] Another set of fortifications meant to co-exist and secure the fertile lands around the Evros river were identified in Thrace.[6] In retrospect, many researchers interpret these endeavours as futile, desperate and hasty. However, when seen from close-up, there is rarely any sign of despair; they were built with adequate resources, evolved defensive features and a sense that their existence would secure prosperity.

The most important category of fortifications from this period is civic walls. In most cases these were mainly additions to older, pre-existing settlements; at these sites older walls were repaired, and autonomous citadels or forts were very often added at the highest/most secure point. These could be protected with minimum forces and could serve as a last refuge against both external assaults and internal (civic) unrest. In the few newly founded settlements (Mystras) a similar care is shown for compartmentalized defence. In all cases these structures underlined the need for increased security from multiple threats.

Another category is the forts/castles (though without the connotation of a feudal lord), whether isolated or related to an unfortified settlement. Many medieval villages were often founded or transferred near the walls of such a castle for protection reasons.

There is a single case of a linear fortification, namely the Hexamilion wall, for whose (re)construction written sources provide detailed accounts.

Fortifications of Asia Minor[7]

In Asia Minor most of the pre-existing **civic centres** (such as Nicaea, Nikomedeia, Magnesia or Smyrna) received additions or repairs during this period. The dating of these structures is often the result of correlating historical sources with masonry styles.

Nicaea (Iznik, Turkey),[8] the temporary capital of the state from 1204, experienced exceptional building activity, related to or explained by the dynamic character of the Lascarid regime. Theodore I Lascaris, the founder of the dynasty, is credited with building some large and powerful towers (based on inscriptions, towers 19 and 106), higher than all the previous ones. They were constructed up to their mid-height with spolia, while the superstructure was built mainly with bricks. Tower 106 is partly built with cloisonné masonry; both use cribwork. However, these did not alter the overall defensive system.

Theodore's successor, however, John III Vatatzes, completely restructured the defences of the city. He added a lower outer wall and an external moat, and he heightened the main (pre-existing) wall (*see* Plate 43). In this way he created a new unified system that was much admired by his contemporaries. The similarity of this system to that of Constantinople was not a coincidence, since Nicaea became, in the minds of its citizens, a miniature of the 'lost City', or a 'capital in exile'.

land walls included the reinforcement of the main wall and towers, the blocking of the lower line of arrow slits and the concentration of fire mainly at battlement level. He related them, potentially, to the wider use of the trebuchet and the crossbow and to the need for protection against (expected) cannon fire, as well as to the diminished number of men available to man the walls.

A series of outer wall towers, situated along the south part of the land walls, were rebuilt following the same architectural plan. They are all rectangular, built exclusively with reused stones. They have a horizontal cornice at their mid-section, a box machicolation at their southern dead angle (where the tower meets the wall), and early cannon-holes on all sides. It is tempting to date them to after the city passed under Ottoman rule, although this cannot be said with certainty.

Similarly, early cannon-holes (with a circular opening on the exterior face, set in an embrasure of the walls) are encountered in several parts of the main land walls. Again their date is debated (whether Byzantine or early Ottoman), although the Byzantines reportedly used also portable/small cannon.

Important information comes from the document known as the 'Dimitriadis plan': executed in the late 19th century by the Ottoman engineer George Dimitriadis, it accurately portrays the (largely lost or altered) Marmara Sea walls.[18] Among them there is a high rectangular tower whose top is protected by continuous machicolation, clearly dated to the 14th century. This is a structure reminiscent of multiple other examples in the Balkans/Aegean and the western European world, proving that Constantinople's walls were updated with advanced defensive forms.

Furthermore, fortified complexes were created along the land walls that could serve as independent strongholds/residences of the political authority (or conflicting political authorities) in times of unrest or peril (coming both from within and outside the city). Starting from the south, the first such fortified residence was at the Golden Gate and it played an important role in the civil wars, changing hands among the contenders.[19] John VI Kantakouzenos (1347–1354) built or reinforced it during the time of the civil wars; John V Palaiologos (1341–1391) enlarged and embellished it by using architectural sculpture from ruined buildings, such as a series of stone reliefs on the façade of the outer wall gate. In 1390 Sultan Bayezid I intervened and demanded the destruction of the fortress, known at the time as the 'small castle' (κασtέλλιον) or small settlement (πολίχνιον); the emperor complied.

A small sea fort built at the southern end of the land walls, known by the popular name *Mermerkule* ('marble tower') has been identified by earlier research as another similar aristocratic residence.[20] With the surrounding area currently filled in, only a large rectangular tower is preserved, as well as a part of the adjoining wall with overlapping platforms for defenders to fire from embrasures and an inner courtyard with three underground cisterns (*see* Plate 46). Its construction extensively used spolia, all coming from a single (unknown) monument. Peschlow

Plate 46. Constantinople. The 'Mermerkule' complex. (*Photo*: David Hendrix)

identified it as the early 15th-century palace of one Theodore Palaiologos Kantakouzenos; Asutay saw it as the sea-part of the Golden Gate complex of John V Palaiologos.

Finally, the Tekfur Saray (known also as the Porphyrogennetos Palace) has been always considered as the sole remaining specimen of Byzantine secular architecture.[21] Dated to the late 13th century, it occupies the space between the main wall and the outer wall of the Theodosian enclosures on a hill overlooking Blachernae Palace. From the original complex is preserved a three-storey wing, along with an adjoining rectangular tower. The wing, whose façades are richly decorated, has a semi-covered vaulted ground floor and two floors with wooden ceilings. Several questions about the complex have not been satisfactorily answered: was this complex private or public, a palace or a manor house? Was it fortified or was it simply 'using' the adjoining walls, etc?

As mentioned above, various sources mention the repairs of the city's walls during its two last centuries under Byzantine rule.[22] Michael VIII Palaiologos (1259–1282), after the reconquest of the city in 1261, ordered that the land walls be heightened, probably meaning to rebuild the battlements; he also repaired the sea walls. In October 1343 an earthquake damaged the land walls, and subsequently the battlements were added to the wall of the moat, up to the height of a person. Another earthquake in 1354 destroyed part of the walls, which were repaired by John V Palaiologos (1341–1391). Inscriptions mentioning Emperor

John VIII Palaiologos (1425–1448) prove that similar repairs took place until the beginning of the 1453 siege. For many of these last repairs, the (by then) impoverished state also had to rely on private donations. Hence, the sea walls were partly funded by powerful magnates, such as Loukas Notaras, Manuel Bryennios and the Serbian despot George Branković, who rebuilt part of the walls and a tower, as related on preserved inscriptions.[23]

The city of **Didymoteichon** (Greece)[24] is situated on a tributary of the Evros (Meriç) river in Thrace. It had been continuously inhabited from at least Late Roman times, but during this period it became a significant centre. The castle occupied a steeply rising oval hill and was therefore naturally defensible, accessible mainly from the north and east sides. It consisted of an enclosure that largely followed the contour of the hill and a citadel at its top. The city walls were strengthened with towers, rectangular, circular (semicircular or U-shaped), and in one case pentagonal, closely placed on the north and east sides and further apart on the south side. To the northwest the wall ran along the river, thus securing the water supply in times of danger. Some of the towers are decorated with the monogram of Constantine Tarchaneiotis (*c*. 1352), general and lord of the city. The more vulnerable northeast side of the walls was further protected with an outer wall and (perhaps) a moat. Some of the gates were larger structures, while others were posterns, perhaps only intended for military use. One of the gates, flanked by pentagonal towers, was later on also protected by a barbican, with a murder hole opening above the barbican gate. The citadel probably rose roughly in the middle of the castle and would have been completely independent from the city walls; no remains are preserved.

The parts of the Didymoteichon walls were variously dated by different researchers (with contradictory views ranging from the Early Byzantine down to the Ottoman period), with the prevailing view being that it was a Justinian fortification but with later additions. Many of the surviving parts (such the section with the monogram towers, the outer wall or the wall along the river) can be securely attributed to the Late Byzantine era (with the barbican being considered as an Ottoman addition during the same period).

The city was occupied by the Crusaders in 1204; they were ousted soon afterwards (1205) by local aristocrats, who then submitted to the Bulgarian emperor Kalojan (1206), who besieged the castle with war machines and tried to divert the river. Didymoteichon was later on (1225) occupied by the Empire of Thessaloniki, then passed to the Bulgarians (1230) and finally to the Empire of Nicaea (1246 onwards). It played an important role in the inner strife of the empire in the 14th century, serving as home, refuge or prison for various members of the imperial family. John VI Kantakouzenos was declared emperor here and used the city as his military and administrative base. In 1360/1361 Didymoteichon fell under Ottoman rule. It is currently believed that members of the elite classes (secular, military and religious) lived within the city walls, while the commanders or the imperial family occupied the citadel. The larger part of the population probably lived outside the walls.

In the walls of **Thessaloniki** (Greece)[25] the parts attributed to this period are built with alternating rows of bricks and stones, in a careless and disorderly way. This masonry has been identified in the northwest city wall, in many parts of the citadel and in the cross-wall between the city and the citadel. In all cases the general disposition of the walls remained the same, but various modifications/restorations/additions were made, including several towers and gates, as well as the (more fragile) upper levels of the walls. Among the preserved inscriptions and monograms, one testifies to repairs during the first period of rule of Manuel II Palaiologos, who was governor of Thessaloniki (1369–1373).

One of the most impressive and best-known parts of the Thessaloniki fortifications is the citadel known as the Heptapyrgion (Seven Towers), a heavily fortified fort with at least ten closely spaced towers built at the highest point of the citadel (see Plate 4). The constant repairs, and various reuses of the complex to the present day, have masked the original structure and its founders. A single inscription above its gate commemorates Sultan Murad II with the date 1430/1431, that is, after Thessaloniki passed to the Ottoman state. The Heptapyrgion may be similar to Yedi-kule ('Seven towers'), the fort Mehmet II built once he occupied Constantinople. Nevertheless, as in the case of Yedi-kule (which was built in the same location as the earlier Golden Gate castle), the Ottoman Heptapyrgion might have replaced or repaired an existing Late Byzantine fort.

In the Macedonian city of **Serres** (Greece),[26] which during the Middle Byzantine period moved to a higher location, part of the citadel belongs to the Late Byzantine period. Situated on the highest ridge of the hill, it is dominated by the so-called Tower of Orestes, a massive rectangular and well-preserved building that probably functioned as a keep and last refuge. The tower was often repaired, and its west façade was decorated with various motifs and with a large brick inscription mentioning the castellan (*kastrophylax*) Orestes, dated *c.*1345–1350.

The city of **Mystras** (Greece),[27] the only new foundation of this period under Byzantine rule, developed and eventually became the capital of the Byzantine dominion in the Peloponnese, later known as the Despotate of Morea, for more than two centuries. The city was built on the hillside of a spur projecting from the Taygetos mountain chain (*see* Plate 47). It therefore offered natural protection and allowed the city to spread over a considerable sloping area.

The fortifications are divided into three parts. The summit of the hill is occupied by the earlier castle, which acted as the citadel. The upper city and the lower city wards encircled two parts of the city along the slope of the hill. The walls of the settlement start from the west side of the citadel, follow the hill slope in a curvilinear direction, and end at the steep slopes of the east side.

The multiple gates of the walls offered both easy circulation within the settlement as well as access to the countryside. The present entrance to the lower

Antique fort. Measuring 105 × 85m, it consists of a main enclosure and a citadel cut off by an internal cross-wall. The citadel was protected by a large pentagonal tower at the apex of the hill and a cylindrical one at the cross-wall. Its interior probably housed the barracks for the garrison.

The castle known as **Gynaikokastro** (Greece)[32] lies 59km north-northwest of Thessaloniki. It is strategically located for the protection of Thessaloniki and its region, since it controlled the Axios valley and the crossings to west Macedonia. It was built on a steep hill, *c.*106m high, on a spot that secured full visual control of the surrounding area.

The castle is oval in shape and surrounds an area of almost 2.5ha; it is strengthened at long intervals with rectangular and semicircular towers. The masonry consists of rubble with the sporadic use of brick. The main gate lies on the smooth, south side of the hill and is nearly destroyed. Excavations proved that it was guarded by a bastion. A second, lesser, gate lies near the northeast corner of the precinct.

The citadel in the northeast part of the castle is divided from the rest of the castle by two walls. The west wall is carefully made and has a series of blind arches on the inner side. The citadel, with an area of *c.*0.2ha, is crowned at the highest point with a rectangular tower.

The tower survives to a height of 7.50m, and the masonry is an irregular cloisonné with bands of all-brick masonry, probably concealing timber cribwork. The remaining parts include the ground floor and the first floor. A traverse wall divides the first floor into two rooms, one of which was transformed into a chapel. Fragments of wall paintings from the chapel preserve the monogram of the Palaiologan dynasty. The ground floor included two brick-vaulted cisterns, covered with double layers of hydraulic mortar. The descent to the cisterns was made from the first-storey floor via a narrow staircase built within the thickness of the partition wall. Communication between the cisterns was achieved through a narrow passage, while the external walls had openings for the circulation of air and light.

The castle was founded by Andronikos III Palaiologos shortly after his ascent to the throne (1328) as part of a programme to strengthen the vulnerable parts of the state with new castles. According to legend, the castle was so strong that even with a female garrison it could withstand all enemy assaults (hence the name *gynaikokastro*, meaning 'the castle of women'). It was used in the civil war between John V and John Kantakouzenos that erupted after the death of Andronikos III (1341). It was occupied by Stefan Dusan but was returned to the Byzantines following negotiations. It was occupied by the Turks in 1373–1374 and was later known as Avret-Hisar.

The castle of **Anaktoroupolis** (Greece)[33] is a naval fort occupying a low hill overseeing a safe harbour that could control the coastline of Thrace and eastern Macedonia. The enclosure surrounded an area of 6ha with a perimeter of 540m.

The wall had rectangular and polygonal towers. The main gate lay at the west side, flanked by two towers. The larger polygonal tower had a narrow and high entrance, which was quickly afterwards filled in and reinforced with a buttress. Communication with the top storey of the tower was via an external staircase.

The enclosure was later reinforced on the east side with an outer wall. Within the castle, another wall was built along an east–west direction that divided the enclosure in two, probably creating a second line of defence. Repairs and later additions are visible in many parts of the walls and towers. The castle was carefully built with masonry consisting of rows of stones and bricks, with large bricks also used at the joints.

Based on the surviving inscription, *Ανδρονίκου Κοντοστεφάνου μεγάλου δουκός μινί Ιουλίω . . . Ι* [*Andronikou Kontostephanou grand duke in the month of July . . .*], the erection of the castle had been dated between 1167 and 1170, but it is currently accepted that it should be dated to 1340, and therefore the castle was part of Andronikos III's building programme. Slightly later it was besieged by the forces of John VI Kantakouzenos, during his campaign against John V Palaiologos.

The single linear fortification known from this period is the rebuilding of **Hexamilion** (Greece)[34] in 1415. The parts attributed to this period are few and consist of mere feeble walls constructed with rubble. Builders reused the older material and followed its line. It is interesting to note that during these works they found the older marble dedicatory inscription from the 6th-century restoration (by Victorinus, under Justinian, see above) and probably reinserted it in the walls as a contemporary invocation to the divine and as a sign of continuation.

Despite its meagre remains, the information concerning this construction is quite rich. The wall was rebuilt at the order of Emperor Manuel II Palaiologos in an operation lasting for forty days. It was praised by contemporaries, including the emperor himself. The endeavour, however, caused a local uprising in the summer of that year, since it was considered too much of a burden for the local population, that is, the local landowning families who contributed funds and workers. Yet despite the belief that the wall would secure the Peloponnese against all assaults, it was easily breached in 1423 and again in 1431 by Ottoman armies. Restored in 1444 by the Byzantines, it was breached again in the winter of 1446 and in October 1452 under the cannonfire of the marching Ottoman army.

Plate 49. Arta. View of the citadel. (*Photo*: David Hendrix)

The Arta walls are attributed to the middle of the 13th century, during the reign of Michael II. He probably reused the ancient or even earlier Byzantine remains. During the 14th century the city was attacked and besieged numerous times by the Byzantines, Franks, Serbs and Albanians.

As already mentioned, the city of **Ioannina** (Greece)[4] was mentioned for the first time in the context of the Komnenian wars. Yet during the despotate period the whole city enclosure was restructured and acquired its present form; it covered a large trapezoidal area whose three sides were surrounded by the Ioannina lake. Two distinct citadels (each a smaller rectangle) occupied the corners of the trapezoid towards the lake (northeast and southeast). The city walls were later incorporated in the 19th-century remodelling: large sections are actually preserved on the inner side of the current Ottoman castle, and they were built with rubble masonry and with broken bricks irregularly filling all the joints. Some of the rectangular towers are also preserved, placed at irregular intervals. A tower-gateway, known as the Thomas Tower (based on its brick inscription), was a later addition and protruded on the inner side of the walls; its façade was constructed with cloisonné masonry with a brick arch around the gate opening. Another tower is decorated with brick crosses on its façade.

From the two citadels (known as the Municipal Museum and Iç Kale), one has been attributed to the 11th century and the other to the despotate period (with different researchers having contradictory views). The Municipal Museum/ northeast one preserves a large oval tower, which can also be attributed to the

Plate 50. Berat. View of the citadel, inner part. (*Photo*: author)

with rectangular and circular towers, placed at regular intervals. There was no moat or outer wall, since the position was naturally defended. The lower city was for the citizens, the upper for the military and the citadel for the ruler. Therefore there were three lines of defence against external enemies, as well as protecting the commander of the citadel against internal unrest.

The lower city wall has not left many traces, so it is impossible to know its plan precisely. It surrounded an area of *c.*7.5ha. The preserved parts are on the north side and along the hill slope. The entrance was at the northwest side of the hill, the only accessible side. The settlement was partially occupied until the early 20th century.

The upper city wall survives in better condition, its plan being polygonal and surrounding an area of *c.*2ha. The walls follow the topography of the ground and are protected by circular and rectangular towers. It was the second defensive line and provided a refuge for the citizens in case the lower city was taken. It was also less densely populated.

The citadel is preserved in a far better condition (*see* Plate 51). Its layout is in the shape of an irregular pentagon, and the walls survive to their full length, surrounding an area of *c.*0.25ha. The rectangular towers are preserved to a considerable height.

Two rectangular towers defended the side towards the upper city; the west tower survives almost to its original height, including the battlements, although the side facing the citadel is completely destroyed. Based on masonry traces, the

despotate period. It also had a gate that originally closed with a portcullis and was flanked by towers.

The extensive rebuilding of the Ioannina walls during this period has been dated to the time of Michael I Komnenos Doukas (1204–1215) based on a contemporary source; additions were also carried out during the 14th century. The Thomas Tower has been attributed either to the Serbian despot Thomas Preliubovic (1367–1384) or to Thomas Komnenos Doukas (1296–1318). The Chronicle of the Morea mentioned the existence of a large moat that covered all the side towards the land, turning the city into an island; a bridge over the moat led to the castle gate, although nothing of that structure is preserved.

The city of **Berat** (Albania),[5] also known as Beligrad or Belegradon in this period, was one of the largest centres in the West Balkans. It was strategically situated on a rocky outcrop above the river Osoum, at the entrance to a fertile valley. The medieval walls rise above the foundations of ancient Antipatrea. Despite its turbulent history, it was continuously a Byzantine administrative and military base for the wider area, initially for the Despotate of Epirus and later on for the Empire of Constantinople.

The city walls covered the plateau; the settlement was at the top of the hill and enclosed a huge area (*c.* 9 ha). They were strengthened with twenty-four towers and had one main entrance and three lesser ones. This enclosure was further expanded to 15 ha by two newly constructed walls that enclosed all the slope down to the river, securing water access in times of peril.

The citadel of the city rested at the higher point of the hill and seems to have been a single-period construction, strengthened by five towers (*see* Plate 50). It was internally divided by a cross-wall, with its best-protected section probably destined for the local governor or imperial representative. An immense underground cistern, covered with brick vaults, was probably part of the palace basement.

The walls of Berat exhibit a variety of structural and formal elements, often copying older techniques or building phases. Various types of tower co-exist, such as round, rectangular, triangular and even pentagonal (prow-shaped). The latter were regarded as reminiscent (or even as a restoration) of Early Byzantine fortifications. In their masonry they extensively use bands of bricks alternating with courses of roughly hewn stones. Older research attributed the Berat walls to the first ruler of Epirus, Michael I (early 13th century), with the citadel being added in the second half of the 13th century. Ćurčić has also pointed out resemblances to the Palaiologan fortifications.

Plate 51. Servia. View of the citadel. (*Photo*: Flora Karagianni)

tower had three storeys. The floors were wooden, as was the roof. The north tower is less well preserved. The towers resemble each other but differ from the rest of the fortification. They both had two small windows overlooking the city and one in the side walls, where their height is considerably diminished due to the ground inclination. Their masonry preserves traces of decoration, with shallow niches and the use of bricks alternating with stones throughout the masonry (*see* Plate 52). This is a well-known Palaiologan masonry style, and the erection or extensive rebuilding of the towers could have taken place in the 14th century. The lime mortar connecting the stones is of particularly good quality, hence the preservation of the masonry despite the rough weather.

The foundation of the castle is tied to the Byzantine-Bulgar conflicts of the 10th and 11th centuries. It was built to ensure the safety of the farmers and shepherds of the surrounding area, occupying a naturally protected and strategic location for access towards the south. In the 10th century it was controlled by the Bulgars, led by Samuel. In 1001 it was captured by Basil II when its commanders were ambushed, a story mentioned by Kekaumenos in his *Strategikon*.[7] In 1018 it was partially destroyed so as not to be used by the Bulgarian army. In the 13th century it was considerably enlarged, being part of the Despotate of Epirus. A faithful and detailed description was given by Emperor John VI Kantakouzenos. In 1393 it was conquered by the Turks.

Plate 52. Servia. Tower of the citadel, masonry detail. (*Photo:* Flora Karagianni)

The town of **Rogon** (Greece)[8] lay on a low hill at the north end of the Louros valley. The impressive walls of the Byzantine period followed the formation of the ancient fortification. On the top of the hill there is a strong wall, enclosing an area of 0.9ha. Its southeast part was cut off with two transverse walls, each strengthened by a projecting tower, so as to create a citadel-refuge in case of siege. On the north and northeast sides there were two more enclosures with towers, which were repaired in the Late Byzantine period, and probably again in the 14th century, when the city began to have an important role in the military campaigns. Indeed, from the 13th century onwards the town of Rogon became one of the key cities of the Despotate of Epirus.

The walled city of **Naupaktos** (Lepanto, Greece),[9] popularly known from the 1571 naval battle, controls one of the most important harbours of the western Balkan coastline. Its imposing fortification is among the best-preserved monuments in the Balkans. The city walls stretched from the harbour upwards, covering the hillside of the nearby spur. The citadel occupies the top of the hill, while two branches of curtain wall descend towards the sea, encircling the harbour. The walled area is divided into five parallel defence zones, further divided by transverse walls that could be separately defended. The three upper zones formed the main Byzantine castle. The two lower zones, which are larger in size, are situated close to the harbour and encircle the main part of the town.

The lower (fifth) zone starts from the harbour and ends with the first transverse wall; it protects the lower town, and its walls were constructed by the Venetians in 1407. The fourth zone protected the part of the settlement known as the upper town. The walls form a trapezoidal area, which was originally sparsely inhabited. These walls are preserved in good condition, with a single arched gate in their eastern part connecting them with the inner city. Another large gateway, known as 'faltsoporti', was decorated with the Venetian emblem and was built next to a later horseshoe-shaped bastion; this gateway allowed for direct communication with the countryside.

The third zone currently preserves a large cistern and storeroom complexes. The current access is on the western walls, formed by a line of gates opening next to a rectangular tower. The second zone is covered by the ruined houses of the Byzantine settlement, with the exception of a church and two cisterns. The final (first) zone includes the citadel, which communicated with the second zone via an arched gate. A secondary gate gave access to the northern, steeper exterior of the castle.

The city, due to its strategic location, was inhabited continuously from pre-historic times. Many of the medieval walls used material from the classical walls or (in the citadel) formed the base of the Byzantine towers. At the end of the 9th century Naupaktos was part of the theme of Nikopolis, and in the early 10th century it became its capital. It is to this period (10th to 11th centuries) that the first structure of a Byzantine fort should be dated. In 1025 it was the seat of a general, and after 1204 it was allocated to Venice. In 1210 it passed under the control of Michael I of Epirus, and in 1294 it was given to the Anjou of Naples as the dowry for Nikephoros' daughter Thamar. The Anjou reportedly repaired the walls, minted coinage and turned the city into a major commercial station. In 1378 Naupaktos was occupied by the Albanian lord Gino Bua Spata. In 1407 it passed under Venetian rule, during which the walls were reinforced once again. Following three failed attempts (1462, 1477, 1485), the city was finally occupied by the Ottomans in 1499.

The city of **Neopatras** (Ypati, Greece)[10] became prominent in the 13th and 14th centuries, first as the capital of the Byzantine (quasi-independent) state of Thessaly/Great Vlachia and later on as the northern epicentre of the Catalan Duchy of Athens. The city occupied the side of a steep hill, on top of which lay the citadel and seat of government. Both the citadel and the city were fortified, although very little remains today from the civic enclosure(s).

The citadel preserves only the lower parts of its walls, currently serving as retaining elements. Its walls followed the irregular contour of the hilltop, with a few rectangular towers irregularly spaced along the vulnerable southern side. It is from this side that access to the citadel was possible. Recent excavations have revealed the traces of the gate, including its threshold, part of the paved street and a water conduit. Within the citadel, there is a large cistern that would have originally been the basement of a (currently lost) central tower. The walls of

surrounded the rock. The outer ward is presently occupied by a modern settlement and has been completely destroyed.

The entrance to the inner castle is from the south, where a heavily altered gate is still preserved. It was 1.75m high and opened between two projections that flanked the area. Walls are interrupted at regular intervals by triangular and semi-circular projections. These projections are solid and fulfill the role of rudimentary towers. They were preferred because construction was easier and because they saved on materials. They have no traces of arrow loops or inner spaces. Defenders fought from the wall-walk level, using these projections for flanking purposes. Later additions or rebuildings are evident in various parts, such as the projection to the west of the entrance gate and the cannon terrace at the west end.

The façades of the walls are built either with roughly hewn stones, set in horizontal courses, or with rubble masonry. Local materials were used, including basalt and schist stones. Smaller stones, pebbles from the Filabonites river, are set in the joints, while the lime mortar was also used to smooth the surfaces. The thickness of the walls varies from 0.75m to 1.25m. They presently survive to a maximum height of 8m.

The castle was one of the key fortresses of the Trebizond Empire and its construction must be attributed to the Grand Komnenoi. The geographer Vital Cuinet noted that he saw two statues of John II Komnenos (1280–1297) and his wife Eudoxia in the castle, which led Bryer and Winfield to consider them as the founders. The city was a personal possession and refuge of the Grand Komnenoi, and during the civil wars Alexios III withdrew to the castle in 1351, abandoning his capital, and four years later he left his wife here for safety.

Trebizond (Trabzon, Turkey)[8] was throughout its history an important administrative and commercial centre. It was founded as Sinope's colony in the 7th century BC, was part of the Roman Empire from 64/63 BC, and became the capital of the theme of Chaldia from the 9th century and of the Empire of the Grand Komnenoi from 1204 onwards. Occupying a naturally fortified hill cut off by gorges, it possessed an important harbour (known as Dafnous), strategically set at the outlet from Armenia and Central Asia to the Black Sea. In its fully developed form, the city had a triangular form, with the tip of the triangle set at the higher point towards the mainland, where the citadel stood. The base of the triangle surrounded the lower city, while a third enclosure, the middle city, lay between the two ends (*see* Plate 55). While the lower city dates from the 14th century, the citadel and middle city were continuously used and repaired from the Roman era down to modern times. In its fully developed form the walled city covered a surface of *c.*22ha.

The lower city ward has a vertical wall strengthened by rectangular towers. The wall-walk was partly supported on blind arches on the inner part of the walls (preserved in a single section of the west wall). The towers were simple flanking projections. The ward may have also had an outer wall (at least on the east and

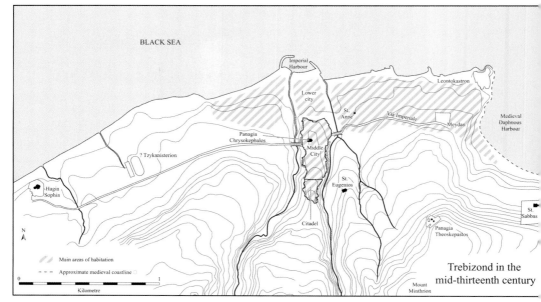

Plate 55. Trebizond (Trabzon). Plan of the city walls. (*Source*: Eastmond et al., *Byzantium's Other Empire*)

west sides), only parts of which are currently preserved on the west side. The southwest tower of the ward is an impressive structure with three storeys and a battlemented terrace. It lies close to one of the most important gates, known today as Zağnos Kapısı. This – currently blocked – monumental structure had a single-stone cover, with an eagle sculpture set above it and an inscription mentioning Emperor Alexios (II). Another surviving gate, known as Molos Kapısı, lies on the north side of the walls, next to a tower that preserves its battlements as well as its machicolation.

These walls are built with a rubble core and a façade of roughly hewn rectangular stones set in horizontal courses with pebbles, bricks and mortar covering the joints. Larger ashlar blocks are used for the corners.

The middle city walls have been seriously altered or reused in modern constructions. Its west wall was built on ancient or Early Byzantine foundations, below a masonry of well-cut blocks, probably dating to Middle Byzantine times. Blind arches on the inner side of the walls are similar to those of the lower city. An all-brick arch in the west corner of the north wall has been attributed to the time of Justinian, while an antique polygonal structure in the southwest corner was used as the foundation for a tower.

The citadel was always the centre of political power (*see* Plate 56). It is an irregular triangular space; only a few building remains are visible, often set against the walls. The oldest part of the citadel occupied its northwest side: it was a monumental rectangular, double-storey structure, whose western part also served as the outer side of the walls. This was identified with the throne room described by Bessarion, and should therefore be dated to the 13th century.

'A Tower of Strength, a Tower of Firmness, a Tower of Life . . .'
(John Geometres, tr. H. Maguire)

This concluding chapter will tackle a number of general themes. Most of these are only gradually appearing in recent studies, and they usually refer only to a single site or to a particular time period. By setting them together, I hope to demonstrate continuities or recurring ideas that may finally help reconstruct how Byzantines not only used but also envisaged and understood their fortifications. We have to remember that despite the fact that 'an axe will always be an axe', the materials, size, decoration, maintenance or wear of fortifications can speak volumes about the social impact that functional structures may have had, as well as about the diverse perceptions they may help to construct within their sociocultural milieus.

The first parts of this chapter will summarize how fortifications functioned when utilized as an integral part of the Byzantine war machine. When I refer to the 'other' fortifications, I have in mind two types. The first is military camps, which played a huge role in every war but barely left a trace afterwards, and the second includes monastic fortifications; these were vital parts of establishments that had an immense impact on Byzantine society as a whole.

Next, I shall focus on the use of the walls during times of peace, practically, aesthetically and, ultimately, metaphysically. These aspects can be traced indirectly through literary sources but also through the various inscriptions and decorative patterns that can still be seen on the walls. A specific feature that stands out in all periods of Byzantine fortifications (and architecture as a whole) is the continuous reuse of ancient material (spolia); this practice is far from being merely utilitarian but has only recently attracted much-deserved attention (see below).

How to Defend or Attack a Byzantine Fortification

Defending or attacking fortresses and cities was an important aspect of the Byzantine art of war. Our knowledge on the subject usually comes from various historical sources, many of which have already been mentioned in the previous chapters. In many instances, however, we are unable to understand accurately the complex images they portray, to check which information they provide is original or simply copied from antique works, or to verify these elements on the ground, based on architectural and archaeological research.[1]

In all aspects, Byzantine strategies do not seem to differ from those of any other medieval state. The main concern of a general was always to minimize losses and improve the prospects of victory. The initial stages of a siege on the part of the attackers would always include cutting off supplies, using starvation to force submission, and waging psychological warfare to persuade garrisons to surrender (demoralizing, frightening, fomenting discord, offering favourable terms, feeding false information, cutting down trees, burning the harvests, etc.). Additionally, many tales recount ruses and stratagems employed to achieve the effortless conquest of a fort, such as sending in soldiers disguised as workers or allies or messengers (as did the Bulgar tsar Samuel when besieging a Byzantine fortress), capturing the leader of the fort when he goes to take his bath outside the walls (as in the case of the city of Servia), and so on.[2]

To defend a fort, it was necessary to prepare the weapon and food stocks, safeguard the water supply, destroy water and food resources available to the enemy, minimize the number of those unable to fight (by sending older men, women and children to other safe places), and be able to send messages for reinforcements. Hunting for information on both sides, plots and spy rings are common narrative subjects, and the conquests of castles are often attributed to treasonous acts (as was allegedly also the case for the Kerkoporta Gate, which was found open and led to the fall of Constantinople in 1453). On the other hand, many stories speak of successful sallies carried out by the besieged, when the attackers were careless and failed to protect their camp (as in the Byzantine siege of Tarsus in 883, or that of Crete in the 820s).[3]

When an outright attack on a fortification was under way, fighting seems to have happened on three levels (above the walls, through the walls, under the walls), varying according to the means of the attackers. As well as the standard offensive tools (bows, swords, daggers, etc.), anti-personnel weapons included a number of biological weapons (beehives, snakes, cadavers, etc.)[4] and combustibles, meant to initiate fire and spread panic, as well as the all-powerful weapon known as 'Greek Fire' or 'Liquid Fire' (see above).

Climbing over the walls with ladders usually resulted in heavier casualties and required a strong attacking force. Utilizing siege towers required intensive preparation and resources, both to construct and to carry the towers to the walls. They were obviously useless when attacking hilltop fortifications. They appear regularly in historical accounts, both for the 6th to early 7th centuries (in Amida, 503; Martyroupolis, 530; Constantinople, 626) and for the 10th to 12th centuries (Kastoria, 1080; Dyrrachion, 1081; various siege scenes discussed in the 12th-century Skylitzes manuscript in Madrid).

Passing through the walls demanded not only the use of siege machines (such as rams and catapults) but also an extended period of time. Tortoise structures (portable penthouses, known as *laisai*) were occasionally used to protect the users of such devices.[5] Missile-projecting and stone-throwing machines are mentioned, but it is hard to visualize their details. As mentioned above, torsion-powered machines (such as the onager) were used only until the 6th century (or slightly before), while tension machines (ballistae in the form of a crossbow that could throw stones or bolts) were widely used until the 9th century. Traction-powered catapults (pulled by people) were introduced in the later 6th century and were used consistently until the late 11th or 12th century, when the more powerful counterweight catapults (trebuchets) were adopted (a change attributed to Emperor Manuel I Komnenos).

Passing under the walls required digging tunnels, filling them with combustibles and setting them on fire, which would cause the walls to collapse and allow attackers to enter. This method is explicitly recommended by Nikephoros Ouranos in his late 10th-century treatise (see above). Mines could only be intercepted by counter-mines, provided that the defenders could detect the parts of the walls that were being mined and that they had adequate forces to dig them out and neutralize them. The discovery of such mines during the excavations of the Doura Europos fortress (which fell to the Sassanids in 256) eloquently testify to the use of these techniques. Defenders could prepare for the breach of the walls, however, by creating earthwork fences on the inner side.

What happened to a city once the walls were breached is usually either summarily passed over (insinuating all were enslaved, everything was destroyed, and the conquerors plundered all the goods, etc.) or is coloured with graphic details of – mostly repeated – events (holy places desecrated, women raped, children slaughtered). However, it seems that a city could also put forward some sort of resistance once the walls fell; fighters could retreat to inner enclaves following a street-by-street fight, which was facilitated by the usually narrow and maze-like street system; in the end, these enclaves could hold on until the attackers promised safe conduct or to spare lives or until some sort of settlement was reached with the official authorities of the conquering army.

This retreat model can be seen in the fall of Constantinople to the armies of the Fourth Crusade (1204), for which we are fortunate to have two eye-witness and trustworthy accounts, by Niketas Choniates and by Geoffrey Villehardouin.[6] Niketas gave a sentimental account of atrocities, which have been repeated henceforth in most textbooks. Geoffrey, on the other hand, details the fight on the sea walls and describes how the attackers scaled them and captured four of the sea towers, then opened three of the gates. Many of the defenders retreated to the Blachernae Palace, which became a rallying point for 'Greek lords' (obviously magnates with their retinues) and could offer independent resistance. Emperor Alexios V had created his own military camp (with tents) on an open area, near the walls where his forces retreated. However, his battalions apparently lost heart in the face of the mounted knights, and the emperor retreated towards the Boukoleon Palace (part of the Great Palace, surrounded by its own walls and served by a harbour).

The Crusaders kept fighting within the city streets, and at the end of the day retreated and camped near the walls they had captured (i.e., at the periphery of the city). Three commanders and their troops camped within the walls: Boniface of Montferrat set up camp near the city centre (probably close to the Great Palace), Baldwin of Flanders took over the military camp deserted by Alexios, and Henry of Flanders settled near the Blachernae Palace. During the night Alexios initially assembled forces for a counterattack but instead fled through the empty streets to the Golden Gate and from there escaped the city. At the same time, the Crusaders set fire to the houses close to their camps to prevent these buildings from being used to mount attacks against their camps. The next day the Crusaders were prepared to continue the battle within the city but they encountered no resistance; Boniface of Montferrat went to the Boukoleon Palace and negotiated the surrender of the 'fortress', sparing the lives of all those within (noblemen related to the imperial family, protected probably by the Varangian guards). Blachernae surrendered to Henry of Flanders on similar terms. Both leaders garrisoned the respective palaces with their people, proclaiming them as their own territories and using them as leverage for the status they hoped to achieve after the end of the war.

Networks of Fortifications; Strategies of Defence

A leitmotif in military history is the role a fortification may play as part of a wider group of similar regional structures within a wider system of defence.[7] Within Roman territory, can fortifications work together as a network to ensure safety? In borderlands, can they control and guard an area? In enemy territory, can they be 'offensive', forcing enemies into submission? In all cases, should they be examined separately, or as parts of multi-task chains (including also the transmission of intelligence)?

For all periods of Byzantine history, various researchers have accepted or spoken in favour of such ideas – some more cautiously, others more convincingly. The idea of networks (especially when combined with watchtowers dotting the territory) is an intriguing and indeed a logical one; furthermore, the notion of a communication system based on fire-signals/beacons is a captivating image, one that was even used in the Trojan War, as perpetuated by Aeschylus.[8]

The Byzantines reportedly had created in the 9th century a similar system of beacons, its organization attributed to Leo the Mathematician and Emperor Theophilos.[9] The system served to give warning of Arab attacks and stretched from the borders of Cilicia all the way to Constantinople, a distance of some 725km. Leo had allegedly devised a code for the interpretation of fire signals and a system that would guarantee their accuracy. Few of these beacons have been identified in Cilicia and Cappadocia, though another such structure serves the idea that the system might have been revived in the 12th century. However, one must take into account the fact that information about Leo's beacons comes exclusively from later sources accusing Michael III of dismantling the system, at a time when it was obviously no longer needed.

A Middle Byzantine inscription, currently relocated from the Peloponnese to Venice, mentions that (an) Emperor Leo has erected a beacon-tower to send fire signals when raiders were approaching. Rife has proposed that the emperor should be Leo VI and the inscription would originally have been erected during the late 9th or early 10th century on one of Acrocorinth's towers.[10]

Examining the fortifications themselves, along with their archaeological evidence, cannot offer, for the time being, conclusive support for or against the existence of defence networks. This lack of clarity is partly related to the uneven degree of archaeological research when it comes to Byzantine fortifications, as well as to the lack of extensive landscape studies, a field that has progressively advanced in the last decades, aided by the use of modern technology (especially GIS-based viewshed analysis that can suggest intervisibility zones among forti-fications).[11] As Haldon rightly pointed out in referring to the Cappadocian fortification network, such 'systems' were never static: they evolved and changed as part of the wider strength and effectiveness of the empire.[12]

Whether as an actor in the hands of a mighty, yet distant, imperial authority, or as a readily available refuge for local inhabitants, each fortification was one more – fully integrated – element within the human and physical landscape (along with roads, water sources, arable land, mines, woods, etc.). To include a specific fort within a larger defensive scheme presupposes an important factor that is almost always absent: the sure knowledge that at any given moment the fortification was manned, prepared and in use. We can be certain about specific sieges and battles; whether walls built centuries apart and situated in rough proximity to one another were also simultaneously used, collaboratively partici-pating in defensive patterns, or even kept in a prepared state, is in each case a matter of further research.

The notion of defensive networks can be more convincingly supported for the cases of island fortifications (especially in the Aegean). An island, due to its very nature, is a restricted landscape, whose relation to the outside world offers clearly defined entry points. At the same time, the habitable areas are also restricted based on the existence of (usually mediocre) agricultural lands. Because of the island's special characteristics, the issue as to whether fortifications could be simultaneously used as part of a regional defensive strategy (in the sense of a customary or logical reaction in the face of imminent danger) can be discussed on more solid grounds.[13]

Marching Camps: the Lost Byzantine Fortifications

Practically all the military handbooks of the 6th to 10th centuries refer extensively to a category of temporary fortifications – the marching camps the army regularly used during military expeditions – that, so far, has not been recognized on the ground.[14] It seems that at least from the later 8th century a system of such camps (known as *aplekta*) was in place, serving as supply or assembly points; they lay at key sites along the military routes leading to the eastern or the northern frontiers.[15]

Great attention was paid to how to choose a site, how to lay out the plans according to the various units, and what provisions would be necessary. Detailed descriptions are offered in the texts concerning their fortifications – ditches, fences, palisades, gates – as well as for its watch systems, which were equipped with guards, passwords, etc. Instructions are also included about the manoeuvres an army must carry out when marching out of a camp or retreating back to it. The diagrams included in the 10th-century manual attributed to Nikephoros Ouranos (see above, ch. 5) are sketchy, oversimplified and probably from a date later than the text they accompany.[16] The text, however, provides detailed descriptions, including the measurements of the camps, the number and location of the gates, and the size of the imperial compound. It was probably addressed to people who would have spent a considerable amount of their serving lives in similar camps.

The idea of marching camps obviously stemmed from and continued along the lines set by their Roman predecessors and, at least according to the manuals, their inner plan followed the Roman prototypes, with the four quadrants separated by centrally crossing paths and leading to entrances in the middle of each side. The imperial tent was at the centre, surrounded by the tents of the thematic troops, forming the arms of a cross, with lightly armed troops occupying one of the corners.

The utter lack of fieldwork in this domain makes it impossible to verify whether these tactics were widespread or actually followed only on special occasions (for instance, when large imperial forces were moving into unsafe territory). The inclusion of many little stories of commanders who failed to take adequate measures, either in choosing or defending a temporary camp, and were thus victims of night attacks or ambushes is evidence that this system was widespread, and practised by the whole military establishment.

Monastic Fortifications

Byzantine religious communities, whether residing within cities or in the countryside, were always surrounded by high walls that cut them off from the world while protecting them against potential intruders. One of the few handbooks dealing with this particular class of buildings is already a century old.[17] It was evident, therefore, from the early stages of Byzantine studies that typified monastic complexes were a class apart and a consistent presence in, and aspect of, Byzantine society throughout its history. Generally, there is a regular plan (rectangular, trapezoid) with the main church (*katholikon*) centrally placed, the secondary buildings set against the inner sides of the walls, and a larger tower-refuge occupying the most protected point of the enclosure. The earliest towers date from the 10th to 11th centuries (Mount Athos) and must have been quite impressive. Later examples always housed a chapel in the upper floors, and they served as the final refuge of the community in times of danger. Many of these towers (starting with the Middle Byzantine Zygos and Hilandar Monasteries) had buttresses/spurs on their exterior walls, probably to support the superstructure.

What separated monastic from other types of non-official fortifications (appearing especially in the Late Byzantine period) was that monasteries were long-lasting, well-established and multi-functional establishments that formed one of the few constants that Byzantine society could rely upon. Their religious buildings closely reflected contemporary 'official' or 'state' architecture, and they very much constitute the bulk of Byzantine structures currently preserved. In the same way, we have to perceive their protective enclosures as going beyond the private sphere; in many cases they resembled public buildings or were even financed by public authorities, including the emperor or those close to him.

For the Early Byzantine period we have a single surviving – and still function-ing – example: the monastery of **St Catherine, Sinai** (Mount Sinai, Egypt).[18] The original structure was a nearly square fortress, surrounding the basilica and the monastic amenities. The strong walls, largely preserved up to battlement level on the three sides, were built with façades of roughly dressed granite stones from local bedrock, covering a core of mortared rubble. The battlements survived by being incorporated into later additions. The walls were strengthened with circular and rectangular towers, and they date from various periods. In the original fortress there were tower-like projections that could provide enfilading fire. The early entrance, currently blocked, was a double one, consisting of a large and imposing portal, and a postern to the left of it. The portal was protected from above by a box machicolation, built with the same granite stones and still bearing a *tabula ansata* with a dedicatory inscription mentioning the founding emperor.

The monastery was created by Justinian in the last years of his reign (between 548 and 560). It is noted specifically by Prokopios that Justinian built it as a fortress to prevent the Saracens from making surprise attacks in Palestine. Workshops, probably from Palestine and Egypt, were commissioned and sent explicitly to construct and decorate the basilica, along with the sturdy rectangular enclosure protecting it. We currently believe that while construction was under way, a military camp was established outside the enclosure to house the workers; this was manned by a garrison sent to secure the unfriendly surrounding territory. Indeed, once the monastery walls were completed, Sinai could be seen not only as a religious house but also as a fort bolstering the Byzantine presence in the area.

For the Middle Byzantine period a number of monastic fortified enclosures, or parts of them, can be attributed to constructions from the 10th to the 12th century. Most of them survive in the Mount Athos community. Among the earlier structures, dated to the late 10th century, are the **Great Lavra**[19] and the **Vatopedi** Monasteries.[20] They were both elongated rectangles, their external walls strengthened with rectangular towers. In Vatopedi there was also a free-standing multi-floored tower, known as the Transfiguration Tower, which was later incorporated into a second phase expansion. The tower had regularly spaced projecting wall buttresses, a feature that was used prolifically in later structures.[21]

The **Zygos** complex,[22] dated to the 10th and 11th centuries, is the only one of the Mount Athos monasteries to have been excavated. The pentagonal walled enclosure was built on relatively flat terrain, with the northern part of the enclosure climbing a steep hillside. All sides were strengthened with rectangular towers, accentuating its military appearance. The gate opened in the south stretch of the enclosure. At the highest point of the hill there was a large tower projecting from the enclosure. It was square and relatively large (10×10m) and had buttresses (projecting spurs) on all sides. It clearly stood out from the rest of the complex, and could have served as a final refuge.

In the area of central Greece a group of monastic complexes seem to have preserved their original layout, with a quadrilateral fortified enclosure (trapezoid or rectangular). The buildings are aligned along the inner sides of the walls, and the *katholikon* is at the centre, free standing. There are few towers, almost always rectangular, placed either on the corners or along the sides. The **Hosios Loukas** complex in Boeotia (Greece)[23] is usually dated to the 11th century. During that period the monastery underwent a major expansion with the addition of a second, huge *katholikon* (the Hosios Loukas church) and a new enclosure expanding towards the south and east of the original nucleus. The fortification walls, mainly built with rubble, included two gatehouses and at least three towers. The gate-houses were located at the two ends of the enclosure. A pre-existing, two-tier chapel next to one of the gates was turned into a high rectangular tower for its protection. A second rectangular tower stood in the middle of the southeast side; it is presently largely restored (with many of its later additions removed). A third semicircular tower was identified at foundation level.

More substantial remains of a monastic enclosure survive at the **Daphni Monastery** near Athens (Greece).[24] It is a rectangle, measuring *c.* 93×100m; its construction date has been greatly disputed, with the 5th, 11th and 13th centuries all proposed as possible dates. The northern half of the enclosure survives today, almost up to the battlements. The walls have blind arches on their interior face, which supported the wall-walk. A few rectangular towers dotted the wall at regular intervals.

The enclosure of the **Hosios Meletios** complex (Attica, Greece)[25] is roughly rectangular (60×50m). Its gate opens to the south, and all the buildings open to the inner courtyard, while the exterior defensive walls have relatively few openings. There are no towers, as was the case in the previous examples. The **Sagmata** Monastery (Boeotia, Greece),[26] dated to the early 12th century, has a similar construction. The rectangular enclosure (45 × 50m) is entered through a gate at the east, and in the southwest corner there is a tower (the current tower is a later construction).

For the Komnenian era, there are two cases which demonstrate how thin the borders became between private and public, monastic and state fortifications. The first involves the monk **Christodoulos,**[27] who acquired a number of properties on the islands of Kos and Leros in the late 11th century. On Leros he held half of the Pateli Castle; on Kos, according to his own words, he constructed a fort in Palio Pyli with his own hands, building it with stones from the bedrock. Afterwards, he exchanged these properties with the state, taking in return the island of Patmos. Here the community built a monastery that is still functioning and is protected by massive walls, although these were extensively restored in later centuries. The Kos properties were in turn ceded to the imperial/Constantinopolitan Pantokrator Monastery. The gate tower of Palio Pyli castle (see above) is one of the finest examples of Komnenian military architecture preserved in the Aegean.

The second case refers to another imperial establishment, the **Kosmosoteira** Monastery in Thrace.[28] The mid-12th century (1152) is the date proposed for the enclosure of the complex, set on a hill overlooking the Evros river valley. Its fortification, enclosing an area of *c.* 0.85ha, was especially strong: it followed an irregular hexagonal plan, probably with towers at all the corners. Three rectangular towers are preserved, built with various techniques: the façade of one features the recessed-brick technique in its simpler, irregular form; the second is built solely with roughly hewn stones; and the third combines stonework with bricks at the joints. The founding charter of the monastery (*typikon*) gives additional information: the fortification had a double (or two-part) enclosure and was built as a castle specifically for the monks, with a tower for suspending the bells and with two gates. From the 13th century onwards the site was turned into a fortress that took part in the civil wars between contenders for the Byzantine throne. By 1355 it had been abandoned by the monks, and turned into a small settlement, passing later to the Ottoman state.

In the Late Byzantine period a concentration of fortified monastic complexes was founded in Mystras and Mount Athos. In **Mystras** (see above) a number of civic religious houses (Peribleptos, Pantanassa, Brontocheion, Metropolis) were strategically placed along or at the corners of the civic walls. While using the city's enclosures and gates to gain easier access to the countryside, they also had their own precinct and, in each case, a central multi-level tower with elaborate façade decoration.

Mount Athos, on the other hand, developed into a multi-ethnic destination, with multiple monasteries housing people from, or under the patronage of,

Constantinople (Vatopedi Monastery), Trebizond (Iviron Monastery), Serbia (Hilandar Monastery) or Bulgaria.[29] At the same time, these monasteries acquired multiple dependencies and lands in various parts of the Balkans and the Aegean. A specific defensive unit, the self-standing tower (with or without external buttresses), became popular over the course of the 14th century:[30] these were built as the last refuge for monastic communities (being found both in the mother houses and dependencies, as in the case of Hilandar), but could also stand independently in the countryside, serving as a residence or storeroom for the local agricultural lands belonging to the monastery (as in the case of the Marianna and Galatista Towers).

Another monastic centre developed towards the end of this period (late 14th to early 15th centuries), with several religious houses taking advantage of the inaccessible rocky landscape of the volcanic rocks of **Meteora** (Greece).[31] These rocks completely protected each community that settled here; perched on these heights, their enclosures served more as fences than walls.

Byzantine Fortifications in Times of Peace

We have very little information regarding the uses of the walls in times of peace, or when there was no imminent danger from enemies. Many countryside forts would obviously be used only in time of danger, and be rarely repaired otherwise. Linear fortifications would also be manned only when under attack, although we would expect guards to secure their entrances and exits (i.e., the gates). The same, however, could not be true for civic fortifications, which were a constant reality within settlements and would be regularly in need of repair if they were to be sustained and ready for action. We can logically assume that their main entry/exit points would be continuously guarded, as they not only controlled circulation but would also facilitate other public functions, such as tax collecting or checking merchandise and incomers.

According to the 5th-century Theodosian law code,[32] regarding the erection of the Constantinople land walls, the owners of the lands on which the defensive towers were erected had the right to use them for private purposes in times of peace; the landowners were also responsible for their maintenance. Their very architecture, as already seen, offered independent use of the ground-floor rooms for storing goods or even housing people. A slightly later law (422) ordered that these ground-floor rooms should house travelling military persons.[33] Furthermore, the land around the walls would continue to be used, either for cultivation, animal husbandry or habitation. The 10th-century poem by John Geometres explicitly mentions the fruit gardens, vegetables and vineyards next to the towers of the capital's land walls (see below), evoking the current conditions in contemporary Istanbul.[34]

Archaeological work at the walls of Hexamilion has proved that when not being used as defences (after the mid-5th century), the walls and towers were turned into residences, while the open space within the fort was used as the cemetery of this minor settlement.

The *Lives* of saints occasionally offer some insight into alternative uses for walls: in Nikomedeia[35] the towers of the Diocletian enclosure were repeatedly mentioned as being home to hermits and monks. In 612, when Theodore of Sykeon was in the city, he visited a number of hermits shut up in buildings along the walls. He met a Syrian monk and a virgin, and went to a wine cellar, kept by the head of the local poorhouse, in one of the towers. In the early 9th century the famous hermit Isaias lived in the tower of 'Saint Diomede' (probably again one of the Diocletian wall towers); there, he received a visit from the iconodule St Ioannikios and foretold the future of Empress Theodora.

Spolia and Decoration

The use of spolia in fortifications was a well-established practice throughout Byzantine history; it is usually attributed to a need to cut down on labour and transport expenses, as there was ready-made material available on site. Alternatively, for the transition period the prolific use of spolia (which was even seen as a criterion for dating a fortification to this period) has been explained based on the model of total collapse, and the resulting hasty erection of walls in the face of imminent danger. Furthermore, it was seen as a self-evident explanation for periods of distress, especially those anticipating or following an enemy attack (such as the building of the Herulian wall in Athens with abundant use of pre-existing stone fragments). Lastly, the disruption of quarry operations at the end of Late Antiquity has been seen as a further reason why each Byzantine monument exhibits a number of reused architectural members.

Nevertheless, our understanding of Byzantium's perceptions and practices in this matter has only lately been readdressed and greatly modified.[36] We are moving away from a purely utilitarian perspective into a more 'organic' and logical interpretation of their use of spolia, one that fits within the wider ideological, social and aesthetic mentalities of Byzantine society. Spoliation was not confined to architecture; indeed, it was a way of thinking, feeling, writing and eventually expressing an identity that was not only restricted to elite layers but rather was widespread, and shared by the whole establishment.

In the field of fortifications, spoliation has been studied only for the early period (especially from the 5th century onwards). Frey[37] has rightly concluded that the use of older architectural and decorative sculpture was prolific, and in ways that could not be compared to other periods. The consistency with which older material was incorporated into fortifications indicates an established and conscious choice on the part of the builders and the viewers. What is even more interesting are the differentiated ways in which older fragments were incorporated into construction, the new functions they were given, and the meaning they acquired by their secondary placement.

Researchers have sought to understand the process of spoliation and the different players involved in this process. Frey examined a limited number of fortifications of similar size and similar date in southern Greece, which helped him to discern three different patterns in the approaches local builders took to reusing architectural elements. In the first case (Aegina), they repaired pre-existing structures and incorporated a number of older inscriptions and decorative blocks (although inconsistently) in the new defences in way that retained their form and character, so that it was, in a sense, a partial restoration of the ancient structure. In the second case (Sparta) they rearranged older decorative material from adjacent buildings in ways that reinterpreted its aesthetic values, while the common provenance of the spolia – and thus their earlier bonds – remained evident. In the third case (Isthmia) builders incorporated spolia into the new structures with indifference, thus rejecting their earlier aesthetics and significance.

Whatever the approach taken in each case, the discussion showed that spoliation in Late Antique fortifications was a distinct and conscious process, which demonstrated more the agency of builders and work crews rather than that of the project coordinator or architect. The masons in each case exhibited a significant freedom in expressing their own aesthetics, and they eventually followed whatever traditions and innovations they deemed effective.

As far as Middle Byzantine structures are concerned, each case or period has been handled very differently. As mentioned above, for the 7th and 8th centuries the use of spolia has been considered as the norm, the sign of an urgent need for ready-made material in the face of adversity. This was promoted as an idea to such a degree that if some parts are strictly built with spolia, then their 'Dark Age' date is almost certainly accepted. Nevertheless, in the 7th-century walls of Nicaea spolia are clearly used with another intention in mind: to promote a sense a monumentality, solidity and luxury. The spolia help these walls to be easily distinguished from earlier structures and would have instilled in the inhabitants a sense of security in the state's ability to protect them.

In 9th-century fortifications the use of spolia is especially distinctive: in massive towers the lower part is constructed almost exclusively with spolia, while the superstructure is made only with bricks (Constantinople, Ankyra). In the Boukoleon Palace the lower parts are again covered with Late Antique spolia, in arrangements that require more study and interpretation. The Theophilos towers along the sea walls of Constantinople are made with spolia in prominent places. Finally, the wall next to the inner ward gate of Ankyra is an exceptional case: it is decorated with a collection of ancient altars set one next to the other.

In the Komnenian and the Palaiologan walls the use of spolia is again prominent: used for structurally sensitive spots (such as tower corners), they are usually mingled along with roughly hewn stones and a variety of brick combinations and integrated within the larger scheme without strikingly standing out. An exceptional case is the 13th-century 'Marble tower' fort in Istanbul, where the whole lower part of the rectangular tower is constructed with reused ashlar blocks from an unknown ancient structure.

A special mention should be made of the use of column shafts. Two examples illustrate the point: in the main gate of Ankyra columns were set horizontally and parallel to one another to form the ceiling of the gateway. In the tower added next to the Anemas complex in Constantinople column shafts were used as brackets to support an open gallery/balcony. In both instances, in addition to structural reasons, columns added an element of luxury and prestige to the structures.

When it comes to decorating the façades of the walls, and especially the gates, there are many examples that testify to the importance the Byzantines placed on these structures and the complex meanings they wanted to convey. The Golden Gate of Constantinople embodies the opulence and political ideology of the empire through its marble façades, inscriptions, gilded doors and statues. The façades of the Ankyra inner ward may serve as another example: besides the section with the altar pieces mentioned above, there are many isolated decorative motifs in brickwork added along the curtain, such as circles with sun rays or crosses. In the latter case (crosses), it is possibly a visual demonstration of how the Byzantines viewed the walls (as expressed in literary sources, see below): as protected by God and a metaphysical boundary that creates and guards a holy space.

The decorative aspect is much more explicit in certain parts of the Komnenian fortifications. The conches with saw-toothed brickwork in the walls of Constantinople and Palio Pyli stand out because they have direct parallels in church architecture and because they animate the entrances of the towers/gateways. The Gyrolimne Gate of Constantinople, with the busts of empresses, may evoke, as a visual concept, a direct link to specific people in the lineage of the imperial family – as suggested for other examples of Komnenian art.[38] In all cases, walls must be seen within the wider context of the artistic production of the day, which was actively used to promote a message of stability, continuity and survival for a state constantly facing perilous adventures.

Dedicatory inscriptions were often combined with spolia and decorative patterns to communicate with the viewers.[39] Besides their aesthetic effects, the commemoration of emperors and government and church officials via inscriptions had strong political, ideological and historical connotations. Inscriptions were usually set on visible points, next to gates or on the façades of prominent towers. They could be carved on stone (in relief, inscribed or inlaid) or made with bricks. The majority simply stated the name of the donor and the year, often with a short invocation to the divine. A few were anonymous invocations for the protection of the walls, providing perennial apotropaic protection.

The Byzantines' Perceptions of Their Walls

The degree to which the Byzantines appreciated and valued their fortifications, and especially the walls surrounding the cities of the empire, can be traced through various threads, which are all basically interlinked and co-exist in the sources. In the minds of the citizens of the empire, their military capacity was not differentiated from divine protection or aesthetic appreciation. All these constituted the distinct identity of Byzantine fortifications, which aimed to instill a sense of security and permanence for the empire.

The first such thread is **semantic**: from the 3rd century onwards, an enormous portion of the available resources was redirected and used in monumental walls and public works.[40] The idea of urban landscape was henceforth closely connected to city walls and monumental gateways. From the end of Late Antiquity, the very word 'castle' (*kastron*) was used interchangeably to denote a 'city';[41] therefore, it was substantially different from the meaning that 'castle' acquired in feudal Western Europe.

In all depictions of cities, whether in murals, floor and wall mosaics, manuscripts, icons, minor objects, seals or coins, the essential component symbolizing a city was its walls.[42] It goes without saying that the bulk of these images refer to the imperial capital, Constantinople; Thessaloniki was also frequently represented. But whenever a city was to be represented, whether existing (in historical accounts) or more fictional (heavenly or earthly Jerusalem, ancient or biblical sites), the main medium was a generic depiction of walls.

Especially in the Late Byzantine period, it seems that castle images were typified and used as symbols for specific cities. In this, they may have followed a process that started in the Mediterranean with the Crusader representations of walls on coins and seals.[43] Consequently, the triple-towered castle was consistently used by the state of Epirus to denote the walls of Thessaloniki; it went as far as to be represented alone on a coin issue, without any inscription or other attribute, being obviously easily understood by all those who handled it. The same came to be with Constantinople and the coinage minted after 1261, when the city was reconquered by the Empire of Nicaea: a circular chain of walls and towers (with repeating triple-towered castles) surrounded the city's patron (the Virgin Mary), and this eloquent image acted as a symbol of the capital.[44]

Walls were also perceived as symbols of power and greatness; they were closely linked to imperial majesty. Written histories, imperial panegyrics, court ceremonies, chronicles, hymns, epigrams and homilies all help to demonstrate how the idea of imperial power was reflected in the defensive greatness of the capital's (and the empire's) walls. At the same time, continuing in the Roman tradition, all celebrations of imperial triumphs, down to the last age of the state, passed through the Golden Gate of Constantinople's land walls.[45] More importantly, the profound symbolic and cultural significance of the *Adventus Domini* ceremonies, which multiplied from the 3rd century onwards, were directly connected to the gates of the major walled cities.[46] It is in their capacity as visual expressions of the empire's strength and opulence, and of the emperor's divine right to rule, that the façade decoration of many such gates should be acknowledged and interpreted.

A second thread we need to follow to understand the walls is **aesthetics**. In literary testimonies the walls are perceived as integrally linked to their landscape, often causing awe and a sense of security in their viewers due to their inaccessible location.[47] They were also places of beauty and delights, appreciated for their aesthetic value, magnificent gateways and well-shaped towers. One such prominent example is the poetic description of a tower in Constantinople by the 10th-century poet John Geometres.[48] He praises this hexagonal tower, pointing out its strength and defensive prowess, as well as its symmetrical plan and fine masonry. It is described as being extremely high and secure, positioned at the meeting point of land and sea (probably at the intersection of the Marmara and land walls). Geometres also praises the landscape, noting it consists of fruit gardens, flowers and vines. It seems also that the tower served as a 'belvedere' point, where people would go in order to admire the wonderful view outside the walls.

Furthermore, within the wider cosmology of Byzantine civilization, the walls had a **metaphysical** connotation:[49] miracles took place next to or on the ramparts of city walls (whether in Constantinople or provincial cities). Countless accounts of divine appearance in times of danger and enemy attacks justified the common notion that the Byzantine walls were 'God-protected'.

A telling example of the perceptions and procedures through which beliefs turned into state ideology was the 626 siege of Constantinople by the Avars/Persians: icons and relics were repeatedly part of the processions along the walls during the siege by Patriarch Sergios. The rescue of the city was attributed to the Virgin Mary, and a celebratory/commemorative service was instituted afterwards, symbolized by the ever-popular *Akathistos* ['Unseated'] hymn (taking its name from the fact that, allegedly, the audience, during its first performance directly after the end of the siege, never sat down so as to show reverence for their divine rescue). In the *Akathistos* the Virgin Mary is clearly portrayed as a protective wall. A similar scene took place during the siege by the Russians in 860, when Patriarch Photios, along with Emperor Michael III, performed a procession around the walls, carrying the Veil of the Virgin (known as *Maphorion*). In Photios's own words, the veil embraced the walls and immediately afterwards their enemies retreated.[50]

A comparable line of divine interventions is recorded for many Byzantine cities, directly relating holy figures to the defences. One of the most telling examples is St Demetrios as the patron and protector of Thessaloniki; his relation to the walls was visually commemorated in mosaics, icons and the city's coinage from Late Antiquity down to the 14th century.[51]

Another case involves the true image of Christ on a cloth (*mandylion*), which was allegedly sent to King Abgar in Edessa (Urfa) and was kept, according to one version, in a conch in the walls above the city gates. According to another version, the letter sent by Jesus to the king was inscribed as a talisman above the gates, while the mandylion was kept in the city's cathedral. It was later taken to Constantinople, in the 10th century.[52] Before that, however, the image was miraculously imprinted on a brick (*keramion*),[53] which lay next to the cloth – perhaps a brick of the walls(?) – thus transferring its holy essence to the clay (and to the fortifications?).

The walls, therefore, functioned as powerful symbolic barriers separating friends from enemies, good from evil, and sacred and holy from heathen and infidel; they were holy spaces, belonging to God. Alexei Lidov has coined the term *hierotopy*, namely, a distinguished sacred place.[54] Especially for Constantinople, the weekly procession and performance of the miracle of the Virgin Hodegetria icon, which took place on the city walls until the 1453 conquest, created and confirmed this metaphysical character. The divine connection was further promoted by some of the inscriptions set on the walls (see above). One of them, set in the Marmara Sea walls erected in the 9th century by Theophilos, functioned as a prayer to Christ for the walls to endure throughout time. The presence of chapels in towers, commonly encountered in monastic fortifications and also in some civic cases (Nicaea, Acrocorinth), not only served the needs of the guards but also sanctified the built borders of the city.

It is within this framework that the crosses (usually made of brick) decorating the façades of many Byzantine walls should be understood. We can envisage armies parading along the walls, or gathered in the open spaces outside them. Whether preparing to campaign, returning victoriously or awaiting incoming enemies, they would carry flags bearing crosses, relics and icons. In the minds of the Byzantines, their state was the universal kingdom of God on earth, their walls were 'God-protected' and their wars were fought in His name.

The composition of a 10th-century religious service,[55] intended specifically to be sung at the moment when the army departed for battle, simply followed an established practice, one that was prescribed as a necessary military preparation in many of the army manuals mentioned in this book. We can only imagine that it would be sung next to (or even on) the walls, with the army attending in formation. It invokes the strength of the Cross, the Virgin Mary and all the Angels as the guardians and defenders of the Byzantine Empire and its fortifications.

Notes

Introduction

1. Herrin, *Byzantium*, 25.
2. Sophocles, Mulroy, & Moon, *Oedipus Rex*, 56.
3. Norwich, *Byzantium*, 1989, 67.

Chapter 1 – The Late Roman Defences (3rd and 4th centuries)

1. From the huge bibliography on the defensive/military conditions of the Roman State during this period, the reader could start with Campbell & Tritle, *The Oxford Handbook of Warfare in the Classical World*, and esp. the article by Howarth, 'War and Warfare in Ancient Rome'. Also, Davies, 'Roman Warfare and Fortification'.
2. See for example Elton, *Frontiers of the Roman Empire*; Symonds, *Protecting the Roman Empire*. There are also various studies for different parts of the frontier zones, such as Petrović, Dušanić, & Arheološki institut, *Roman Limes on the Middle and Lower Danube*.
3. Lander, *Roman Stone Fortifications*; Richardson, *Theoretical Aspects of Roman Camp and Fort Design*; Gregory, 'Not "Why Not Playing Cards?" But "Why Playing Cards in the First Place?"'
4. From the multiple sources for the monument and its history, see Hingley, *Hadrian's Wall*; Goldsworthy, *Hadrian's Wall*.
5. For the latest bibliography on the various frontier lines of the Roman Empire, and their defences, see Sarantis, 'Fortifications in the East'; Sarantis, 'Fortifications in Africa'; Sarantis & Christie, 'Fortifications in the West'. For a description of the geo-topography and the Roman efforts on the Eastern Roman frontier zone, see Howard-Johnston, 'Military Infrastructure in the Roman Provinces North and South of the Armenian Taurus in Late Antiquity', 857–61, 864–7.
6. See the standard references: Winter, *Greek Fortifications*; Lawrence, *Greek Aims in Fortification*; and more recently, Souza, 'Greek Warfare and Fortification'. Also, Müth, *Ancient Fortifications*.
7. For more details, see Lander, *Roman Stone Fortifications*.
8. For Gerasa, see Mango, *Byzantine Architecture*, 20–3.
9. For Philippopolis, see Topalilov, 'Philippopolis: The City from the 1st to the Beginning of the 7th c.', 374, 411–12. For Bizye, see Beygo, 'The Historical Topography of a Provincial Byzantine City in Thrace with Special Attention to the Fortifications: Vize (Bizye)', 71–3.
10. Hekster, *Rome and Its Empire, AD 193–284*; Southern, *The Roman Empire from Severus to Constantine*.
11. Such as the extensive earthworks, under which many houses neighbouring the walls were buried to improve the defensive capacity of the walls against ballistic weapons; or the excavation of mines and countermines dug under the walls during the siege, and still containing the skeletal remains of the soldiers who fought there. For the excavations and material from Doura-Europos, see http://media.artgallery.yale.edu/duraeuropos/dura.html (accessed 17 March 2020); Brody et al., *Dura-Europos*; Baird, *Dura-Europos*; also Haldon, The Byzantine Wars, 47.
12. From the huge bibliography on Diocletian and Constantine the Great, the reader could see: Cameron, *The Later Roman Empire, AD 284–430*, 30–65; Norwich, *Byzantium*, 1989, 33–50.

13. Norwich, *Byzantium*, 1989, 85–6; Norwich, *A Short History of Byzantium*, 22–3. For the reign of Julian, see Cameron, *The Later Roman Empire, AD 284–430*, 85–98.
14. Norwich, *Byzantium*, 1989, 96–8.
15. Norwich, *A Short History of Byzantium*, 29. Howard-Johnston, 'Military Infrastructure in the Roman Provinces North and South of the Armenian Taurus in Late Antiquity', 871–2.
16. Norwich, *Byzantium*, 1989, 103–8.
17. For the events in the period of Theodosios, see Williams, *Theodosius*; Norwich, *Byzantium*, 1989, 109–18.
18. Kelly, *Ammianus Marcellinus*; Barnes, *Ammianus Marcellinus and the Representation of Historical Reality*; Whately, 'War in Late Antiquity', 121–5.
19. Belcher, 'Ammianus Marcellinus and the Nisibene Handover of A.D. 363'.
20. Vegetius Renatus, *Epitoma Rei Militaris*; Vegetius Renatus, *Vegetius, Epitome of Military Science*. See also Allmand, *The De Re Militari of Vegetius*.
21. Giardina, ed., Anonimo. *Le cose della guerra*; Coulston, 'Arms and Armour of the Late Roman Army', 4.
22. For the organization of the Late Roman Army, see Jones, *The Later Roman Empire, 284–602*, chap. 17; Coulston, 'Arms and Armour of the Late Roman Army', 4, with previous bibliography. For strategies in relation to fortification usage and the supply and training of the armies, see Sarantis, 'Waging War in Late Antiquity', 7–18, 36–40, 44–5.
23. For the frontier areas in Late Antiquity and their military preparations, see Whately, 'Strategy, Diplomacy and Frontiers', 246–54.
24. For the weaponry of the Late Roman army, see Sarantis, 'Military Equipment and Weaponry'. For experimental reproductions, see Conyard, 'Recreating the Late Roman Army'.
25. Coulston, 'Arms and Armour of the Late Roman Army', 16–17. For the equipment of the Late Roman soldiers (and especially of the Tetrarchic period), see Coulston, 'Late Roman Military Equipment Culture'.
26. Sarantis, 'Military Equipment and Weaponry', 170–1; Whitby, 'Siege Warfare and Counter-Siege Tactics in Late Antiquity (ca. 250–640)', 447–53.
27. Coulston, 'Arms and Armour of the Late Roman Army', 16.
28. Coulston, 'Arms and Armour of the Late Roman Army', 15.
29. The chapter deals only with monuments that were constructed in the lands that later became part of the Eastern Roman Empire, even if during this period there was no such notion.
30. Sarantis & Christie, 'Fortifications in the West', 256.
31. Rizos, 'New Cities and New Urban Ideas, AD 250–350', esp. 36–8.
32. Ćurčić, *Architecture in the Balkans from Diocletian to Süleyman the Magnificent*, 15. See also Dey, *The Afterlife of the Roman City*, 33–4.
33. Dey, *The Aurelian Wall and the Refashioning of Imperial Rome, AD 271–855*, esp. 17–32; Richmond, *The City Wall of Imperial Rome*; Todd, *The Walls of Rome*; Ćurčić, *Architecture in the Balkans from Diocletian to Süleyman the Magnificent*, 17; Sarantis & Christie, 'Fortifications in the West', 283; Dalyancı-Berns, 'An Exceptional City Wall?', 81–2.
34. For some twenty examples of cities that were either built or radically rebuilt and expanded during this period coming also from the Eastern frontier provinces and Anatolia, see Rizos, 'New Cities and New Urban Ideas, AD 250–350'.
35. Petrova, *Stobi*; Ćurčić, *Architecture in the Balkans from Diocletian to Süleyman the Magnificent*, 32, 110.
36. Ćurčić, *Architecture in the Balkans from Diocletian to Süleyman the Magnificent*, 51–2; Rizos, 'New Cities and New Urban Ideas, AD 250–350', 24–5.
37. Traulos, *Poleodomiki exelixis ton Athinon*; Ćurčić, *Architecture in the Balkans from Diocletian to Süleyman the Magnificent*, 17; Theocharaki, 'The Ancient Circuit Wall of Athens', 84, 131–4.

38. Spieser, *Thessalonique et ses monuments du IVe au VIe siècle*; Velenis, *Ta teichi tis Thessalonikis*; Kourkoutidou-Nikolaidou, *Wandering in Byzantine Thessaloniki*; Ćurčić, *Architecture in the Balkans from Diocletian to Süleyman the Magnificent*, 17–18, 102; Dey, *The Afterlife of the Roman City*, 38–44; Rizos, 'The Late-Antique Walls of Thessalonica and Their Place in the Development of Eastern Military Architecture'.

39. For Crow referring to Ćurčić's dates as 'radical' and 'singular' without dismissing them, see Crow, 'A Balkan Trilogy', 969–70.

40. Ćurčić, *Architecture in the Balkans from Diocletian to Süleyman the Magnificent*, 23–25; Dey, *The Afterlife of the Roman City*, 53–6; Crow, 'Power and Glory', 67–8.

41. Ćurčić, *Architecture in the Balkans from Diocletian to Süleyman the Magnificent*, 26–9; Dey, *The Afterlife of the Roman City*, 49–53.

42. From the bibliography on Constantinian Constantinople, see Mango, *Byzantine Architecture*, 24–34.

43. Sarantis, 'Fortifications in the East', 319–20.

44. Ćurčić, *Architecture in the Balkans from Diocletian to Süleyman the Magnificent*, 46; Rizos, 'New Cities and New Urban Ideas, AD 250–350', 31–2.

45. Moutsopoulos, *Rentina II*; Museum of Byzantine Culture, 'From Macedonian to Thessalian Tempi: From Rentina to Velika'.

46. Ćurčić, *Architecture in the Balkans from Diocletian to Süleyman the Magnificent*, 47–8.

47. For Xanthos, see Des Courtils, Cavalier, & Lemêtre, 'Le rempart de Xanthos', 130–1. For Ankyra, see Peschlow, 'Ancyra', 351.

48. Schneider, *Die Stadtmauer von Iznik (Nicaea)*; Foss, *Byzantine Fortifications*, 100, 113; Dalyancı-Berns, 'An Exceptional City Wall?', 77–80. For Nicaea in general, see Foss, 'Nicaea'.

49. Foss, *Survey of Medieval Castles of Anatolia II. Nicomedia*, 1–43.

50. Dey, *The Afterlife of the Roman City*, 21–4.

51. Gabriel, *Voyages Archéologiques Dans La Turquie Orientale*; Crow, 'Amida and Tropaeum Traiani'; Dalkılıç & Nabikoğlu, 'The Architectural Features of the Diyarbakir City Walls'; Dalyancı-Berns, 'An Exceptional City Wall?', 82–3; Gregory, *Roman Military Architecture on the Eastern Frontier*, vol. 2, 59–65; Assénat & Pérez, 'La Topographie Antique d'Amida (IIIe Siècle Après J.-C.–VIe Siècle Après J.-C.) d'après Les Sources Littéraires'.

52. Sarantis, 'Fortifications in the East', 348–50, 353. Howard-Johnston, 'Military Infrastructure in the Roman Provinces North and South of the Armenian Taurus in Late Antiquity', 868–71.

53. Parker, *The Roman Frontier in Central Jordan*; Whately, 'El-Lejjūn', 901–8.

54. Sarantis, 'Fortifications in the East', 350; Rizos, 'New Cities and New Urban Ideas, AD 250–350', 20–1; Intagliata, 'Palmyra and Its Ramparts during the Tetrarchy'.

55. Sarantis, 'Fortifications in the East', 355.

Chapter 2 – The Fortifications of the 5th and 'Long' 6th Centuries

1. For the historical facts, see Norwich, *Byzantium*, 1989, 120–33.

2. Norwich, *Byzantium*, 1989, 152–9.

3. Norwich, *Byzantium*, 1989, 177–80.

4. For these events, see Howard-Johnston, 'Military Infrastructure in the Roman Provinces North and South of the Armenian Taurus in Late Antiquity', 872–4.

5. For the battle of Dara, see Haldon, The Byzantine Wars, 27–33. For a discussion on Prokopios' account, see Lillington-Martin, 'Procopius on the Struggle for Dara in 530 and Rome in 537–38', 601–11.

6. Norwich, *Byzantium*, 1989, 228–33.

7. For the events of these years and the battle of Solachon, see Haldon, The Byzantine Wars, 52–7.

8. For the events of the African expedition, see Norwich, *Byzantium*, 1989, 206–11.

9. For the historical events of the Italian campaigns, see Haldon, The Byzantine Wars, 33–42; Norwich, *Byzantium*, 1989, 212–26, 235–44, 252–3, 268–9. For other aspects of the campaigns, see Kouroumali, 'The Justinianic Reconquest of Italy'.

10. For a discussion of Prokopios' account, see Lillington-Martin, 'Procopius on the Struggle for Dara in 530 and Rome in 537–38', 611–27.

11. Louth, 'Byzantium Transforming (600–700)', 226; Norwich, *Byzantium*, 1989, 273–8.

12. For the Perso-Byzantine wars of 602–27 and the Herakleios expeditions, see Louth, 'Byzantium Transforming (600–700)', 226–7; Norwich, *Byzantium*, 1989, 280–301.

13. For the historical events of the Arab conquest, see Louth, 'Byzantium Transforming (600–700)', 229–30; Norwich, *Byzantium*, 1989, 304–10.

14. For the military events and the battle of Yarmuk, see Haldon, The Byzantine Wars, 57–65.

15. Norwich, *Byzantium*, 1989, 314–15.

16. Rufus et al., *Maurice's Strategikon*.

17. Whately, 'War in Late Antiquity', 118–20.

18. Whately, 'War in Late Antiquity', 121–3, 125.

19. For more information on the subject, see Haldon, The Byzantine Wars, 21–7.

20. Haldon, The Byzantine Wars, 45.

21. Sarantis, 'Tactics', 185–8.

22. Haldon, The Byzantine Wars, 43. For further discussion on the subject, see Curta, 'Horsemen in Forts or Peasants in Villages?', 809–22. For a challenging view on how stirrups changed the medieval art of war, see White, *Medieval Technology and Social Change*.

23. Whitby, 'Siege Warfare and Counter-Siege Tactics in Late Antiquity (ca. 250–640)', 448–53.

24. Haldon, The Byzantine Wars, 48.

25. Whately, 'Organisation and Life in the Late Roman Military', 211–20.

26. Whately, 'El-Lejjūn', 908–17.

27. Accomplished through the establishment of the new field command, quaestura exercitus, by Justinian, comprising under the same authority the Danube areas and the Aegean coastline provinces: Haldon, The Byzantine Wars, 22; Sarantis, 'Military Encounters and Diplomatic Affairs in the North Balkans during the Reigns of Anastasius and Justinian', 787–8.

28. For a general overview of recruitment in Late Antiquity, see Whately, 'Organisation and Life in the Late Roman Military', 227–30.

29. See Sarantis, 'Fortifications in the East', 321. with previous bibliography. Ćurčić, on the opposite side, saw a decline in the volume of military architecture for the 5th century, which he interpreted within the wider political climate of a state where matters were gradually slipping out of its control. Ćurčić, *Architecture in the Balkans from Diocletian to Süleyman the Magnificent*, 76. For a general overview of this period's fortifications, see Crow, 'Fortification and the Late Roman East'.

30. Rizos, 'The Late-Antique Walls of Thessalonica and Their Place in the Development of Eastern Military Architecture', 462–5.

31. Avraméa, *Le Péloponnèse du IVe au VIIIe siècle*.

32. For an overview of this programme, see Howard-Johnston, 'Military Infrastructure in the Roman Provinces North and South of the Armenian Taurus in Late Antiquity', 874–81.

33. For an overview of the Balkan fortifications in the late 5th and 6th centuries, see Sarantis, 'Military Encounters and Diplomatic Affairs in the North Balkans during the Reigns of Anastasius and Justinian', 777–87.

34. We have unfortunately no archival evidence about the size of the garrisons, and only speculations may be attempted at the moment.

35. Mango, *Byzantine Architecture*, 57–8.

36. Veikou, 'Byzantine Histories, Settlement Stories'.

37. From the huge bibliography on the walls of Istanbul, we can cite: Foss, *Byzantine Fortifications*, 9ff.; Müller-Wiener, *Bildlexikon zur Topographie Istanbuls*, 286–319; Freely, *Byzantine Monuments*

of Istanbul, 26, 44–7, 49–54; Asutay-Effenberger, *Landmauer von Konstantinopel-İstanbul*; Crow, 'Power and Glory', 65–7.

38. Crow & Ricci, 'Anastasian Wall Project', 14; Rizos & Sayar, 'Urban Dymanics in the Bosphorus Region during Late Antiquity', 89–91.

39. http://www.ancient-nessebar.com/html/main_en.php?menu=sights_wall (accessed 30 March 2020).

40. For Komotini, see Tsouris, *I Ochyrosi tou Didymoteichou*, 277–78. For Drama, Tsouris, 'Paratiriseis sti Chronologisi tis Ochyroseos tis Dramas'.

41. Koukoulē-Chrysanthakē, *Philippi*, 18; Dadaki, Lychounas, & Tsouris, 'Ochyroseis stis Paruphes tis Euryteris Periadas ton Philippon', 122.

42. Snively, 'Golemo Gladište at Konjuh'.

43. Mango, *Byzantine Architecture*, 24–5; Duval et al., *Caričin Grad*; Ćurčić, *Architecture in the Balkans from Diocletian to Süleyman the Magnificent*, 209–14; Dey, *The Afterlife of the Roman City*, 105–7; Ivanišević, 'Main Patterns of Urbanism in Caričin Grad (Justiniana Prima)'; Snively, 'Caričin Grad'.

44. Ćurčić, *Architecture in the Balkans from Diocletian to Süleyman the Magnificent*, 184; Gregory, 'Dyrrachion'.

45. Bowden, *Epirus Vetus*, 91–3; Hodges et al., 'Late-Antique and Byzantine Butrint', 214.

46. Bowden, *Epirus Vetus*, 87–8; Hodges et al., 'Late-Antique and Byzantine Butrint', 217, 230–1.

47. Chrysostomou, *Nikopolis*; Bowden, *Epirus Vetus*, 89–91; Ćurčić, *Architecture in the Balkans from Diocletian to Süleyman the Magnificent*, 131.

48. Theocharaki, 'The Ancient Circuit Wall of Athens', 135–7.

49. Gregory, 'The Late Roman Wall at Corinth'; Gregory, 'Fortification and Urban Design in Early Byzantine Greece', 51–3; Ćurčić, *Architecture in the Balkans from Diocletian to Süleyman the Magnificent*, 126; Athanasoulis, *The Castle of Acrocorinth and Its Enhancement Project (2006–2009)*, 26–9.

50. Carpenter, *The Defenses of Acrocorinth and the Lower Town*; Athanasoulis, *The Castle of Acrocorinth and Its Enhancement Project (2006–2009)*, 26–33.

51. Georgopoulou-Verra, *The Kastro at Patras*.

52. Gregory, 'Fortification and Urban Design in Early Byzantine Greece', 54–5, 57.

53. Gregory, *The Hexamilion and the Fortress*.

54. Cherf, 'The Dhema Pass and Its Early Byzantine Fortifications'; Cherf, 'Procopius, Lime-Mortar C14 Dating and the Late Roman Fortifications of Thermopylai'.

55. Museum of Byzantine Culture, 'From Macedonian to Thessalian Tempi: From Rentina to Velika'.

56. Freely, *Byzantine Monuments of Istanbul*, 72–3; Whitby, 'The Long Walls of Constantinople'; Crow & Ricci, 'Investigating the Hinterland of Constantinople', 239–53; Crow & Ricci, 'Anastasian Wall Project', 12–13; Ćurčić, *Architecture in the Balkans from Diocletian to Süleyman the Magnificent*, 173–4; Crow, 'Fortification and the Late Roman East', 415–18.

57. Crow, 'Fortification and the Late Roman East', 420–1.

58. Ćurčić, *Architecture in the Balkans from Diocletian to Süleyman the Magnificent*, 174. See also Crow, 'Crow, 'A Balkan Trilogy – Slobodan Ćurčić, Architecture in the Balkans from Diocletian to Süleyman the Magnificent', 972.

59. See more details in Gregory, *Roman Military Architecture on the Eastern Frontier*.

60. Crow, 'Dara, a Late Roman Fortress in Mesopotamia'; Croke & Crow, 'Procopius and Dara'; Whitby, 'Procopius' Description of Dara (Buildings II.1–3)'; Foss, *Byzantine Fortifications*, 9; Gregory, *Roman Military Architecture on the Eastern Frontier*, vol. 2, 80–8; Keser-Kayaalp & Erdoğan, 'Recent Research on Dara/Anastasiopolis'. For the history of the place, see Haldon, The Byzantine Wars, 27–33.

61. Crow, 'New Cities of Late Antiquity: Theodosiopolis in Armenia'.

62. Foss, *Byzantine Fortifications*, 8, 10; Mango, *Byzantine Architecture*, 24, 29; Lauffray, 'Ḥalabiyya-Zenobia, place forte du limes oriental et la Haute-Mésopotamie au VIe siècle'; Mango, 'Zenobia'; Dey, *The Afterlife of the Roman City*, 103–4; Blétry, 'The Fortifications of Zenobia Reinterpreted'. Blétry, 'L'urbanisme et l'habitat de La Ville de Zénobia-Halabiya'.

63. Karnapp, *Die Stadtmauer von Resafa in Syrien*; Foss, *Byzantine Fortifications*, 9; Mango, 'Sergiopolis'; Hof, 'The Revivification of Earthen Outworks in the Late Eastern Empire'; Gussone & Sack, 'Resafa/Syrien'.

64. Arthur, *Byzantine and Turkish Hierapolis (Pamukkale)*, 42–3, 129–30.

65. Lightfoot, *Amorium*, 45–7, 76–9, 104–17.

66. Balance, 'Kayseri'.

67. Posamentir, 'Anazarbos in Late Antiquity'.

68. Crow, 'Fortification and the Late Roman East', 400–8. With previous bibliography.

69. For a general discussion on the state of research and previous bibliography, see Sarantis, 'Fortifications in Africa', esp. 305–10. The basic source for this material is Pringle, *The Defence of Byzantine Africa from Justinian to the Arab Conquest*.

70. Pringle, *The Defence of Byzantine Africa from Justinian to the Arab Conquest*, 94–109.

71. Pringle, *The Defence of Byzantine Africa from Justinian to the Arab Conquest*.

72. Pringle, *The Defence of Byzantine Africa from Justinian to the Arab Conquest*, 179–81.

73. Pringle, *The Defence of Byzantine Africa from Justinian to the Arab Conquest*, 238–42.

74. Goodchild & Ward Perkins, 'The Roman and Byzantine Defences of Lepcis Magna'; Pringle, *The Defence of Byzantine Africa from Justinian to the Arab Conquest*, 208–11.

75. Pringle, *The Defence of Byzantine Africa from Justinian to the Arab Conquest*, 232–6; Lassus, *La forteresse byzantine de Thamugadi*.

76. Pringle, *The Defence of Byzantine Africa from Justinian to the Arab Conquest*, 214–16.

77. Pringle, *The Defence of Byzantine Africa from Justinian to the Arab Conquest*, 212–14.

Chapter 3 – What Makes an 'Early Byzantine' Fortification?

1. For Drama, see Tsouris, 'Paratiriseis sti Chronologisi tis Ochyroseos tis Dramas'.

2. For studies on the bricks of the Early Byzantine architecture, their size, system of manufacture, stamping etc., see for example Bardill, *Brickstamps of Constantinople*; Gerolymou, 'Sphragismata se Keramous kai Plinthous apo ti Nikopoli'.

3. Pringle, *The Defence of Byzantine Africa from Justinian to the Arab Conquest*, 133.

4. Sarantis & Christie, 'Fortifications in the West', 256.

5. Foss, *Byzantine Fortifications*, 30–1.

6. Ćurčić, *Architecture in the Balkans from Diocletian to Süleyman the Magnificent*, 174; Rizos, 'The Late-Antique Walls of Thessalonica and Their Place in the Development of Eastern Military Architecture', 459–65. with further examples.

7. Rizos, 'The Late-Antique Walls of Thessalonica and Their Place in the Development of Eastern Military Architecture', 458–61.

8. Based on these features, the addition of marble facings in the Porta Appia of Roma (with similar works done to the Portae Flaminia, Tiburtina and Praenestina-Labicana) has recently been attributed to the efforts of Narses, after 552, emulating the imperial gate of Constantinople: Dey, *The Aurelian Wall and the Refashioning of Imperial Rome, AD 271–855*, 292–7; Crow, 'Power and Glory', 70.

9. Examples of spiral staircases can be observed in contemporary secular architecture; for example, see the gallery access to Lausos Palace, Constantinople.

Chapter 4 – The Fortifications from the 7th to the 9th Centuries

1. Louth, 'Byzantium Transforming (600–700)', 224, 232; Norwich, *Byzantium*, 1989, 320–2.

2. Norwich, *Byzantium*, 1989, 334.

3. Gregory, 'Cyprus'.
4. Louth, 'Byzantium Transforming (600–700)', 230–1, 232–3; Norwich, *Byzantium*, 1989, 315, 323–4.
5. Louth, 'Byzantium Transforming (600–700)', 235.
6. Ćurčić, *Architecture in the Balkans from Diocletian to Süleyman the Magnificent*, 249.
7. Louth, 'Byzantium Transforming (600–700)', 231; Norwich, *Byzantium*, 1989, 320, 329.
8. Louth, 'Byzantium Transforming (600–700)', 233; Haldon, *The Byzantine Wars*, 73–4; Norwich, *Byzantium*, 1989, 325–6.
9. Norwich, *Byzantium*, 1989, 352–3. For the wars with the Arabs, see Auzépy, 'State of Emergency (700–850)', 255–6.
10. Norwich, *Byzantium*, 1989, 363.
11. Norwich, *Byzantium*, 1989, 348, 363–4, 368.
12. Norwich, *Byzantium*, 1989, 364–5.
13. Norwich, *Byzantium*, 1991, 6.
14. Norwich, *Byzantium*, 1991, 6.
15. For the campaigns of Nikephoros against the Bulgarians and the Battle of Pliska, see Haldon, The Byzantine Wars, 74–8.
16. For the battle of Versinikia, 813, see Haldon, The Byzantine Wars, 79–82.
17. Norwich, *Byzantium*, 1991, 7–9, 13–20; Ćurčić, *Architecture in the Balkans from Diocletian to Süleyman the Magnificent*, 265.
18. Norwich, *Byzantium*, 1991, 108–9.
19. Norwich, *Byzantium*, 1991, 32–6.
20. For the Arab emirate of Crete, see Christides, *The Conquest of Crete by the Arabs (ca. 824)*; Miles, *The Coinage of the Arab Amirs of Crete*. For Theoktistos, see Hollingsworth, 'Theoktistos'.
21. Norwich, *Byzantium*, 1991, 36–8, 93, 109.
22. Norwich, *Byzantium*, 1991, 45–9. For the events of 838, see Haldon, The Byzantine Wars, 82–6.
23. Haldon, The Byzantine Wars, 87–8. Norwich, *Byzantium*, 1991, 60–1, 93.
24. Gregory, 'Cyprus'.
25. Dennis, *Three Byzantine Military Treatises*, 1–136. For the redating, see Haldon, 'Information and War', 381. With previous bibliography.
26. Dennis, *Three Byzantine Military Treatises*, vii, 3.
27. Dennis, *Three Byzantine Military Treatises*, 22–3.
28. Dennis, *Three Byzantine Military Treatises*, 28–31.
29. Dennis, *Three Byzantine Military Treatises*, 30–43.
30. For war tactics during this period, see Haldon, The Byzantine Wars, 70–2.
31. For the themes and their gradual appearance, see Louth, 'Byzantium Transforming (600–700)', 239; Haldon, The Byzantine Wars, 65–6, 68–70.
32. Kontogiannis, *Venetian and Ottoman Heritage in the Aegean*, 24–5.
33. Kontogiannis, 'Euripos-Negroponte-Eğrıboz', 31.
34. Foss, *Byzantine Fortifications*, 140–2.
35. For the decline of archery during this period, and its reintroduction after the 9th-century encounters with Turkish armies, see Haldon, The Byzantine Wars, 86.
36. McGeer, Kazhdan, & Cutler, 'Weaponry'.
37. For Greek Fire, see Haldon, The Byzantine Wars, 49; Haldon, '"Greek Fire" Revisited'; McGeer, 'Greek Fire'. with previous bibliography. For the First Arab Siege, see Jankowiak, 'The First Arab Siege of Constantinople'.
38. For Chalcis and Thebes, see Kontogiannis, *Venetian and Ottoman Heritage in the Aegean*, 24–5., with previous bibliography. For Thessaloniki, the repairs of the west walls were documented by an inscription dated to 862 and mentioning the two government officials (*protospatharios* Marinos

and *strator* Kakikis) who were responsible for the repairs (Ćurčić, *Architecture in the Balkans from Diocletian to Süleyman the Magnificent*, 278.)

39. Foss, *Byzantine Fortifications*, 50, 53–5, 70–1; Müller-Wiener, *Bildlexikon zur Topographie Istanbuls*, 288, 293, 301–3, 308, 313; Freely, *Byzantine Monuments of Istanbul*, 156–7, 161–2, 164–5; Ćurčić, *Architecture in the Balkans from Diocletian to Süleyman the Magnificent*, 252–3, 268, 270; Berger, 'The Byzantine Court as a Physical Space', 8–9.
40. Mango, 'The Palace of the Boukoleon'.
41. Mexia, 'I Vasiliki sto Tigani tis Mesa Manis', with previous bibliography.
42. *Abdera-Polystylon*.
43. Kollias, 'Topographika provlimata tis mesaionikis agoras, 85–98, 101, 106; Kollias, *The Medieval City of Rhodes and the Palace of the Grand Master*, 13, 73–7, 89, 143–8, 151; Kollias, 'I Palaiochristianiki kai Vyzantini Rodos', 303–5; Manousou-Della, 'I proimi mesaioniki ochyrosi tis polis tis Rodou', 332, 334–36. Manousou-Della, *Mesaioniki poli Rodou*, 10.
44. Hill, Roland, & Odegard, 'The Kastro Apalirou Project'; Roland, 'The Fortifications at Kastro Apalirou'; Hill, Roland, & Odegard, 'Kastro Apalirou, Naxos, a Seventh-Century Urban Foundation'.
45. Andrianakis, 'Oi Ochyroseis ton Chalion, ', 20–3; Andrianakis, 'To Ergo tis Epitropis Syntirisis, Stereosis, Apokatastasis kai Anadeiksis, ', 475, 482.
46. Tsigonaki, 'Poleon Anelpistois Metavolais', 80–8.
47. Tsigonaki, 'Poleon Anelpistois Metavolais', 89–98.
48. Foss, *Byzantine Fortifications*, 140–2.
49. For Xanthos, see Foss, 'The Lycian Coast in the Byzantine Age', 11–12; Des Courtils, 'Nouvelles données sur le rempart de Xanthos', 293; Des Courtils, Cavalier, & Lemêtre, 'Le rempart de Xanthos', 130–1. For Patara and Side, see Peschlow, 'Patara'; Piesker, 'Side'. For the other sites, see below.
50. For Telmessos-Makre (Fethiye, Turkey), see Foss & Kazhdan, 'Makre'; Foss, 'The Lycian Coast in the Byzantine Age', 5; Crow, 'Fortifications', 102.
51. Foss, *Byzantine Fortifications*, 79–120, esp. 80–2, 100–2, 104, 110–12.
52. Butler, *The Excavations*, 21–5, figs 8, 13–15; Hanfmann, 'The Third Campaign at Sardis (1960)', 32–7; Hanfmann, 'The Thirteenth Campaign at Sardis (1970)', 12, fig. 8; Hanfmann, *Letters from Sardis*, 286–7, fig. 218; Foss, *Byzantine and Turkish Sardis*, 57–9; Foss, *Byzantine Fortifications*, 131–2; Vann, *The Unexcavated Buildings of Sardis*, 21–2, 87–8; Dey, *The Afterlife of the Roman City*, 205–6.
53. Foss, *Byzantine Fortifications*, 133.
54. Foss, *Byzantine Fortifications*, 132–3; Dey, *The Afterlife of the Roman City*, 202–4; Crow, 'Power and Glory', 70–2.
55. Foss, *Byzantine Fortifications*, 137–8; Dey, *The Afterlife of the Roman City*, 204–5.
56. Foss, *Byzantine Fortifications*, 133–6, 143–4; Foss, 'Late Antique and Byzantine Ankara'; Lawrence, 'A Skeletal History of Byzantine Fortification', 204–9; Peschlow, *Ankara*; Peschlow, 'Ancyra', 349–51, 356–60.
57. Crow & Hill, 'The Byzantine Fortifications of Amastris in Paphlagonia'.
58. Foss & Fursdon, *Survey of Medieval Castles of Anatolia*.
59. Lightfoot, *Amorium*, 48–59, 72–3, 144–9.
60. Dey, *The Afterlife of the Roman City*, 206–9.
61. Foss, 'The Lycian Coast in the Byzantine Age', 33–4; Morganstern, *The Fort at Dereağzi, and Other Material Remains in Its Vicinity*; Crow, 'Fortifications', 100–2.

Chapter 5 – The Fortifications of the 10th and 11th Centuries

1. Haldon, The Byzantine Wars, 90–3; Norwich, *Byzantium*, 1991, 128–9, 132–4.
2. Norwich, *Byzantium*, 1991, 150–2.

30. Provost, 'Esquisse du paysage urbain entre le IXe s. et le XIIe s. d'après les sources archéologiques', 221–2.
31. Ćurčić, *Architecture in the Balkans from Diocletian to Süleyman the Magnificent*, 512.
32. Ćurčić, *Architecture in the Balkans from Diocletian to Süleyman the Magnificent*, 513–14.
33. Kakouris, 'Anaktoropoli. Istorikes Plirophories kai Archaiologika Dedomena'; Ćurčić, *Architecture in the Balkans from Diocletian to Süleyman the Magnificent*, 514; Tsouris, *I Ochyrosi tou Didymoteichou*, 279–80.
34. Gregory, *The Hexamilion and the Fortress*; Ćurčić, *Architecture in the Balkans from Diocletian to Süleyman the Magnificent*, 510–11; Bakirtzis, 'Ta teichi ton Vyzantinon Poleon', 157–8; Frey, 'Disuse, Re-Use, and Misuse of the Early Byzantine Fortress at Isthmia', 147–9.

Chapter 10 – The Empire of Thessaloniki/the Despotate of Epirus/ Duchy of Thessaly

1. Nicol, *The Despotate of Epiros, 1267–1479*. See also Fine, *The Late Medieval Balkans*, 65–9, 112–16, 119–28, 133–5, 156–65, 168–70, 235–43. The following section is based on these sources, unless otherwise stated. For the empire of Thessaloniki, in particular, see Bredenkamp, 'The Byzantine Empire of Thessaloniki (1224–1242)'.
2. For these events and the history of the Catalan Duchy of Athens, see Nicol, *The Despotate of Epiros, 1267–1479*, 74; Setton, *Catalan Domination of Athens, 1311–1388*.
3. Orlandos, 'To Kastron tis Artis'; Papadopoulou, 'Nea Archaiologika Stoicheia gia tin Vyzantini Poli tis Artas', 378–9, 390; Ephorate of Antiquities of Arta, 'The Castle of Arta'.
4. Tsouris, 'I Vyzantini Ochyrosi ton Ioanninon'; Papadopoulou, 'Kastro Ioanninon. I Istoria ton Ochyroseon kai tou Oikismou', 51–63.
5. Ćurčić, Chatzētryphōnos & Aimos, Society for the Study of the Medieval Architecture in the Balkans and its Preservation, *Secular Medieval Architecture in the Balkans 1300–1500 and its Preservation*, 114.
6. Theologidou, 'Servia'.
7. Kekaumenos, *Vademecum des byzantinischen Aristokraten*.
8. Ćurčić, *Architecture in the Balkans from Diocletian to Süleyman the Magnificent*, 518.
9. Vikatou, Chamilaki & Katsouli, *The Castle of Naupaktos*; Korre, Mamaloukos & Papavarnavas, 'The Venetian Fortifications of Lepanto'.
10. Smpyraki-Kalantzi & Kakavas, '24th EBA', 79.
11. 19th Ephorate of Byzantine Antiquities, 'Castle of Fanari at Karditsa'.

Chapter 11 – The Empire of Trebizond

1. Bryer, *The Byzantine Monuments and Topography of the Pontos*.
2. Eastmond, *Art and Identity in Thirteenth-Century Byzantium*. See also the project East of Byzantium, https://eastofbyzantium.org/about/ (accessed 15 April 2020); the recent exhibition Byzantium's Other Empire: Trebizond (Anamed, Istanbul, 2016), https://anamed.ku.edu.tr/en/events/byzantiums-other-empire-trebizond/ (accessed 15 April 2020), and its accompanying catalogue, Eastmond et al., *Byzantium's Other Empire*.
3. For the historical facts related to the Empire of Trebizond, see Nicol, *The Last Centuries of Byzantium, 1261–1453*, 401–9; variously in Bryer, *The Empire of Trebizond and the Pontos*; Eastmond, 'The Empire of Trebizond'.
4. The main source for this section is the work of Winfield & Bryer in Bryer, *The Byzantine Monuments and Topography of the Pontos*.
5. Foss, *Byzantine Fortifications*, 150, 151.
6. Bryer, *The Byzantine Monuments and Topography of the Pontos*, 126–32.
7. Bryer, *The Byzantine Monuments and Topography of the Pontos*, 138–42.

8. Bryer, *The Byzantine Monuments and Topography of the Pontos*, 178–95.
9. Bryer, *The Byzantine Monuments and Topography of the Pontos*, 331–4.
10. Bryer, *The Byzantine Monuments and Topography of the Pontos*, 310–11.
11. Bryer, *The Byzantine Monuments and Topography of the Pontos*, 312.

Chapter 12 – What Makes a 'Late Byzantine' Fortification?

1. For the two known examples from 15th-century Constantinople (the palaces of Goudelis and Notaras), see Ganchou, 'La tour d'Irène (Eirene Kulesi) à Istanbul: le palais de Loukas Notaras?', 189–99. For the houses of Mystras, see Orlandos, *Ta palatia kai ta spitia tou Mystra*.
2. For specimens from the Byzantine lands, see Ćurčić, *Architecture in the Balkans from Diocletian to Süleyman the Magnificent*, 518–27; Ousterhout, 'Life in a Late Byzantine Tower'.
3. Tsouris, 'I Vyzantini Ochyrosi ton Ioanninon', 148–51.
4. For Smederevo, see Foss, *Byzantine Fortifications*, 30; Ćurčić, *Architecture in the Balkans from Diocletian to Süleyman the Magnificent*, 628–31.
5. Akyürek, *The Panorama of the Marmara Sea Walls by Dimitriadis Efendi*.

Chapter 13 – Byzantine Walls: Functions, Perceptions and 'Other' Fortifications

1. For an effort to gather historical evidence and to recreate Byzantine siege and defensive strategies, see Haldon, The Byzantine Wars, 45–51. See also Sullivan, 'Tenth Century Byzantine Offensive Siege Warfare'; McGeer, 'Byzantine Siege Warfare in Theory and Practice'. For the Late Antique period, see Sarantis, 'Waging War in Late Antiquity', 55–60; Sarantis, 'Tactics', 193–9; and esp. Whitby, 'Siege Warfare and Counter-Siege Tactics In Late Antiquity (ca. 250–640)'.
2. See various examples in Germanidou, 'Mia morphi 'perivallontikou' polemou sto Vyzantio'.
3. Haldon, The Byzantine Wars, 51.
4. Germanidou, 'Martyries istorikon pigon kai archaiologikon evrimaton gia mia morphi 'viologikou' polemou me ti chrisi ton melisson sto Vyzantio'.
5. Haldon, The Byzantine Wars, 49–50.
6. For Choniates, see Choniates, *Nicetae Choniatae Historia*; Choniates, *O City of Byzantium*. For Villehardouin see Villehardouin, *Chronicles of the Crusades*. For English versions of both texts, see https://sourcebooks.fordham.edu/source/4cde.asp and https://sourcebooks.fordham.edu/basis/villehardouin.asp (accessed 19 April 2020).
7. For Late Antiquity, for example, see Sarantis, 'Waging War in Late Antiquity', 30–3; Sarantis, 'Fortifications in the East', 358–60.
8. For the Byzantine era, see Haldon, 'Information and War', 387. For Clytemnestra's beacon speech in Aeschylus (Agam. 281ff.), see Quincey, 'The Beacon-Sites in the Agamemnon'.
9. Foss, 'Beacon'; Pattenden, 'The Byzantine Early Warning System'.
10. Rife, 'Leo's Peloponnesian Fire-Tower and the Byzantine Watch-Tower on Acrocorinth'.
11. See, for example, Turchetto & Salemi, 'Hide and Seek. Roads, Lookouts and Directional Visibility Cones in Central Anatolia'.
12. Haldon, 'Information and War', 380. For an overview of the (Cappadocian) frontier defensive networks, see Haldon, 'Information and War', 382–5.
13. The best studied case for the Aegean concerns the Dodecanese Islands under Hospitaller rule, with many of the defensive installations dating back to the Byzantine era; see Heslop, 'The Search for the Defensive System of the Knights in the Dodecanese', Part I (Chalki, Symi, Nisyros and Tilos) and Part II (Leros, Kalymnos, Kos and Bodrum).
14. On the subject of Byzantine marching camps, see Kolias, 'Peri Apliktou', 144–84; Haldon, The Byzantine Wars, 72–3.
15. Haldon, 'Information and War', 379.

16. Dennis, *Three Byzantine Military Treatises*, 329–35.
17. Orlandos, *Monastic Architecture*.
18. Forsyth, 'The Monastery of St Catherine at Mount Sinai', 4–7; Myriantheos-Koufopoulou, 'Vyzantina kai Metavyzantina Parekklisia tis Monis Sina', 31–5.
19. Ćurčić, *Architecture in the Balkans from Diocletian to Süleyman the Magnificent*, 302–3; Voyadjis, Sotiris & Sythiakaki-Kritsimalli, *To katholiko tis Ieras Monis Meyistis Lauras sto Ayion Oros*.
20. Mylonas, *Moni Vatopediou*; Mamaloukos, 'To Katholiko tis Monis Vatopediou'.
21. Ćurčić, *Architecture in the Balkans from Diocletian to Süleyman the Magnificent*, 304–6.
22. Ćurčić, *Architecture in the Balkans from Diocletian to Süleyman the Magnificent*, 392.
23. Ćurčić, *Architecture in the Balkans from Diocletian to Süleyman the Magnificent*, 383–4; Stikas, *To Oikodomikon Chronikon tis Monis Osiou Louka Phokidos*.
24. Bouras, 'The Daphni Monastic Complex Reconsidered'; Ćurčić, *Architecture in the Balkans from Diocletian to Süleyman the Magnificent*, 140–1.
25. Ćurčić, *Architecture in the Balkans from Diocletian to Süleyman the Magnificent*, 390–1.
26. Voyadjis, 'Paratiriseis stin Oikodomiki Istoria tis Monis Sagmata sti Voiotia'.
27. Tsouris, 'To Kastro sto Palio Pyli kai o Osios Christodoulos o Latrinos', 365, 371–2.
28. Sinos, *Die Klosterkirche der Kosmosoteira in Bera (Vira)*; Tsouris & Brikas, *To Frourio tou Pythiou kai to Ergo tis Apokatastaseos tou*, 22; Tsouris & Brikas, 'Vyzantines Ochyroseis ston Evro 1', 186–90.
29. Mylonas, *Bildlexikon Des Heiligen Berges Athos*, vol. 1.
30. For these towers, see Ćurčić, *Architecture in the Balkans from Diocletian to Süleyman the Magnificent*, 519–27; Androudis, 'Fortified Towers of the 16th Century in the Monasteries of Mount Athos'.
31. Choulia & Albani, *Meteora*.
32. Pharr, Davidson & Pharr, *The Theodosian Code*, 459.
33. Pharr, Davidson & Pharr, *The Theodosian Code*, 167.
34. Ricci, 'A Resilient Landscape'.
35. Foss, *Survey of Medieval Castles of Anatolia II. Nicomedia*, 12–13, 18.
36. See, for example, Bakirtzis, 'Ta Teichi ton Vyzantinon Poleon', 144–50; Barsanti et al., *Spolia Reincarnated*.
37. Frey, *Spolia in Fortifications and the Common Builder in Late Antiquity*.
38. As in the Kosmosoteira murals, where in the facial features of the soldier-saints people have seen portraits of the ruling dynasty.
39. Bakirtzis, 'Ta Teichi ton Vyzantinon Poleon', 150–4.
40. Dey, *The Afterlife of the Roman City*, 11.
41. Bakirtzis, 'Ta Teichi ton Vyzantinon Poleon', 140; Haldon, 'Information and War', 381.
42. For mosaics, see the 6th-century 'Madaba Map' in Jordan; representations in Sant' Apollinare Nuovo and San Vitale in Ravenna; Santa Maria Maggiore and San Vincenzo in Rome; and Hagia Sophia in Constantinople (see Dey, *The Afterlife of the Roman City*, 11–13, 120–6.). For manuscripts, see the illustrations in copies of the 5th-century *Notitia Dignitatum*: Dey, *The Afterlife of the Roman City*, 120.
43. Morrisson, 'The Emperor, the Saint, and the City'; Kontogiannis, 'Translatio Imaginis'.
44. Hilsdale, 'The Imperial Image at the End of Exile', 189–90.
45. Among the numerous descriptions of such ceremonies, one can see those celebrated by Theophilos in 830 or by Michael VIII in 1261. Norwich, *Byzantium*, 1991, 45–7.
46. Smith, *Architectural Symbolism of Imperial Rome and the Middle Ages*, chs 1–3; Dey, *The Afterlife of the Roman City*, 59–63.
47. Bakirtzis, '*The Afterlife of the Roman City*', 141–4.
48. Maguire, 'The Beauty of Castles'.
49. See Tomadaki, 'Literary Depictions of the Constantinopolitan Walls in Byzantium'; Bakirtzis, '*The Afterlife of the Roman City*', 157–8.
50. Norwich, *Byzantium*, 1991, 66–7.

51. Morrisson, 'The Emperor, the Saint, and the City'.
52. Ševčenko, 'Mandylion'; Mango, 'Edessa'; Jensen & Nicholson, 'Mandylion of Edessa'. See also Nicolotti, *From the Mandylion of Edessa to the Shroud of Turin*.
53. Ševčenko, 'Keramion'.
54. Lidov, ed., *Ierotopiia*.
55. Pertusi, 'Una Acolouthia Militare Inedita Del X Secolo'.

Bibliography

19th Ephorate of Byzantine Antiquities. 'Castle of Fanari at Karditsa.' Trikala: Ministry of Culture and Sports, n.d.

Abdera-Polystylon. Komotini: ITH' Ephoreia Proistorikon kai Klasikon Archaiotiton Komotinis, 2001.

Acheimastou-Potamianou, Myrtalē. *Mystras: Historical and Archaeological Guide*. Monuments and Museums of Greece. Athens: Hesperos Editions, 2003.

Ahrweiler, Hélène. *Byzance et La Mer: La Marine de Guerre, La Politique et Les Institutions Maritimes de Byzance Aux VIIe–XVe Siècles [Byzantium and the Sea: The Naval Forces, the Politics and the Maritime Institutions of Byzantium from the 7th to the 15th Centuries]*. Bibliothèque Byzantine Études 5. Paris: Presses universitaires de France, 1966.

Akyürek, Engin. *The Panorama of the Marmara Sea Walls by Dimitriadis Efendi*. İstanbul: GABAM, 2020.

Allmand, C.T. *The De Re Militari of Vegetius: The Reception, Transmission and Legacy of a Roman Text in the Middle Ages*. Cambridge, UK/New York: Cambridge University Press, 2011.

Andrianakis, Michalis. 'To Ergo tis Epitropis Syntirisis, Stereosis, Apokatastasis kai Anadeixis tou Vyzantinou Perivolou kai ton Enetikon Ochyroseon tis Palaias Polis ton Chanion' [The Work of the Committee for the Conservation, Stabilization and Enhancement of the Byzantine Enclosure and the Venetian Fortifications of the Old City of Chania], in *To Ergo ton Epistimonikon Epitropon Anastilosis, Syntirisis kai Anadeixis Mnimeion [The Work of the Scientific Committees for Restoration, Conservation and Enhancement of Monuments]*, 475–85. Athens: Ministry of Culture, Finance Management Fund for Archaeological Projects, 2006.

———. 'Oi Ochyroseis ton Chanion, Parelthon, Paron kai Mellon' [The Fortifications of Chania, Past, Present and Future]. *Ereisma Periodiki Ekdosi Logou Kai Texnis [Ereisma Periodical Edition of Speech and Art]*, 38–9 (2007): 14–33.

Androudis, Paschalis. 'Fortified Towers of the 16th Century in the Monasteries of Mount Athos', in *To Ayion Oros ston 15o kai 16o Aiona, Praktika St' Diethnous Epistimonikou Synedriou [Mount Athos in the 15th and 16th Century, Proceedings of the 6th International Scientific Congress]*, 487–515. Thessaloniki: Aristoteleio Panepistimio Thessalonikis, 2012.

Angold, Michael. *A Byzantine Government in Exile: Government and Society under the Laskarids of Nicaea, 1204–1261*. Oxford Historical Monographs. London: Oxford University Press, 1975.

Arthur, Paul. *Byzantine and Turkish Hierapolis (Pamukkale): An Archaeological Guide*. Istanbul: Ege Yayınları, 2006.

Asp-Talwar, Annika. 'The Chronicle of Michael Panaretos', in *Byzantium's Other Empire: Trebizond: Exhibition June 24–September 18 2016, Koç University, Research Center for Anatolian Civilizations (RCAC)*, edited by Antony Eastmond, et al., 173–212. Koç Üniversitesi Yayınları. İstanbul: Koç Üniversitesi Research Center for Anatolian Civilizations, 2016.

Assénat, Martine, and Antoine Pérez. 'La Topographie Antique d'Amida (IIIe Siècle Après J.-C. – VIe Siècle Après J.-C.) d'après Les Sources Littéraires' [The Ancient Topography of Amida (3rd C. AD – 6th C. AD) according to Litterary Sources], in *New Cities in Late Antiquity: Documents and Archaeology*, edited by Efthymios Rizos, 57–70. Bibliothèque de l'Antiquité Tardive 35. Turnhout, Belgium: Brepols, 2017.

Asutay-Effenberger, Neslihan. 'Wer Erbaute Mermer-Kule?' [Who Built Mermer-Kule?]. *Byzantion (Bruxelles)* 72, no. 1 (2002): 270–75.

———. *Landmauer von Konstantinopel-İstanbul: Historisch-Topographische Und Baugeschichtliche Untersuchungen* [*The Landwalls of Constantinople-Istanbul: Historical-Topographical and Architectural Research*]. Millennium-Studien Bd. 18. Berlin/New York: Walter De Gruyter, 2007.

Athanasopoulos, Antonis. 'Episkeuazontas ta Teichi tis Konstantinoupolis: Autokratorikes Protovoulies kata tin Ysteri Vyzantini Period' [Repairing the Walls of Constantinople: Imperial Initiatives during the Late Byzantine Period], *Byzantina Symmeikta* 27 (2017): 111–28.

Athanasoulis, Demetrios. *The Castle of Acrocorinth and Its Enhancement Project (2006–2009)*. Ancient Corinth: Hellenic Ministry of Culture and Tourism/25th Ephorate of Byzantine Antiquities, 2009.

Avraméa, Anna. *Le Péloponnèse du IVe au VIIIe siècle: changements et persistances* [*The Peloponnese from the 4th to the 8th Century: Changes and Continuities*]. Paris, 1997. Available at: http://ark.bnf.fr/ark:/12148/bpt6k33841218.

Auzépy, Marie-France. 'State of Emergency (700–850)', in *The Cambridge History of the Byzantine Empire c. 500–1492*, edited by Jonathan Shepard, 251–91. Cambridge, UK/New York: Cambridge University Press, 2008. Available at: http://nrs.harvard.edu/urn-3:hul.ebookbatch.CAMHI_batch:9780511756702.

Baird, Jennifer A. *Dura-Europos*. Archaeological Histories. London/New York: Bloomsbury Academic, 2018.

Bakirtzis, Nicholas. 'Ta Teichi ton Vyzantinon Poleon: Aisthitiki, ideoloyies kai symvolismoi' [The Walls of Byzantine Cities: Aesthetics, Ideologies and Symbolisms], in *Byzantine Cities, 8th–15th Centuries*, edited by T. Kioussopoulou, 73–100. Rethymno: Publications of the Faculty of Philosophy of the University of Crete, 2012.

Balance, M. 'Kayseri.' *Anatolian Archaeology* 2 (1996): 13–14.

Bardill, Jonathan. *Brickstamps of Constantinople*. Oxford Monographs on Classical Archaeology. Oxford/New York: Oxford University Press, 2004.

Barnes, H. & Mark Whittow. 'Medieval Castles.' *Anatolian Archaeology* 2 (1996): 14–15.

———. 'Medieval Castles: Antioch-on-the-Maeander.' *Anatolian Archaeology* 4 (1998): 17–18.

Barnes, Timothy D. *Ammianus Marcellinus and the Representation of Historical Reality*. Vol. 56. Cornell University Press, 1998. Available at: https://doi.org/10.7591/j.cttq45g1.

Barsanti, Claudia, et al. (eds.) *Spolia Reincarnated: Afterlives of Objects, Materials, And Spaces in Anatolia from Antiquity to the Ottoman Era*. İstanbul: Koç University Research Center for Anatolian Civilizations, 2018.

Bartusis, Mark C. *The Late Byzantine Army: Arms and Society, 1204–1453*. Middle Ages Series. Philadelphia: University of Pennsylvania Press, 1992.

Bassett, Sarah, et al. *Archaeology and the Cities of Asia Minor in Late Antiquity*. Kelsey Museum Publication 6. Ann Arbor, MI: Kelsey Museum of Archaeology, University of Michigan, 2011.

Belcher, Susannah. 'Ammianus Marcellinus and the Nisibene Handover of A.D. 363.' *Late Antique Archaeology* 8, no. 2 (2013): 631–52. Available at: https://doi.org/10.1163/22134522-90000020.

Berg, Hilda van den. 'Anonymus De obsidione toleranda: editio critica [Anonymous: Sustaining Sieges: Critical Edition].' Dissertationes inaugurales Batavae ad res antiquas pertinentes 4. Leyden: E.J. Brill, 1947.

Berger, Albrecht. 'The Byzantine Court as a Physical Space', in *The Byzantine Court: Source of Power and Culture: Papers from the Second International Sevgi Gönül Byzantine Studies Symposium, Istanbul, 21–23 June 2010*, 3–12. Istanbul: Koç University Press, 2013.

Beygo, A. 'The Historical Topography of a Provincial Byzantine City in Thrace with Special Attention to the Fortifications: Vize (Bizye).' Ph.D Thesis, Istanbul Technical University, 2015.

Bianca, Stefano, and Aga Khan Trust for Culture. *Syria: Medieval Citadels between East and West*. Turin: Umberto Allemandi for The Aga Khan Trust for Culture, 2007.

Birkenmeier, John W. *The Development of the Komnenian Army: 1081–1180*. History of Warfare 5. Leiden/Boston: Brill, 2002.

Blétry, Sylvıe. 'L'urbanisme et l'habitat de La Ville de Zénobia-Halabiya: Résultats de La Mission Franco-Syrienne (2006–10)', in *New Cities in Late Antiquity: Documents and Archaeology*, edited by Efthymios Rizos, 137–52. Bibliothèque de l'Antiquité Tardive 35. Turnhout, Belgium: Brepols, 2017.

———. 'The Fortifications of Zenobia Reinterpreted.' Oxbow Books, 2020. Available at: https://doi.org/10.2307/j.ctv138wsz8.18.

Boase, Thomas, Sherrer Ross, ed. *The Cilician Kingdom of Armenia*. Edinburgh: Scottish Academic Press, 1978.

Borkopp-Restle, Birgitt, et al. *Studien zur byzantinischen Kunstgeschichte: Festschrift für Horst Hallensleben zum 65. Geburtstag* [*Studies in Byzantine History of Art: in honor of Horst Hallensleben for his 65th Birthday*]. Amsterdam: Adolf M. Hakkert, 1995.

Bouras, Charalampos. 'The Daphni Monastic Complex Reconsidered', in *Aetos: Studies in Honour of Cyril Mango, Presented to Him on April 14, 1998*, edited by Irmgard Hutter, and Ihor Sevcenko, 1–14. Stuttgart: B.G. Teubner, 1998.

Bowden, William. *Epirus Vetus: The Archaeology of a Late Antique Province*. London: Duckworth, 2003.

Brand, Charles M. 'Tzachas', in *The Oxford Dictionary of Byzantium*. Oxford University Press, 2005. Available at: https://www.oxfordreference.com/view/10.1093/acref/9780195046526.001.0001/acref-9780195046526-e-5634.

Bredenkamp, Francois. 'The Byzantine Empire of Thessaloniki (1224–1242).' History Center, 1996.

Brody, Lisa R. et al. *Dura-Europos: Crossroads of Antiquity*. Chestnut Hill, MA/Chicago, IL: McMullen Museum of Art, Boston College/University of Chicago Press, 2011.

Bryer, Anthony. *The Byzantine Monuments and Topography of the Pontos*. Dumbarton Oaks Studies 20. Washington, DC: Dumbarton Oaks Research Library and Collection, 1985. Available at: http://nrs.harvard.edu/urn-3:hul.ebookbatch.ACLS_batch:MIU01000000000000005122677.

———. *The Empire of Trebizond and the Pontos*. Collected Studies; CS117. London: Variorum Reprints, 1980. Available at: http://nrs.harvard.edu/urn-3:hul.ebookbatch.ACLS_batch:MIU01000000000000005861820.

Butler, Howard Crosby. *The Excavations*. Sardis 1. Leyden: E.J. Brill, 1922.

Cameron, Averil. *The Later Roman Empire, AD 284–430*. Cambridge, MA/Harvard University Press, 1993.

Campbell, Janet B., and Lawrence A. Tritle, eds. *The Oxford Handbook of Warfare in the Classical World*. E-book. Oxford Handbooks Online-Classical Studies. Oxford: Oxford University Press, 2013.

Carpenter, Rhys. *The Defenses of Acrocorinth and the Lower Town*. Corinth, v. 3, Pt 2. Cambridge, MA, published for the American School of Classical Studies at Athens, Harvard University Press, 1936.

Chatzelis, Georgios. *Byzantine Military Manuals as Literary Works and Practical Handbooks: The Case of the Tenth-Century Sylloge Tacticorum*. Abingdon/New York: Routledge, Taylor & Francis Group, 2019.

Chatzelis, Georgios, and Jonathan Harris. *A Tenth-Century Byzantine Military Manual: The Sylloge Tacticorum*. Birmingham Byzantine and Ottoman Studies, v. 22. London/New York: Routledge, Taylor & Francis Group, 2017.

Chatzidakis, Manolis. *Mystras: historia, mnēmeia, technē* [*Mystras: History, Monuments, Art*]. Athens: Phoivos Papachrysanthou, 1948.

———. *Mystras: The Medieval City and the Castle: A Complete Guide to the Churches, the Palaces, and the Castle*. Athens: Ekdotike Athenon, 1985.

Cherf, W. 'The Dhema Pass and Its Early Byzantine Fortifications.' Loyola University Chicago, 1983. Available at: https://ecommons.luc.edu/luc_diss/2474.

———. 'Procopius, Lime-Mortar C14 Dating and the Late Roman Fortifications of Thermopylai'. *American Journal of Archaeology* 88 (1984): 594–8.

Cheynet, Jean-Claude, et al. *Ou dōron eimi tas graphas blepōn noei: mélanges Jean-Claude Cheynet* [*Studies in honor of Jean-Claude Cheynet*]. Travaux et mémoires. Centre de recherche d'histoire et civilisation de Byzance (Paris, France) 21. Paris: Association des amis du Centre d'histoire et civilisation de Byzance, 2017.

Choniates, Nicetas. *Nicetae Choniatae Historia* [*History of Nicetas Choniates*]. Corpus fontium historiae Byzantinae, v. 11, 1–2. Berlin/New York: de Gruyter, 1975.

——. *O City of Byzantium: Annals of Niketas Choniatēs*. Byzantine Texts in Translation. Detroit: Wayne State University Press, 1984.

Choulia, Suzana, and Jenny Albani. *Meteora: Architektoniki – Zographiki* [*Meteora: Architecture – Painting*]. Athens: Adam editions, 1999.

Christides, Vassilios. *The Conquest of Crete by the Arabs (ca. 824): A Turning Point in the Struggle between Byzantium and Islam*. Athēnai: Akadēmia Athēnōn, 1984.

Chrysostomou, Paulos. *Nikopolis*. Athens: Ministry of Culture, Archaeological Receipts Fund, 2001.

Conyard, John. 'Recreating the Late Roman Army.' *Late Antique Archaeology* 8, no. 2 (2013): 523–67. Available at: https://doi.org/10.1163/22134522-90000017.

Coulston, J.C.N. 'Late Roman Military Equipment Culture.' *Late Antique Archaeology* 8, no. 2 (2013): 461–92. Available at: https://doi.org/10.1163/22134522-90000015.

Coulston, Jon. 'Arms and Armour of the Late Roman Army', in *A Companion to Medieval Arms and Armour*, edited by David Nicolle, 3–24. Woodbridge, UK/Rochester, NY: Boydell Press, 2002.

Courault, Christopher, Simon J. Barker, and Emanuele Intagliata. *City Walls in Late Antiquity: An Empire-Wide Perspective*. Oxbow Books, Oxbow, 2020. Available at: https://doi.org/10.2307/j.ctv138wsz8.

Croke, Brian, and James Crow. 'Procopius and Dara.' *The Journal of Roman Studies* 73 (1983): 143–59. Available at: https://doi.org/10.2307/300078.

Crow, James. 'Dara, a Late Roman Fortress in Mesopotamia.' *Yayla* 4 (1981): 11–20.

——. 'Amida and Tropaeum Traiani: A Comparison of Late Antique Fortress Cities on the Lower Danube and Mesopotamia', in *The Transition to Late Antiquity: on the Danube and Beyond*, edited by A.G. Poulter. British Academy, 2007. Available at: https:// DOI:10.5871/bacad/9780197264027. 003.0017.

——. 'A Balkan Trilogy – Slobodan Ćurčić, Architecture in the Balkans from Diocletian to Süleyman the Magnificent' (New Haven: Yale University Press, 2010). Review in *Journal of Roman Archaeology* 25 (2012): 969–73. Available at: https://doi.org/10.1017/S104775940000218X.

——. 'Fortification and the Late Roman East: from Urban Walls to Long Walls.' *Late Antique Archaeology* 8, no. 2 (2013): 395–432. Available at: https://doi.org/10.1163/22134522-90000013.

——. 'Fortifications', in *The Archaeology of Byzantine Anatolia: From the End of Late Antiquity until the Coming of the Turks*, edited by Philipp Niewöhner. Oxford University Press, 2017. Available at: https://doi.org/10.1093/acprof:oso/9780190610463.003.0008.

——. 'New Cities of Late Antiquity: Theodosiopolis in Armenia', in *New Cities in Late Antiquity: Documents and Archaeology*, edited by Efthymios Rizos, 101–15. Bibliothèque de l'Antiquité Tardive 35. Turnhout, Belgium: Brepols, 2017.

——. 'Power and Glory: Ceremonial Gates in Constantinople and the Balkans: Prototypes and Legacy', in *City Walls in Late Antiquity: an empire-wide perspective*, edited by Emanuele Intagliata, Simon Barker, and Christopher Courault, 65–76. Oxbow Books, 2020. Available at: https://doi.org/10.2307/j.ctv138wsz8.11.

Crow, James, and David Hill. *Naxos and the Byzantine Aegean: Insular Responses to Regional Change*. Papers and Monographs from the Norwegian Institute at Athens, v. 7. Athens: Norwegian Institute at Athens, 2018.

Crow, James, and Stephen Hill. 'The Byzantine Fortifications of Amastris in Paphlagonia.' *Anatolian Studies* 45 (1995): 251–65. Available at: https://doi.org/10.2307/3642924.

Crow, James, and Alessandra Ricci. 'Anastasian Wall Project.' *Anatolian Archaeology* 1 (1995): 12–14.

————. 'Investigating the Hinterland of Constantinople: Interim Report on the Anastasian Long Wall.' *Journal of Roman Archaeology* 10 (1997): 235–62. Available at: https://doi.org/10.1017/S1047759400014811.

Ćurčić, Slobodan. *Architecture in the Balkans from Diocletian to Süleyman the Magnificent*. New Haven: Yale University Press, 2010.

Ćurčić, Slobodan, Euangelia Chatzētryphōnos, and Aimos, Society for the Study of Medieval Architecture in the Balkans and its Preservation, eds. *Secular Medieval Architecture in the Balkans 1300–1500 and its Preservation*. Thessaloniki: Aimos, Society for the Study of Medieval Architecture in the Balkans and its Preservation, 1997.

Ćurčić, Slobodan, et al. *Architecture as Icon: Perception and Representation of Architecture in Byzantine Art*. New Haven: Princeton University Art Museum, 2010.

Curta, Florin. 'Horsemen in Forts or Peasants in Villages? Remarks on the Archaeology of Warfare in 6th to 7th C. Balkans.' *Late Antique Archaeology* 8, no. 2 (2013): 809–50. Available at: https://doi.org/10.1163/22134522-90000026.

Cyprus Monuments: New Illustrated Series, No. 3–7. Nicosia: Government Printing Office, 1929.

Dadaki, Stavroula, Michalis Lychounas, and Konstantinos Tsouris. 'Ochyroseis stis Paruphes tis Euryteris Pediadas ton Philippon' [Fortifications at the Fringes of the Wider Valey of Philippoi], in *I Drama kai I Periochi tis, Istoria kai Politismos, D'Epistimoniki Synantisi, Drama 16–19 Maiou 2002* [*Drama and her Regions, History and Culture, 4th Scientific Meeting, Drama 16–19 May 2002*], 117–36. Drama, 2006.

Dalkılıç, Neslihan, and Adnan Nabikoğlu. 'The Architectural Features of the Diyarbakir City Walls: A Report on Current Status and Issues of Conservation.' *Mediterranean Archaeology and Archaeometry* 12, no. 2 (2012): 171–82.

Dalyancı-Berns, Ayşe. 'An Exceptional City Wall?: Re-Thinking the Fortifications of Nicaea in an Empire-Wide Context.' Oxbow Books, 2020. Available at: https://doi.org/10.2307/j.ctv138wsz8.12.

Davies, Gwyn. 'Roman Warfare and Fortification', in *The Oxford Handbook of Engineering and Technology in the Classical World*, 30 December 2009. Available at: https://doi.org/10.1093/oxfordhb/9780199734856.013.0028.

Dennis, George T. 'Flies, Mice, and the Byzantine Crossbow.' *Byzantine and Modern Greek Studies* 7 (ed. 1981): 1–5. Available at: https://doi.org/10.1179/030701381790206571.

————. *Three Byzantine Military Treatises*. Dumbarton Oaks Texts 9. Washington, DC: Dumbarton Oaks, Research Library and Collection, 1985.

Des Courtils, Jacques. 'Nouvelles données sur le rempart de Xanthos.' *Revue des études anciennes* 96, no. 1 (1994): 285–98. Available at: https://doi.org/10.3406/rea.1994.4577.

Des Courtils, Jacques, Laurence Cavalier, and Séverine Lemêtre. 'Le rempart de Xanthos: Recherches 1993–2010' [The Walls of Xanthos: Studies 1993–2010], in *Turm und Tor: Siedlungsstrukturen in Lykien und benachbarten Kulturlandschaften: Akten des Gedenkkolloquiums für Thomas Marksteiner in Wien, November 2012*, 103–31. Forschungen in Limyra, Bd. 7. Wien: Österreichisches Archäologisches Institut, 2015.

Dey, Hendrik W. *The Afterlife of the Roman City: Architecture and Ceremony in Late Antiquity and the Early Middle Ages*. New York: Cambridge University Press, 2015.

————. *The Aurelian Wall and the Refashioning of Imperial Rome, AD 271–855*. Cambridge University Press, 2011.

Diaconu, Petre. *Păcuiul lui Soare*. Biblioteca de arheologie 18. București: Editura Academiei Republicii Socialiste România, 1972.

Dimitriadis Efendi [G.A. Demetriades], *The panorama of the Marmara Sea Walls by Dimitriadis Efendi. Texts and The Panorama* [*Dimitriadis Efendi'nin Marmara Sahil Surlari panoramasi. Yazilar and Panorama*]. Koç Üniversitesi Stavros Niarchos Vakfi Geç Antik Çag ve Bizans Arastirmalari Merkezi, 2019.

Duval, Noël, Vladislav Popović, Bernard Bavant, Jean-Pierre Caillet, Vladimir Kondić, J.-M. Spieser. *Caričin Grad*. Collection de l'École française de Rome 75. Belgrade/Rome: Institut archéologique de Belgrade/Ecole française de Rome, 1984.

Eastmond, Antony. 'The Empire of Trebizond', in *Byzantium's Other Empire: Trebizond: Exhibition June 24–September 18 2016, Koç University, Research Center for Anatolian Civilizations* (RCAC), edited by Antony Eastmond, et al., 31–57. Koç Üniversitesi Yayınları. İstanbul: Koç Üniversitesi Research Center for Anatolian Civilizations, 2016.

Eastmond, Antony,. *Art and Identity in Thirteenth-Century Byzantium: Hagia Sophia and the Empire of Trebizond*. Birmingham Byzantine and Ottoman Monographs, v. 10. England: Ashgate/Variorum, 2004.

Eastmond, Antony, et al., eds. *Byzantium's Other Empire: Trebizond: Exhibition June 24–September 18 2016, Koç University, Research Center for Anatolian Civilizations* (RCAC). Koç Üniversitesi Yayınları. İstanbul: Koç Üniversitesi Research Center for Anatolian Civilizations, 2016.

Edwards, Robert W. *The Fortifications of Armenian Cilicia*. Dumbarton Oaks Studies 23. Washington, D.C.: Dumbarton Oaks Research Library and Collection, 1987.

Elton, Hugh. *Frontiers of the Roman Empire*. Bloomington: Indiana University Press, 1996.

Ephorate of Antiquities of Arta. 'The Castle of Arta.' Arta, 2015.

Eugenidou, Despoina. *Monemvasia: Artefacts, Environment, History, the Archaeological Collection*. Athens: Archaeological Receipts Fund, 2001.

Fasolio, Marco. 'I Vassalli e Le Comunita Renitenti Agli Obblighi Militari Nei Documenti Del Marchese Teodoro I Paleologo Di Monferrato' [The vassals and the communities who resist military obligations in the documents of the Marquis Theodore I Palaiologos of Montferrat]. *Bollettino Storico-Bibliografico Subalpino* 113, no. 2 (2015): 315–58.

Fine, John V.A. *The Late Medieval Balkans: A Critical Survey from the Late Twelfth Century to the Ottoman Conquest*. Ann Arbor: University of Michigan Press, 1987.

Forsyth, George. 'The Monastery of St Catherine at Mount Sinai: The Church and Fortress of Justinian.' *Dumbarton Oaks Papers* 22 (1968): 1.

Foss, Clive. *Byzantine and Turkish Sardis*. Archaeological Exploration of Sardis Monographs. Cumberland: Harvard University Press, 1975.

———. *Byzantine Fortifications: An Introduction*. Studia (University of South Africa) 22. Pretoria: University of South Africa, 1986.

———. 'Late Antique and Byzantine Ankara.' *Dumbarton Oaks Papers* 31 (1977): 27–87. Available at: https://doi.org/10.2307/1291403.

———. 'The Lycian Coast in the Byzantine Age.' *Dumbarton Oaks Papers* 48 (1994): 1–52. Available at: https://doi.org/10.2307/1291721.

———. *Survey of Medieval Castles of Anatolia II. Nicomedia*. British Institute of Archaeology at Ankara Monograph 21. Oxford: British Institute of Archaeology at Ankara, 1996.

———. 'Beacon', in *The Oxford Dictionary of Byzantium*. Oxford University Press, 2005. Available at: https://www.oxfordreference.com/view/10.1093/acref/9780195046526.001.0001/acref-9780195046526-e-0692.

———. 'Nicaea', in *The Oxford Dictionary of Byzantium*. Oxford University Press, 2005. Available at: https://www.oxfordreference.com/view/10.1093/acref/9780195046526.001.0001/acref-9780195046526-e-3773.

Foss, Clive, and Alexander Kazhdan. 'Makre', in *The Oxford Dictionary of Byzantium*. Oxford University Press, 2005. Available at: https://www.oxfordreference.com/view/10.1093/acref/9780195046526.001.0001/acref-9780195046526-e-3263.

Foss, Clive, and Robin Fursdon. *Survey of Medieval Castles of Anatolia*. BAR International Series 261. Oxford: BAR, 1985.

Freely, John. *Byzantine Monuments of Istanbul*. Cambridge/New York: Cambridge University Press, 2004.

Freely, John, and Ahmet S. Çakmak. *Byzantine Monuments of Istanbul*, 2004.

Freeman, Philip, and D. L. Kennedy. *The Defence of the Roman and Byzantine East: Proceedings of a Colloquium Held at the University of Sheffield in April 1986*. BAR International Series 297. Oxford: BAR, 1986.

French, D.H., and C.S. Lightfoot. *The Eastern frontier of the Roman Empire: Proceedings of a Colloquium Held at Ankara in September 1988*. BAR International Series 553. Oxford: BAR, 1989.

Frey, Jon M. *Spolia in Fortifications and the Common Builder in Late Antiquity*. Mnemosyne, Bibliotheca Classica Batava. Supplementum. History and Archaeology of Classical Antiquity, 389. Leiden/ Boston, MA: Brill, 2016.

———. 'Disuse, Re-Use, and Misuse of the Early Byzantine Fortress at Isthmia', in *City Walls in Late Antiquity: an empire-wide perspective*, edited by Intagliata, Emanuele, Simon Barker and Christopher Courault, 147–56. Oxbow Books, 2020. Available at: https://doi.org/10.2307/j.ctv138wsz8.19.

Gabriel, Albert. *Voyages Archéologiques Dans La Turquie Orientale*. Paris: E. de Boccard, 1940.

Ganchou, Thierry. 'La tour d'Irène (Eirene Kulesi) à Istanbul: le palais de Loukas Notaras?' [The Tower of Irene in Istanbul: the Palace of Loukas Notaras?], in *Ou dōron eimi tas graphas blepōn noei: mélanges Jean-Claude Cheynet* [Studies in honor of Jean-Claude Cheynet], edited by Béatrice Caseau-Chevallier, Vivien Prigent, and Alessio Sopracasa, 169–256. Travaux et mémoires. Centre de recherche d'histoire et civilisation de Byzance (Paris, France) 21. Paris: Association des amis du Centre d'histoire et civilisation de Byzance, 2017.

Georgopoulou-Verra, Myrto. *The Kastro at Patras*. Athens: Ministry of Culture, Archaeological Receipts Fund, 2000.

Germanidou, Sophia. 'Martyries istorikon pigon kai archaiologikon evrimaton gia mia morphi "viologikou" polemou me ti chrisi ton melisson sto Vyzantio' [Testimonies of Historical Sources and Archaeological Finds for a Form of 'Biological' War with the Use of Bees in Byzantium]. *Byzantina Symmeikta* 23, (2013): 91–104. Available at: https://doi.org/10.12681/byzsym.1046.

———. 'Mia morphi "perivallontikou" polemou sto Vyzantio: Georgikes Doliophthores kai Agrotika Ergaleia os Phonika Opla' [A Form of 'Environmental' War in Byzantium: Agricultural Sabotage and Farm Tools as Killing Weapons]. *Byzantina Symmeikta* 27, (2017): 145–72. Available at: https://doi.org/10.12681/byzsym.1215.

Gerolymou, Konstantina. 'Sphragismata se Keramous kai Plinthous apo ti Nikopoli. Symboli sti Meleti ton Ensphragiston Oikodomikon Proionton tis Protobyzantinis Periodou' [Brickstamps on Tiles and Bricks from Nicopolis. Contribution to the Study of Stamped Building Materials of the Early Byzantine Period]. PhD Thesis, Aristotle University of Thessaloniki, n.d.

Giardina, Andrea, ed. Anonimo. *Le cose della guerra* [The Things of War]. Milano: Fondazione Lorenzo Valla, A Mondadori, 1989.

Gigourtakis, Nikos M. 'Vyzantines Ochyroseis stin Kriti kata ti B' Byzantini Periodo (961–1204).' [Byzantine Fortifications in Crete during the Second Byzantine Period (961–1204)]. MA, University of Crete, 2004.

Goldsworthy, Adrian. *Hadrian's Wall*. New York: Basic Books, 2018.

Goodchild, R.G., and J.B. Ward Perkins. 'The Roman and Byzantine Defences of Lepcis Magna.' *Papers of the British School at Rome* 21 (1953): 42–73.

Grandin, Thierry. 'Introduction to the Citadel of Salah Al-Din', in *Syria: Medieval Citadels between East and West*, edited by Stefano Bianca, 139–80. Turin: Umberto Allemandi for The Aga Khan Trust for Culture, 2007.

———. *The Castle of Salah Ad-Din, Description, History, Site Plan & Visitor Tour*. Geneva: The Aga Khan Trust for Culture, 2008.

Gregory, Shelagh. 'Not "Why Not Playing Cards?" But "Why Playing Cards in the First Place?"' In *The Eastern Frontier of the Roman Empire: Proceedings of a Colloquium Held at Ankara in September 1988*, edited by D.H. French and C.S. Lightfoot, 169–75. BAR International Series 553. Oxford: BAR, 1989.

———. *Roman Military Architecture on the Eastern Frontier*. Amsterdam: A.M. Hakkert, 1995.

Gregory, T.E. 'The Late Roman Wall at Corinth.' *Hesperia* 48, no. 3 (1979): 264–80.

———. 'Fortification and Urban Design in Early Byzantine Greece', in *City, Town, and Countryside in the Early Byzantine Era*, edited by Robert L. Hohlfelder, 43–64. East European Monographs, no. 120. Boulder NY: East European Monographs; distributed by Columbia University Press, 1982.

———. *The Hexamilion and the Fortress*. Isthmia, v. 5. Princeton, NJ: American School of Classical Studies at Athens, 1993.

———. 'Cyprus', in *The Oxford Dictionary of Byzantium*. Oxford University Press, 2005. Available at: https://www.oxfordreference.com/view/10.1093/acref/9780195046526.001.0001/acref-9780195046526-e-1317.

———. 'Dyrrachion', in *The Oxford Dictionary of Byzantium*. Oxford University Press, 2005. Available at: https://www.oxfordreference.com/view/10.1093/acref/9780195046526.001.0001/acref-9780195046526-e-1589.

Gussone, Martin, and Dorothée Sack. 'Resafa/Syrien. Städtebauliche Entwicklung Zwischen Kultort Und Herrschaftssitz' [Resafa in Syria. Urban Development between Cult Place and Mansion], in *New Cities in Late Antiquity: Documents and Archaeology*, edited by Efthymios Rizos, 117–36. Bibliothèque de l'Antiquité Tardive 35. Turnhout, Belgium: Brepols, 2017.

Haldon, John. '"Solenarion" – the Byzantine Crossbow?' *University of Birmingham Historical Journal* 12 (1969/1970): 155–7.

———. *The Palgrave Atlas of Byzantine History*. New York: Palgrave Macmillan, 2005.

———. '"Greek Fire" Revisited: Recent and Current Research', in *Byzantine Style, Religion and Civilization: In Honour of Sir Steven Runciman*, edited by Elizabeth Jeffreys, 290–325. Cambridge/New York: Cambridge University Press, 2006.

———. *The Byzantine Wars*. Stroud, Gloucestershire: History Press, 2008.

———. 'Information and War: Some Comments on Defensive Strategy and Information in the Middle Byzantine Period (ca. AD 660–1025).' *Late Antique Archaeology* 8, no. 2 (2013): 371–93. Available at: https://doi.org/10.1163/22134522-90000012.

———. *A Critical Commentary on the Taktika of Leo VI*. Dumbarton Oaks Studies 44. Washington DC: Dumbarton Oaks Research Library and Collection, 2014.

———. *Byzantine Warfare*. The International Library of Essays on Military History. Ashgate: Routledge, Taylor & Francis, 2017.

Hanfmann, George. 'The Third Campaign at Sardis (1960).' *Bulletin of the American Schools of Oriental Research* 0, 162 (1961): 8.

———. 'The Thirteenth Campaign at Sardis (1970).' *BASOR*, no. 203 (1971): 5–22.

———. *Letters from Sardis*. Harvard College Library Preservation Digitization Program. Cambridge, MA: Harvard University Press, 1972. Available at: http://nrs.harvard.edu/urn-3:FHCL:29066987.

Hekster, Olivier. *Rome and Its Empire, AD 193–284*. Debates and Documents in Ancient History. Edinburgh: Edinburgh University Press, 2008.

Herrin, Judith. *Byzantium: The Surprising Life of a Medieval Empire*. Princeton: Princeton University Press, 2007.

Heslop, Michael. 'The Search for the Defensive System of the Knights in the Dodecanese (Part I: Chalki, Symi, Nisyros and Tilos)', in *On the Margins of Crusading, The Military Orders, the Papacy and the Christian World*, edited by Helen J. Nicholson, 139–66. Farnham: Ashgate, 2011.

———. 'The Search for the Defensive System of the Knights in the Dodecanese (Part II: Leros, Kalymnos, Kos and Bodrum)', in *Archaeology and Architecture of the Military Orders*, edited by M. Piana and C. Carlsson, 29–67. London: Ashgate, 2014.

Hill, David, Hakon Roland, and Knut Odegard. 'Kastro Apalirou, Naxos, a Seventh-Century Urban Foundation', in *New Cities in Late Antiquity: Documents and Archaeology*, edited by Efthymios Rizos, 281–91. Bibliothèque de l'Antiquité Tardive 35. Turnhout, Belgium: Brepols, 2017.

———. 'The Kastro Apalirou Project', in *Naxos and the Byzantine Aegean: Insular Responses to Regional Change*, edited by James Crow and David Hill, 3–7. Papers and Monographs from the Norwegian Institute at Athens, v. 7. Athens: Norwegian Institute at Athens, 2018.

Hilsdale, Cecily J. 'The Imperial Image at the End of Exile: The Byzantine Embroidered Silk in Genoa and the Treaty of Nymphaion (1261).' *Dumbarton Oaks Papers* 64 (2010): 151–99.

Hingley, Richard. *Hadrian's Wall: A Life*. Oxford/New York: Oxford University Press, 2012. Available at: http://nrs.harvard.edu/urn-3:hul.ebookbatch.GEN_batch:EDZ000010737820160628.

Hodges, R., et al. 'Late-Antique and Byzantine Butrint: Interim Report on the Port and Its Hinterland (1994–95).' *Journal of Roman Archaeology* 10 (1997): 207–34. Available at: https://doi.org/10.1017/S104775940001480X.

Hof, Catharine. 'The Revivification of Earthen Outworks in the Late Eastern Empire: The Case Study of Resafa, Syria.' Oxbow Books, 2020. Available at: https://doi.org/10.2307/j.ctv138wsz8.17.

Hohlfelder, Robert L. *City, Town, and Countryside in the Early Byzantine Era*. East European Monographs, no. 120. Boulder, NY: East European Monographs, distributed by Columbia University Press, 1982.

Hollingsworth, Paul A. 'Theoktistos', in *The Oxford Dictionary of Byzantium*. Oxford University Press, 2005. Available at: https://www.oxfordreference.com/view/10.1093/acref/9780195046526.001.0001/acref-9780195046526-e-5427.

Howard-Johnston, James. 'Military Infrastructure in the Roman Provinces North and South of the Armenian Taurus in Late Antiquity.' *Late Antique Archaeology* 2013, 8, no. 2 (2013): 851–91. Available at: https://doi.org/10.1163/22134522-90000027.

Howarth, Randall S. 'War and Warfare in Ancient Rome.' *The Oxford Handbook of Warfare in the Classical World*, 9 January 2013. Available at: https://doi.org/10.1093/oxfordhb/9780195304657.013.0002.

Intagliata, Emanuele. 'Palmyra and Its Ramparts during the Tetrarchy', in *New Cities in Late Antiquity: Documents and Archaeology*, edited by Efthymios Rizos, 71–83. Bibliothèque de l'Antiquité Tardive 35. Turnhout, Belgium: Brepols, 2017.

Ivanišević, Vujadin. 'Main Patterns of Urbanism in Caričin Grad (Justiniana Prima)', in *New Cities in Late Antiquity: Documents and Archaeology*, edited by Efthymios Rizos, 221–32. Bibliothèque de l'Antiquité Tardive 35. Turnhout, Belgium: Brepols, 2017.

Ivanov, Rumen. *Roman Cities in Bulgaria*. Bulgarian first edition. Corpus of Ancient and Medieval Settlements in Modern Bulgaria, vol. 1. Sofia: Prof Marin Drinov Academic Publishing House, 2012.

Jankowiak, Marek. 'The First Arab Siege of Constantinople.' *Travaux et Mémoires* 17 (2013): 237–320.

Jeffery, G. *The Hilltop Castles of Hilarion, Buffavento and Kantara, and the Lesser Forts and Watch Towers of the Ancient Kingdom of Cyprus*. Cyprus Monuments. Historical and Architectural Buildings. Illustrated Series 6. Nicosia: Cyprus G.P.O, 1935.

Jensen, Robin, and Oliver Nicholson. 'Mandylion of Edessa.' Oxford University Press, 2018. Available at: http://www.oxfordreference.com/view/10.1093/acref/9780198662778.001.0001/acref-9780198662778-e-2949.

Jones, A.H.M. *The Later Roman Empire, 284–602: A Social Economic and Administrative Survey*. Baltimore, MD: Johns Hopkins University Press, 1986.

Kakouris, Isidore. 'Anaktoropoli. Istorikes Plirofories kai Archaiologika Dedomena' [Anaktoropoli. Historical Information and Archaeological Data], in *I Kavala kai i Periochi tis, A' Topiko Symposio, Kavala, 18–20/4/1977 [Kavala and its Region, First Local Symposium, Kavala 18–20/4/1977]*. Thessaloniki, 1980.

Kanellopoulos, Nikolaos. 'Peri tis Stratiotikis Ekgumnasis kai Ekpaideusis sto Vyzantio kata tin Ysteri Periodo (1204–1453)' [About Military Training and Education in Byzantium during the Late Period]. *Byzantina Symmeikta* 22 (2012): 157–71. Available at: https://doi.org/10.12681/byzsym.1056.

Karnapp, Walter. *Die Stadtmauer von Resafa in Syrien* [*The City Walls of Resafa in Syria*]. Denkmäler antiker Architektur 11. Berlin: Wde Gruyter, 1976.

Kazhdan, Alexander. 'Domestikos Ton Scholon', in *The Oxford Dictionary of Byzantium*. Oxford University Press, 2005. Available at: https://www.oxfordreference.com/view/10.1093/acref/97801 95046526.001.0001/acref-9780195046526-e-1528.

———. 'Komnene, Anna', in *The Oxford Dictionary of Byzantium*. Oxford University Press, 2005. Available at: https://www.oxfordreference.com/view/10.1093/acref/9780195046526.001.0001/acref-9780195046526-e-2901.

———. 'Choniates, Niketas', in *The Oxford Dictionary of Byzantium*. Oxford University Press, 2005. Available at: https://www.oxfordreference.com/view/10.1093/acref/9780195046526.001.0001/acref-9780195046526-e-1032.

Kazhdan, Alexander, and Eric McGeer. 'Praecepta Militaria', in *The Oxford Dictionary of Byzantium*. Oxford University Press, 2005. Available at: https://www.oxfordreference.com/view/10.1093/acref/9780195046526.001.0001/acref-9780195046526-e-4441.

Kazhdan, Alexander, and Ellen C. Schwartz. 'Păcuiul Lui Soare', in *The Oxford Dictionary of Byzantium*. Oxford University Press, 2005. Available at: https://www.oxfordreference.com/view/10.1093/acref/9780195046526.001.0001/acref-9780195046526-e-4011.

Kekaumenos. *Vademecum des byzantinischen Aristokraten: das sogenannte Strategikon des Kekaumenos* [*A handbook of the Byzantine Aristocrats: the so-called Strategikon of Kekaumenos*]. Byzantinische Geschichtsschreiber, 5. Graz: Verlag Styria, 1956.

Kelly, Gavin. *Ammianus Marcellinus: The Allusive Historian*. Cambridge Classical Studies. Cambridge/New York: Cambridge University Press, 2008.

Kennedy, Scott, ed. *Two Works on Trebizond*. Dumbarton Oaks Medieval Library 52. Cambridge, MA: Harvard University Press, 2019.

Keser-Kayaalp, Elif, and Nihat Erdoğan. 'Recent Research on Dara/Anastasiopolis', in *New Cities in Late Antiquity: Documents and Archaeology*, edited by Efthymios Rizos, 153–75. Bibliothèque de l'Antiquité Tardive 35. Turnhout, Belgium: Brepols, 2017.

Knowles, Christine. 'Les Enseignements de Théodore Paléologue.' *Byzantion* 22 (1952): 389–94.

Kolias, Georgios T. 'Peri Apliktou' [About Military Camps]. *Epetiris Etaireias Vyzantinon Spoudon* 17 (1941): 144–84.

Kollias, Ēlias. *The Medieval City of Rhodes and the Palace of the Grand Master*. 2nd edn. Athens: Archaeological Receipts Fund, Direction of Publications, 1998.

———. 'I Palaiochristianiki kai Vyzantini Rodos. I Antistasi mias Ellinistikis Polis' [Early Christian and Byzantine Rhodes. The Resistance of a Hellenistic City], in *Rodos 2.400 Chronia. I Poli tis Rodou apo tin Idrysi tis mechri tin katalipsi apo tous Tourkous (1523). Diethnes Epistimoniko Synedrio, Rodos, 24–29 Oktovriou 1993. Praktika Tomos B* [Rhodes 2,400 years. The City of Rhodes from its Foundation to its Conquest by the Turks (1523). International Scientific Congress, Rhodes, 24–29 October 1993. Proceedings, Volume B], edited by Diana Zapheiropoulou, 299–308. Athens: Ministry of Culture/12 Ephorate of Prehistoric and Classical Antiquities/4th Ephorate of Byzantine Antiquities, 2000.

———. 'Topographika Provlimata tis Mesaionikis Agoras tis Rodou kai tou Notiou Teichous tou Kollakiou, "versus civitatem"' [Topographical Issues of the Medieval Agora of Rhodes and the South Wall of Kollakio, 'versus civitatem'], in *Istoria kai Provlimata syntirisis tis mesaionikis polis tis Rodou: epistimoniki synantisi 27–29 Noemvriou 1986. Praktika* [History and Conservation Problems of the Medieval City of Rhodes: Scientific Meeting 27–29 November 1986. Proceedings], edited by Municipality of Rhodos, 81–108. Athens: Municipality of Rhodes/Office of the Medieval City of Rhodes, 1992.

Kondyli, Fotini. 'Lords at the end of the Empire: Negotiating Power in the Late Byzantine Frontiers (fourteenth-fifteenth centuries).' *The Annual of the British School at Athens* 112 (2017): 309–39. Available at: https://doi.org/10.1017/S0068245417000077.

Kontogiannis, Nikos D. *Mesaionika kastra kai ochyroseis tis Ko.* Athens: Dēmos Hērakleidōn: Dēmos Dikaiou, 2002.

———. 'Translatio Imaginis: Assimilating the Triple-Towered Castle in Late Byzantine Coinage.' *Byzantinische Zeitschrift* 106, no. 2 (2013): 713–44. Available at: https://doi.org/10.1515/bz-2013-0024.

———. 'Euripos-Negroponte-Eğriboz: Material Culture and Historical Topography of Chalcis from Byzantium to the End of the Ottoman Rule.' *Jahrbuch Der Österreichischen Byzantinistik* 62 (2012): 29–56.

Kontogiannis, Nikos D. and Stefania S. Skartsis, eds. *Venetian and Ottoman Heritage in the Aegean: The Bailo House in Chalcis, Greece.* Turnhout: Brepols Publishers, 2020.

Korre, Katerina B., Stavros Mamaloukos, and Michail Papavarnavas. 'The Venetian Fortifications of Lepanto. Archival Documents, Architecture, Perspectives.' *Thesaurismata* 47 (2017).

Koukoulē-Chrysanthakē, Chaidō. *Philippi.* 2nd edn. Athens: Ministry of Culture, Archaeological Receipts Fund, 1997.

Kourkoutidou-Nikolaidou, Eutychia. *Wandering in Byzantine Thessaloniki.* Athens: Kapon Editions, 1997.

Kouroumali, Maria. 'The Justinianic Reconquest of Italy: Imperial Campaigns and Local Responses.' *Late Antique Archaeology* 2013, 8, no. 2 (2013): 969–99. Available at: https://doi.org/10.1163/2213 4522-90000030.

Kyriakidis, Savvas. *Warfare in Late Byzantium, 1204–1453.* History of Warfare, v. 67. Leiden/Boston: Brill, 2011.

Laiou, A.E. 'A Byzantine Prince Latinized: Theodore Palaeologus, Marquis of Montferrat.' *Byzantion* 38, no. 2 (1968): 386–410.

———. *Constantinople and the Latins: The Foreign Policy of Andronicus II, 1282–1328.* Cambridge, MA: Harvard University Press, 1972.

Lander, James. *Roman Stone Fortifications: Variation and Change from the First Century A.D. to the Fourth.* BAR International Series 206. Oxford: BAR, 1984.

Lassus, Jean. *La fortresse byzantine de Thamugadi.* Études d'antiquités africaines. Paris: Editions du Centre national de la recherche scientifique, 1981.

Lauffray, J. *Ḥalabiyya-Zenobia, place forte du limes oriental et la Haute-Mésopotamie au VIe siècle* [*Ḥalabiyya-Zenobia, stronghold of the Eastern Limes and the Upper Mesopotamia in the 6th Century*]. Bibliothèque archéologique et historique, 119, 138. Paris: Librorientaliste P Geuthner, 1983.

Lawrence, A.W. 'A Skeletal History of Byzantine Fortification.' *Annual of the British School at Athens* 78 (1983): 171–227.

———. *Greek Aims in Fortification.* Oxford/New York: Clarendon Press/Oxford University Press, 1979.

Lee, A.D. 'The Empire at War', in *The Cambridge Companion to the Age of Justinian*, edited by Michael Maas, 113–33. Cambridge Companions to the Ancient World. Cambridge: Cambridge University Press, 2005.

Lemerle, Paul. 'Le château de Philippes au temps de Nicéphore Phocas (pl XIV).' *Bulletin de Correspondance Hellénique* 61, no. 1 (1937): 103–8. Available at: https://doi.org/10.3406/bch.1937.2726.

———. *Philippes et la Macédoine orientale à l'époque chrétienne et byzantine; recherches d'histoire et d'archéologie* [*Philippoi and the eastern Macedonia in the Christian and Byzantine Period; Researches of History and Archaeology*]. Bibliothèque des écoles françaises d'Athènes et de Rome, 158. Paris: Ede Boccard, 1945.

Leo VI, Emperor of the East. *The Taktika of Leo VI.* Revised edition/text, Translation, and Commentary by George T. Dennis. Dumbarton Oaks Texts 12. Washington, DC: Dumbarton Oaks, 2014.

Lidov, Aleksei, ed. *Ierotopiia: sozdanie sakral'nykh prostranstv v Vizantii i drevnei Rusi* [*Hierotopy: the Creation of Sacred Spaces in Byzantium and Medieval Russia*]. Moscow: Indrik, 2006.

Lightfoot, C.S. 'Amorium.' *Anatolian Archaeology* 2 (1996): 8–9.

―――. *Amorium: A Byzantine City in Anatolia*. Homer Archaeological Guides 5. İstanbul: Homer Kitabevi, 2007.

Lillington-Martin, Christopher. 'Procopius on the Struggle for Dara in 530 and Rome in 537–38: Reconciling texts and landscapes.' *Late Antique Archaeology* 8, no. 2 (2013): 599–630. Available at: https://doi.org/10.1163/22134522-90000019.

Louth, Andrew. 'Byzantium Transforming (600–700)', in *The Cambridge History of the Byzantine Empire c. 500–1492*, edited by Jonathan Shepard, 221–48. Cambridge/New York: Cambridge University Press, 2008. Available at: http://nrs.harvard.edu/urn-3:hul.ebookbatch.CAMHI_batch:9780511756702.

Lowry, Heath W. *The Nature of the Early Ottoman State*. SUNY Series in the Social and Economic History of the Middle East. Albany: State University of New York Press, 2003.

Maas, Michael. *The Cambridge Companion to the Age of Justinian*. Cambridge Companions to the Ancient World. Cambridge: Cambridge University Press, 2005.

McGeer, Eric. 'Byzantine Siege Warfare in Theory and Practice', in *Byzantine Warfare*, edited by John Haldon, 519–25. Routledge, 2007. Available at: https://doi.org/10.4324/9781315261003-36.

―――. 'De Obsidione Toleranda', in *The Oxford Dictionary of Byzantium*. Oxford University Press, 2005. Available at: https://www.oxfordreference.com/view/10.1093/acref/9780195046526.001.0001/acref-9780195046526-e-1422.

―――. 'De Re Militari', in *The Oxford Dictionary of Byzantium*. Oxford University Press, 2005. Available at: https://www.oxfordreference.com/view/10.1093/acref/9780195046526.001.0001/acref-9780195046526-e-1427.

―――. 'Greek Fire', in *The Oxford Dictionary of Byzantium*. Oxford University Press, 2005. Available at: https://www.oxfordreference.com/view/10.1093/acref/9780195046526.001.0001/acref-9780195046526-e-2152.

―――. 'Ouranos, Nikephoros', in *The Oxford Dictionary of Byzantium*. Oxford University Press, 2005. Available at: https://www.oxfordreference.com/view/10.1093/acref/9780195046526.001.0001/acref-9780195046526-e-3998.

―――. 'Taktika of Leo VI', in *The Oxford Dictionary of Byzantium*. Oxford University Press, 2005. Available at: https://www.oxfordreference.com/view/10.1093/acref/9780195046526.001.0001/acref-9780195046526-e-5291?rskey=MJBQPH&result=2

―――. *Sowing the Dragon's Teeth: Byzantine Warfare in the Tenth Century*. Dumbarton Oaks Studies 33. Washington, DC: Dumbarton Oaks Research Library and Collection, 1995.

McGeer, Eric, Alexander Kazhdan, and Anthony Cutler. 'Weaponry', in *The Oxford Dictionary of Byzantium*. Oxford University Press, 2005. Available at: https://www.oxfordreference.com/view/10.1093/acref/9780195046526.001.0001/acref-9780195046526-e-5806.

Maguire, Henry. 'The Beauty of Castles: A Tenth Century Description of a Tower at Constantinople.' *Deltion Christianikis Archaeologikis Etaireias* 35 (1994): 21. Available at: https://doi.org/10.12681/dchae.1086.

Mamaloukos, Stavros. 'To Katholiko tis Monis Vatopediou: Istoria kai Architektoniki.' [The Katholikon of the Vatopedi Monasteri: History and Architecture]. PhD diss., Ethniko Metsovio Polytechnio, 2001.

Mango, Cyril. 'The Palace of the Boukoleon.' *Cahiers Archéologiques* 45 (1997): 41–50.

―――. *Byzantine Architecture*. Milan: faber and faber/Electra, 1986.

Mango, Marlia M. 'Edessa', in *The Oxford Dictionary of Byzantium*. Oxford University Press, 2005. Available at: https://www.oxfordreference.com/view/10.1093/acref/9780195046526.001.0001/acref-9780195046526-e-1606.

―――. 'Sergiopolis', in *The Oxford Dictionary of Byzantium*. Oxford University Press, 2005. Available at: https://www.oxfordreference.com/view/10.1093/acref/9780195046526.001.0001/acref-9780195046526-e-4913.

———. 'Zenobia', in *The Oxford Dictionary of Byzantium*. Oxford University Press, 2005. Available at: https://www.oxfordreference.com/view/10.1093/acref/9780195046526.001.0001/acref-978019504 6526-e-5885.

Manousou-Della, Aikaterini. 'I proimi mesaioniki ochirosi tis polis tis Rodou' [The early medieval fortification of the city of Rhodes], in *15 Chronia Ergon Apokatastasis sti Mesaioniki Poli tis Rodou: Praktika tou Diethnous Epistimonikou Synedriou* [*15 years of restoration in the medieval town of Rhodes: proceedings of the international symposium*], *Rhodes 14–18 November 2001*, edited by Elias E. Kollias, 331–40. Athens: Ministry of Culture, 2007.

———. *Mesaioniki Poli Rodou: Erga Apokatastasis (1985–2000)* [*The Medieval City of Rhodes: Restoration Works (1985–2000)*]. Athens: Ministry of Culture, 2001.

Marinou, G. 'Oi para ta teichi tis polis Vyzantines Mones tou Mystra kai oi ochyroseis toys' [The next-to-the-city walls, Byzantine Monasteries of Mystras and their fortifications], in *15 Chronia Ergon Apokatastasis sti Mesaioniki Poli tis Rodou: Praktika tou Diethnous Epistimonikou Synedriou* [*15 years of restoration in the medieval town of Rhodes: proceedings of the international symposium*], *Rhodes 14–18 November 2001*, edited by Elias E. Kollias, 412–21. Athens: Ministry of Culture, 2007.

Marksteiner, Thomas, et al. *Turm und Tor: Siedlungsstrukturen in Lykien und benachbarten Kultur-landschaften: Akten des Gedenkkolloquiums für Thomas Marksteiner in Wien, November 2012* [Tower and Gate: Settlement structures in Lycia and neighbouring cultural landscapes: Proceedings of the memorial colloquium for Thomas Marksteiner in Vienna]. Forschungen in Limyra, 7. Wien: Österreichisches Archäologisches Institut, 2015.

Matthew, Donald. *The Norman Kingdom of Sicily*. Cambridge University Press, 1992. Available at: https://doi.org/10.1017/CBO9781139167741.

Mavritsaki, Maria. 'Frourio Temenos Nikiphorou Phoka' [The Fortress Temenos of Nikephoros Phokas], in *Archaiologiko Ergo Kritis 2, Praktika tis 2is Synantisis, Rethymno, 26–28 Noemvriou 2010* [*Archaeological Work of Crete 2, Proceedings of the Second Meeting, Rethymno, 26–28 November 2010*], edited by Michalis Andrianakis, Petroula Varthalitou, and Iris Tzahili, 374–81. Rethymnon: Ekdoseis Philosophikis Scholis Panepistimiou Kritis, 2012.

Mexia, Angeliki. 'I Vasiliki sto Tigani tis Mesa Manis, Symvoli stin Oikodomiki Istoria tou Naou' [The Basilica at Tigani of Mesa Mani, Contribution to the Architectural History of the Church], in *Aphieroma ston Akadimaiko Panayioti L. Vokotopoulo* [*Dedication to the Academician Panayioti L. Vokotopoulo*], edited by Vasilis Katsaros and Anastasia Tourta, 57–66. Athens: 2015.

Miles, George Carpenter. *The Coinage of the Arab Amirs of Crete*. Numismatic Notes & Monographs, no. 160. New York: American Numismatic Society, 1970.

Millingen, Alexander van. *Byzantine Constantinople. The Walls of the City and Adjoining Historical Sites*. London: J. Murray, 1899.

Morganstern, James. *The Fort at Dereağzi, and Other Material Remains in Its Vicinity: From Antiquity to the Middle Ages*. Istanbuler Forschungen, Bd. 40. Tübingen: Wasmuth, 1993.

Morrisson, Cécile. 'The Emperor, the Saint, and the City: Coinage and Money in Thessalonike from the Thirteenth to the Fifteenth Century.' *Dumbarton Oaks Papers* 57 (2003): 173–203. Available at: https://doi.org/10.2307/1291880.

Moutsopoulos, Nikolaos K. *Rentina II: to Vyzantino kastro tis mygdonikis Rentinas: i ochyrosi kai i ydreusi tou oikismou* [*Rentina II: the Byzantine Castle of the Mygdonian Rentina: the Fortification and Water Supply of the Settlement*]. Athens: Techniko Epimelitirio Helladas, 2001.

Müller-Wiener, Wolfgang. *Bildlexikon zur Topographie Istanbuls: Byzantion, Konstantinupolis, Istanbul bis zum Beginn d. 17. Jh* [*Pictorial Dictionary for the Topography of Istanbul: Byzantion, Constantinople, Istanbul up to the early 17th Century*]. Tübingen: Wasmuth, 1977.

Museum of Byzantine Culture. 'From Macedonian to Thessalian Tempi: From Rentina to Velika.' Available at: https://www.mbp.gr/en/exhibitions/%E2%80%9C-macedonian-thessalian-tempi-rentina-velika%E2%80%9D.

Müth, Silke. *Ancient Fortifications: A Compendium of Theory and Practice*. Ancient Fortifications Studies, vol. 1. Oxford/Philadelphia, PA: Oxbow Books, 2016.

Mylonas, Paul M. *Bildlexikon Des Heiligen Berges Athos* [*Pictorial Dictionary of the Holy Mountain Athos*], *v.1:1 in 3 Fascicles: Atlas of the Twenty Sovereign (Ruling) Monasteries*. Tübingen: Wasmuth, 2000.

Mylonas, Paul M. *Moni Vatopediou* [*Vatopedi Monastery*]. Pragmateiai tis Akadimias Athinon 58. Athens: Academy of Athens, 2003.

Myriantheos-Koufopoulou, Marina. 'Vyzantina kai Metavyzantina Parekklisia tis Monis Sina, Istoria kai Architektoniki' [Byzantine and Post-Byzantine Chapels of the Sinai Monastery, History and Architecture]. PhD Thesis, Athens National Technical University, 2015.

Nicol, Donald MacGillivray. *The Despotate of Epiros*. Oxford: Blackwell, 1957.

———. *The Despotate of Epiros, 1267–1479: A Contribution to the History of Greece in the Middle Ages*. Cambridge/New York: Cambridge University Press, 1984.

———. *The Last Centuries of Byzantium, 1261–1453*. 2nd edn. Cambridge/New York: Cambridge University Press, 1993.

Nicolle, David, ed. *A Companion to Medieval Arms and Armour*. Woodbridge/Rochester, NY: Boydell Press, 2002.

Nicolotti, Andrea. *From the Mandylion of Edessa to the Shroud of Turin: The Metamorphosis and Manipulation of a Legend*. Art and Material Culture in Medieval and Renaissance Europe, 1. Boston: Brill, 2014.

Niewöhner, Philipp. 'Houses', in *The Archaeology of Byzantine Anatolia: From the End of Late Antiquity until the Coming of the Turks*, edited by Philipp Niewöhner, 109–18. Oxford: Oxford University Press/OSO, 2017. Available at: https://doi.org/10.1093/acprof:oso/9780190610463.001.0001.

Norwich, John Julius. *Byzantium: The Early Centuries*. 1st American edn. New York: Knopf, 1989.

———. *Byzantium: The Apogee*. London/New York: Viking, 1991.

———. *A Short History of Byzantium*. New York: Knopf, 1997.

Oikonomidès, Nicolas. 'La Décomposition de l'empire Byzantin à La Veille de 1204 et Les Origines de l'empire de Nicée: À Propos de La Partitio Romaniae.' In *Byzantium from the Ninth Century to the Fourth Crusade: Studies, Texts, Monuments*, 3–28. Collected Studies; CS369. Gower House, Hampshire/Brookfield, VT: Variorum, 1992.

Orlandos, Anastasios K. *Monastic Architecture*. 1926.

———. *Ta palatia kai ta spitia tou Mystra* [*The Palaces and Houses of Mystras*]. Vivliothiki tis en Athinais Archaiologikis Etaireias, 203. Athens: I en Athinais Archaiologiki Etaireia, 2000.

———. 'To Kastron tis Artis' [The Castle of Arta]. *Arxeion ton Vyzantinon Mnimeion tis Ellados* 2 (1936): 151–60.

Ousterhout, Robert. 'Life in a Late Byzantine Tower: Examples from Northern Greece.' Routledge, 2012. Available at: https://doi.org/10.4324/9781315262307-19.

The Oxford Handbook of Engineering and Technology in the Classical World. Oxford University Press, 2009. Available at: https://doi.org/10.1093/oxfordhb/9780199734856.001.0001.

Oxford Handbook of Engineering and Technology in the Classical World, The. Oxford University Press, 2009. Available at: https://doi.org/10.1093/oxfordhb/9780199734856.001.0001.

Papadopoulou, Varvara. 'Kastro Ioanninon. I Istoria ton Ochyroseion kai tou Oikismou' [Castle of Ioannina. The History of the Fortifications and the Settlement], in *To Kastro ton Ioanninon* [*The Castle of Ioannina*], edited by Varvara Papadopoulou, 36–103. Ioannina: Ministry of Culture, 8th Ephorate of Byzantine Antiquities, 2009.

———. 'Nea Archaiologika Stoicheia gia tin Vyzantini Poli tis Artas' [New Archaeological Evidence for the Byzantine City of Arta], in *Praktika Diethnous Symposiou gia to Despotato tis Ipeirou (Arta, 27–31 Maiou 1990)* [*Proceedings of the International Symposium for the Despotate of Epirus (Arta, 27–31 May 1990)*], edited by Evangelos Chrysos, 375–400. Athens: 1992.

Parani, Maria G. *Reconstructing the Reality of Images, Byzantine Material Culture and Religious Iconography (11th–15th Centuries)*. The Medieval Mediterranean 41. Leiden-Boston: Brill, 2003.

Pattenden, Philip. 'The Byzantine Early Warning System.' *Byzantion (Bruxelles)* 53, no. 1 (1983): 258–99.

Pertusi, Agostino. 'Una Acolouthia Militare Inedita Del X Secolo' [An Unpublished Military Liturgy of the 10th Century]. *Aevum* 22, no. 2/4 (1948): 145–68.

Peschlow, Urs. 'Mermerkule – Ein spatbyzantinischer Palast in Konstantinopel' [Mermerkule – a Late Byzantine Palace in Constantinople], in *Studien zur byzantinischen Kunstgeschichte: Festschrift für Horst Hallensleben zum 65. Geburtstag* [*Studies in Byzantine History of Art: in honor of Horst Hallensleben for his 65th Birthday*], 93–7. Amsterdam: Adolf M. Hakkert, 1995.

———. *Ankara: Die bauarchaologischen Hinterlassenschaften aus römischer und byzantinischer Zeit.* Vienna: Phoibos Verlag, 2015.

———. 'Patara', in *The Archaeology of Byzantine Anatolia: From the End of Late Antiquity to the Coming of the Turks*, edited by Philipp Niewöhner, 280–90. Oxford University Press, 2017. Available at: https://doi.org/10.1093/acprof:oso/9780190610463.003.0025.

———. 'Ancyra', in *The Archaeology of Byzantine Anatolia: From the End of Late Antiquity to the Coming of the Turks*, edited by Philipp Niewöhner, 349–60. Oxford University Press, 2017. Available at: https://doi.org/10.1093/acprof:oso/9780190610463.003.0025.

Petre, James Scott. *Crusader Castles of Cyprus: The Fortifications of Cyprus under the Lusignans, 1191–1489.* Texts and Studies of the History of Cyprus 69. Nicosia: Cyprus Research Centre, 2012.

Petrova, Eleonora. *Stobi: Vodič.* Skopje: Museum of Macedonia, 2003.

Petrović, Petar, Slobodan Dušanić, and Arheološki institut. *Roman Limes on the Middle and Lower Danube.* Đerdapske Sveske. Posebna Izdanja 2. Belgrade: Archaeological Institute, 1996.

Pharr, Clyde, Theresa Sherrer Davidson, and Mary Brown Pharr. *The Theodosian Code. A Translation, with Annotations, of All the Source Material of Roman Law.* Corpus of Roman Law, v. 1. Nashville, TN: Department of Classics, Vanderbilt University, 1944.

Philippides, Marios. *The Siege and the Fall of Constantinople in 1453: Historiography, Topography, and Military Studies.* Farnham/Burlington, VT: Ashgate Pub. Co., 2011.

Phillips, Jonathan. *The Fourth Crusade and the Sack of Constantinople.* New York: Penguin Books, 2004.

Piesker, Katja. 'Side', in *The Archaeology of Byzantine Anatolia: From the End of Late Antiquity to the Coming of the Turks*, edited by Philipp Niewöhner, 294–301. Oxford University Press, 2017. Available at: https://doi.org/10.1093/acprof:oso/9780190610463.003.0027.

Posamentir, Richard. 'Anazarbos in Late Antiquity', in *Archaeology and the Cities of Asia Minor in Late Antiquity*, edited by Ortwin Dally and Christopher John Ratté. Kelsey Museum Publication 6. Ann Arbor, MI: Kelsey Museum of Archaeology, University of Michigan, 2011.

Pringle, Denys. *The Defence of Byzantine Africa from Justinian to the Arab Conquest: An Account of the Military History and Archaeology of the African Provinces in the Sixth and Seventh Centuries.* BAR International Series 99. Oxford: BAR, 1981.

Provost, Samuel. 'Esquisse du paysage urbain entre le IXe s. et le XIIe s. d'après les sources archéologiques' [Outline of the Urban Landscape Between the 9th and the 12th Century According to Archaeological Sources], in *Philippes, de la préhistoire à Byzance: études d'archéologie et d'histoire* [*Philippoi from Prehistory to Byzantium: Studies in Archaeology and History*], edited by Julien Fournier, 217–44. BCH supplément 55. Athens: École française d'Athènes, 2016.

Quincey, J.H. 'The Beacon-Sites in the Agamemnon.' *The Journal of Hellenic Studies* 83 (1963): 118–32. Available at: https://doi.org/10.2307/628457.

Ricci, Alessandra. 'A Resilient Landscape: The Land Walls of Constantinople and Their Surroundings.' *Deltion tis Christianikis Archaiologikis Etaireias* 39 (2018): 125. Available at: https://doi.org/10.12681/dchae.18479.

Richardson, Alan. *Theoretical Aspects of Roman Camp and Fort Design.* BAR International Series 1321. Oxford: John and Erica Hedges, 2004.

Richmond, I.A. *The City Wall of Imperial Rome.* Yardley, PA: Westholme, 2013.

Rife, Joseph L. 'Leo's Peloponnesian Fire-Tower and the Byzantine Watch-Tower on Acrocorinth', in *Archaeology and History in Roman, Medieval and Post-Medieval Greece*, edited by William Caraher, Linda Hall and R. Scott Moore. Routledge, 2008. Available at: https://doi.org/10.4324/978131 5262277-28.

Riley-Smith, Jonathan, ed. *The Oxford Illustrated History of the Crusades*. Oxford Illustrated Histories. GB: Oxford University Press, Oxford University Press, Incorporated, 1995.

Rizos, Efthymios. 'The Late-Antique Walls of Thessalonica and Their Place in the Development of Eastern Military Architecture.' *Journal of Roman Archaeology* 24 (2011): 450–68. Available at: https://doi.org/10.1017/S1047759400003469.

———. 'New Cities and New Urban Ideas, AD 250–350', in *New Cities in Late Antiquity: Documents and Archaeology*, edited by Efthymios Rizos. Bibliothèque de l'Antiquité Tardive 35. Turnhout, Belgium: Brepols, 2017.

———, ed. *New Cities in Late Antiquity: Documents and Archaeology*. Bibliothèque de l'Antiquité Tardive 35. Turnhout, Belgium: Brepols, 2017.

Rizos, Efthymios, and Mustafa Hamdi Sayar. 'Urban Dynamics in the Bosphorus Region during Late Antiquity', in *New Cities in Late Antiquity: Documents and Archaeology*, edited by Efthymios Rizos. Bibliothèque de l'Antiquité Tardive 35. Turnhout, Belgium: Brepols, 2017.

Roland, Hakon. 'The Fortifications at Kastro Apalirou', in *Naxos and the Byzantine Aegean: Insular Responses to Regional Change*, edited by James Crow and David Hill, 89–103. Papers and Monographs from the Norwegian Institute at Athens, v. 7. Athens: Norwegian Institute at Athens, 2018.

Rufus, Orbicius, George T. Dennis, and Emperor of the East Maurice. *Maurice's Strategikon: Handbook of Byzantine Military Strategy*. Middle Ages. Philadelphia: University of Pennsylvania Press, 1984.

Runciman, Steven, and Elizabeth Jeffreys. *Byzantine Style, Religion and Civilization: In Honour of Sir Steven Runciman*. Cambridge/New York: Cambridge University Press, 2006.

Sarantis, Alexander. 'Fortifications in Africa: a Bibliographic Essay.' *Late Antique Archaeology* 8, no. 1 (2013): 297–315. Available at: https://doi.org/10.1163/22134522-90000009.

———. 'Fortifications in the East: a Bibliographic Essay.' *Late Antique Archaeology* 8, no. 1 (2013): 317–70. Available at: https://doi.org/10.1163/22134522-90000010.

———. 'Military Encounters and Diplomatic Affairs in the North Balkans during the Reigns of Anastasius and Justinian.' *Late Antique Archaeology* 8, no. 2 (2013): 759–808. Available at: https://doi.org/10.1163/22134522-90000025.

———. 'Military Equipment and Weaponry: a Bibliographic Essay.' *Late Antique Archaeology* 8, no. 1 (2013): 153–75. Available at: https://doi.org/10.1163/22134522-90000004.

———. 'Tactics: a Bibliographic Essay.' *Late Antique Archaeology* 8, no. 1 (2013): 177–207. Available at: https://doi.org/10.1163/22134522-90000005.

———. 'Waging War in Late Antiquity.' *Late Antique Archaeology* 8, no. 1 (2013): 1–98. Available at: https://doi.org/10.1163/22134522-90000002.

Sarantis, Alexander, and Neil Christie. 'Fortifications in the West: a Bibliographic Essay.' *Late Antique Archaeology* 8, no. 1 (2013): 255–96. Available at: https://doi.org/10.1163/22134522-90000008.

———, eds. *War and Warfare in Late Antiquity*. Late Antique Archaeology, vol. 8.1–8.2. Leiden/Boston: Brill, 2013.

Schneider, Alfons Maria. *Die Stadtmauer von İznik (Nicaea)*. [*The City Walls of Iznik (Nicaea)*]. Istanbuler Forschungen 9. Berlin: Archäologisches Institut des Deutschen Reiches, 1938.

Second International Sevgi Gönül Byzantine Studies Symposium. *The Byzantine Court: Source of Power and Culture: Papers from the Second International Sevgi Gönül Byzantine Studies Symposium, Istanbul, 21–23 June 2010*. Istanbul: Koç University Press, 2013.

Setton, Kenneth M. *Catalan Domination of Athens, 1311–1388*. Rev. edn. London: Variorum Revised Editions, 1975. Available at: http://nrs.harvard.edu/urn-3:hul.ebookbatch.ACLS_batch:MIU010 0000000000005122054.

Ševčenko, Nancy Patterson. 'Keramion', in *The Oxford Dictionary of Byzantium*. Oxford University Press, 2005. Available at: https://www.oxfordreference.com/view/10.1093/acref/9780195046526. 001.0001/acref-9780195046526-e-2832.

———. 'Mandylion', in *The Oxford Dictionary of Byzantium*. Oxford University Press, 2005. Available at: https://www.oxfordreference.com/view/10.1093/acref/9780195046526.001.0001/acref-978019 5046526-e-3296.

Shepard, Jonathan. *The Cambridge History of the Byzantine Empire c. 500–1492*. Cambridge/New York: Cambridge University Press, 2008. Available at: http://nrs.harvard.edu/urn-3:hul.ebookbatch. CAMHI_batch:9780511756702.

Sinos, Stefan. *Die Klosterkirche der Kosmosoteira in Bera (Vira)* [*The Monastic Church of Kosmosoteira in Bera (Vira)*]. Byzantinisches Archiv 16. München: CHBeck, 1985.

Smith, E. Baldwin (Earl Baldwin). *Architectural Symbolism of Imperial Rome and the Middle Ages*. Princeton Monographs in Art and Archaeology 30. Princeton: University Press, 1956.

Smpyraki-Kalantzi, Aikaterini, and George Kakavas. '24th EBA', in *2000–2010 Apo to Anaskaphiko Ergo ton Ephoreion Archaiotiton* [*2000–2010 From the Excavation Works of the Ephorates of Antiquities*]. Athens: Ministry of Culture and Tourism, 2012. Available at: https://www.culture.gov.gr/el/ service/SitePages/view.aspx?iiD=1436

Snively, Carolyn S. 'Golemo Gladište at Konjuh: A New City or a Relocated One?' In *New Cities in Late Antiquity: Documents and Archaeology*, edited by Efthymios Rizos, 205–19. Bibliothèque de l'Antiquité Tardive 35. Turnhout, Belgium: Brepols, 2017.

———. 'Caričin Grad', in *The Oxford Dictionary of Late Antiquity*. Oxford University Press, 2018.

Sophocles, David D. Mulroy, and Warren G. Moon. *Oedipus Rex*. Wisconsin Studies in Classics. Madison, WI: University of Wisconsin Press, 2011.

Southern, Pat. *The Roman Empire from Severus to Constantine*. London/New York: Routledge, 2001.

Souza, Philip de. 'Greek Warfare and Fortification', in *The Oxford Handbook of Engineering and Technology in the Classical World*, 30 December 2009. Available at: https://doi.org/10.1093/oxfordhb/ 9780199734856.013.0027.

Spieser, J.-M. *Thessalonique et ses monuments du IVe au VIe siècle: contribution a l'étude d'une ville paléochrétienne* [*Thessaloniki and its monuments from the 4th to the 6th Century: Contribution to the Study of an Early Christian City*]. Bibliothèque des écoles françaises d'Athènes et de Rome, 254. Athens/Paris: Ecole française d'Athènes; Dépositaire, Diffusion de Boccard, 1984.

Spiteri, Stephen C. *Fortresses of the Cross: Hospitaller Military Architecture (1136–1798)*. Valletta, Malta: Heritage Interpretation Services, 1994.

Stikas, Eustathios G. *To Oikodomikon Chronikon tis Monis Osiou Louka Phokidos* [*The Architectural Chronicle of the Hosios Loukas Monastery in Phokis*]. Vivliothiki tis en Athinais Archaiologikis Etaireias 65. Athens: I en Athinais Archaiologiki Etaireia, 1970.

Sullivan, Denis. 'Tenth Century Byzantine Offensive Siege Warfare: Instructional Prescriptions and Historical Practice', in *Byzantine Warfare*, edited by John Haldon. The International Library of Essays on Military History. Ashgate: Routledge, Taylor & Francis, 2017. Available at: https://doi.org/10.4324/9781315261003.

Sullivan, Denis, and Heron of Byzantium. *Siegecraft: Two Tenth-Century Instructional Manuals*. Dumbarton Oaks Studies 36. Washington, DC: Dumbarton Oaks Research Library and Collection, 2000.

Symonds, Matthew F.A. *Protecting the Roman Empire: Fortlets, Frontiers, and the Quest for Post-Conquest Security*. Cambridge, UK/New York, NY: Cambridge University Press, 2018.

Theocharaki, Anna Maria. 'The Ancient Circuit Wall of Athens: Its Changing Course and the Phases of Construction.' *Hesperia* 80, no. 1 (2011): 71–156. Available at: https://doi.org/10.2972/ hesp.80.1.71.

Theologidou, K. 'Servia.' *Archaiologiko Deltio* 50 (1995): 600–1.

Todd, Malcolm. *The Walls of Rome*. Archaeological Sites. London: PElek, 1978.

Tomadaki, Maria. 'Literary Depictions of the Constantinopolitan Walls in Byzantium.' Istanbul City Walls Project (Koc University), n.d.

Topalilov, I. 'Philippopolis: The City from the 1st to the Beginning of the 7th c', in *Roman Cities in Bulgaria*, edited by Rumen Ivanov, Bulgarian first edn, 363–438. Corpus of Ancient and Medieval Settlements in Modern Bulgaria, vol. 1. Sofia: Prof Marin Drinov Academic Publishing House, 2012.

Traulos, Ioannis N. *Poleodomiki exelixis ton Athinon: apo ton proistorikon chronon mechri ton archon tou 19ou aionos* [*Urban Evolution of Athens: from Prehistoric Times until the early 19th Century*]. 2nd edn. Athens: KAPON, 1993.

Tsamakda, Vasiliki. *The Illustrated Chronicle of Ioannes Skylitzes in Madrid*. Leiden: Alexandros, 2002.

Tsigonaki, Christina. 'Poleon Anelpistois Metavolais: Istorikes kai Archaiologikes Martyries apo ti Gortyna kai thn Eleutherna tis Kritis (4os–8os ai.)' [The Unexpected Changes of Cities: Historical and Archaeological Testimonies from Gortyna and Eleutherna in Crete (4th–8th C.)', in *Byzantine Cities, 8th–15th Centuries*, edited by T. Kioussopoulou, 73–100. Rethymno: Publications of the Faculty of Philosophy of the University of Crete, 2012.

Tsouris, K. 'I Vyzantini Ochyrosi ton Ioanninon' [The Byzantine Fortification of Ioannina]. *Ipeirotika Chronika* 25 (1983).

———. *I Ochyrosi tou Didymoteichou* [*The Fortification of Didymoteichon*]. Kavala: Saita Publications, 2015.

———. 'Paratiriseis sti Chronologisi tis Ochyroseos tis Dramas' [Observation for the Chronology of the Drama Fortification], in *I Drama kai i Periochi tis, Istoria kai Politismos, C' Epistimoniki Synantisi, Drama 21–24 Maiou 1998* [*Drama and its Region, History and Culture, Third Scientific Meeting, Drama 21–24 May 1998*], 113–18. Drama, 2002.

———. 'To Kastro sto Palio Pyli kai o Osios Christodoulos o Latrinos' [The Castle at Palio Pyli and the Blessed Christodoulos from Latros], in *Istoria-Techni-Archaiologia, A' Diethnes Epistimoniko Synedrio, Kos 2–4 Maiou 1997* [*History-Art-Archaeology, First International Scientific Congress, Kos 2–4 May 1997*], edited by G. Kokkorou-Aleura, A.A. Laimou, and E. Simantoni-Bournia. Athens: 2001.

Tsouris, K. and A. Brikas. *To Frourio tou Pythiou kai to Ergo tis Apokatastaseos tou, Prokatarktiki Anakoinoni* [*The Fortress of Pythion and its Restoration, Preliminary Report*]. Kavala: Ministry of Culture, 12th Ephorate of Byzantine Antiquities, 2002.

———. 'Vyzantines Ochyroseis ston Evro 1. Messimvria – Potamos – Avas – Traianoupolis – Pheres' [Byzantine Fortifications in the Evros 1. Messimvria – Potamos – Avas – Traianoupolis – Pheres]. *Byzantina* 26 (2006): 153–209.

Turchetto, Jacopo and Giuseppe Salemi. 'Hide and Seek. Roads, Lookouts and Directional Visibility Cones in Central Anatolia.' *Open Archaeology (Berlin, Germany)* 3, no. 1 (2017): 69–82. Available at: https://doi.org/10.1515/opar-2017-0004.

Tzompanaki, Chrysoula. *Chandakas, i Poli kai ta Teichi* [*Chandakas, the City and the Walls*]. Irakleio: Etaireia Kritikon Istorikon Meleton, 1996.

Vann, Robert Lindley. *The Unexcavated Buildings of Sardis*. BAR International Series 538. Oxford: BAR, 1989.

Vegetius Renatus, Flavius. *Epitoma Rei Militaris*. Scriptorum Classicorum Bibliotheca Oxoniensis. Oxford/New York: Clarendon Press/Oxford University Press, 2004.

———. *Vegetius, Epitome of Military Science*. Translated Texts for Historians, v. 16. Liverpool: Liverpool University Press, 1993.

Veikou, Myrto. '"Rural Towns" and "In-between" or "Third" Spaces: Settlement Patterns in Byzantine Epirus (7th–11th Centuries) from an Interdisciplinary Approach.' *Archeologia Medievale*, 2009.

———. 'Byzantine Histories, Settlement Stories: Kastra, "Isles of Refuge", and "Unspecified Settlements" as In-between or Third Spaces,' in *Byzantine Cities, 8th–15th Centuries*, edited by

T. Kioussopoulou, 159–206. Rethymno: Publications of the Faculty of Philosophy of the University of Crete.

Velenis, George. *Ta teichi tis Thessalonikis, apo ton Kassandro os ton Irakleio* [*The Walls of Thessaloniki, from Kassandros to Herakleios*]. Thessaloniki: University Studio Press, 1998.

Vikatou, Olympia, Aikaterini Chamilaki, and Eleni Katsouli. *The Castle of Naupaktos, Partial Reconstruction, Structural Reinforcement, and Enhancement of the Archaeological Site.* Mesolongi: Ephoreia Archaiotiton Aitoloakarnanias kai Leukadas, 2015.

Villehardouin, Geoffrey. *Chronicles of the Crusades.* Dover Military History, Weapons, Armor. New York: Dover Publications, 2007.

Vokotopoulos, Panagiotis. 'The Concealed Course Technique: Further Examples and a Few Remarks.' *Jahrbuch Des Osterreichischen Byzantinistik* 28 (1979): 247–60.

Voyadjis, Sotiris, 'Paratiriseis stin Oikodomiki Istoria tis Monis Sagmata sti Voiotia' [Observations for the Architectural History of Sagmata Monastery in Boeotia]. *Deltio tis Christianikis Archaiologikis Etaireias* 18 (1995): 49–69.

Voyadjis, Sotiris, and Vasiliki Sythiakaki-Kritsimalli, *To katholiko tis Ieras Monis Meyistis Lauras sto Ayion Oros: Istoria kai Architektoniki* [*The Katholikon of the Monastery Megistis Lauras in Mount Athos: History and Architecture*]. Athens KAPON, 2019.

Vranousē, Era L., et al. *Vyzantina engrapha tēs Monēs Patmou.* Diplōmatikē ekd [*Byzantine Documents of the Patmos Monastery. Diplomatic Edition*]. Athens: Ethnikon Hidryma Ereunōn, 1980.

Whately, Conor. 'El-Lejjün: Logistics and Localisation on Rome's Eastern Frontier in the 6th C. A.D.' *Late Antique Archaeology* 2013, 8, no. 2 (2013): 893–924. Available at: https://doi.org/10.1163/22134522-90000028.

———. 'Organisation and Life in the Late Roman Military: a Bibliographic Essay.' *Late Antique Archaeology* 8, no. 1 (2013): 209–38. Available at: https://doi.org/10.1163/22134522-90000006.

———. 'Strategy, Diplomacy and Frontiers: a Bibliographic Essay.' *Late Antique Archaeology* 8, no. 1 (2013): 239–54. Available at: https://doi.org/10.1163/22134522-90000007.

———. 'War in Late Antiquity: Secondary Works, Literary Sources and Material Evidence.' *Late Antique Archaeology* 8, no. 1 (2013): 99–151. Available at: https://doi.org/10.1163/22134522-90000003.

Whitby, Michael. 'Procopius' Description of Dara (Buildings II.1–3)', in *The Defence of the Roman and Byzantine East: Proceedings of a Colloquium Held at the University of Sheffield in April 1986*, edited by Philip Freeman and D.L. Kennedy, 737–83. BAR International Series 297. Oxford: BAR, 1986.

———. 'Siege Warfare and Counter-Siege Tactics in Late Antiquity (ca. 250–640).' *Late Antique Archaeology* 8, no. 2 (2013): 433–59. Available at: https://doi.org/10.1163/22134522-90000014.

———. 'The Long Walls of Constantinople.' *Byzantion* 55, no. 2 (1985): 560–83.

White, Lynn Townsend. *Medieval Technology and Social Change.* London: Oxford University Press, 1976.

Williams, Stephen. *Theodosius: The Empire at Bay.* New Haven: Yale University Press, 1995.

Winter, Frederick E. *Greek Fortifications.* Phoenix. Supp. vol. 9. Toronto: University of Toronto Press, 1971.

———. 'The Chronology of the Ancient Defenses of Acrocorinth: A Reconsideration.' *American Journal of Archaeology* 95, no. 1 (1991): 109–21. Available at: https://doi.org/10.2307/505159.

Index

Historical Figures and Officials

Michael III, emperor, 4, 91, 93, 102–3, 109, 111, 217, 227
Michael VIII Palaiologos, emperor, 160, 172, 174, 184
Michael Panaretos, author, 158
Michael Prosouh, 136
Mu'awiya, caliph, 85
Murad II, sultan, 176, 196

Nicholas Orsini, despot, 185
Nikephoros I, emperor, 87, 109
Nikephoros II Phokas, emperor, 114, 117–18, 120–1, 124
Nikephoros III Botaneiates, emperor, 126
Nikephoros (Komnenos Doukas), despot, 184, 192
Nikephoros Gregoras, author, 158
Nikephoros Melissinos, 126
Nikephoros Ouranos, general and author, 117–18, 215, 218
Niketas Choniates, author, 132, 215

Oedipus, 1
Odo de Deuil, author, 143, 169
Orestes, castellan, 176
Ormisdas, 22

Petronas, general, 120
Philip, emperor, 27
Philip of Taranto, prince, 184
Philippikos, emperor, 87
Phokas, emperor, 33
Phokas, family, 117
Photios, patriarch, 227
Postumus, 13
Probus, emperor, 17
Prokopios, author, 3, 31, 34–5, 37, 39, 50, 54–5, 59–60, 66, 68–70, 74, 202, 219

Ramon Muntaner, author, 158
Roger de Lluria, 161, 164
Romanos IV Diogenes, emperor, 115
Romanos, general, 121
Romula, 23
Rufinus, 31

Saladin, sultan, 126
Samuel, tsar, 114–15, 152, 190, 214
Septimius Severus, emperor, 24
Sergios, patriarch, 227

Sergios, saint, 61
Shapur, shah, 13
Solomon, patrician and prefect, 69–71
Sphrantzes, author, 158
Stefan Dusan, emperor, 164, 181
Svjatoslav, prince, 114, 123
Symeon, tsar, 88, 113–14
Syrgiannes Philanthropenos, 185
Syrianos Magister, author, 34, 88

Thamar, princess, 184, 192
Theodora, empress, 70, 223
Theodore I Lascaris, 163, 166, 195, 197
Theodore II Lascaris, 168
Theodore Doukas, sebastokrator, 184
Theodore Komnenos Doukas, emperor, 183
Theodore Mankaphas, 163
Theodore Palaiologos, marquis, 158–9
Theodore Palaiologos Kantakouzenos, 174
Theodore of Sykeon, saint, 223
Theodosios I, emperor, 3, 13–14, 22–3, 43, 66
Theodosios II, emperor, 32, 36, 43, 51, 54, 60
Theoktistos, 88
Theophilos, emperor, 88, 91, 93, 120, 216, 224, 228
Thomas, despot, 185
Thomas Komnenos Doukas, 188
Thomas Preliubovic, despot, 188
Thomas the Slav, 88
Tiberios II, emperor, 92
Totila, 50
Tzachas, emir, 130

Valens, emperor, 13
Valentinian, emperor, 13
Valerian, emperor, 18
Vegetius, Publius Vegetius Renatus, author, 14
Victorinus, praetorian prefect, 54, 182
Vital Cuinet, geographer, 199
Vitruvius, author, 51, 76

William Villehardouin, prince, 164, 184

Yolanda of Montferrat, empress, 158

Zeno, emperor, 50, 65

Historical Places and Monuments